"Valuable corrective to contemporary political discourse about settler colonialism, which is usually framed in binary terms. In contrast, Esteban Rozo shows how indigeneity in the Colombian Amazon emerged in relation to state formation, evangelization, and economic interests, as well as choices made by indigenous peoples themselves."

Stuart Kirsch, *University of Michigan, USA*

"Esteban Rozo offers a powerful intervention in the ways that states, Christian missionaries, and industries of capitalist extraction impinge on indigenous life in the Colombian Amazon. Pushing against the figuration of indigenous groups as passive victims of outside encroachments, Rozo shows how *indígenas* selectively appropriated Catholic and then evangelical Christianities to define their own identities and advance their own interests."

Paul Christopher Johnson*, University of Michigan, USA*

"This outstanding historical ethnography analyzes the relational construction of indigeneity in the Colombian Amazon frontier. With interpretative fluidity, the study looks at the social and cultural processes that linked indigenous peoples to Christianity, the nation-state, narratives of modernity, and development politics."

César Ceriani Cernadas*, CONICET – UBA, Argentina*

Remaking Indigeneity in the Amazon

Drawing on archival and ethnographic work, this book analyzes how indigeneity, Christianity and state-making became intertwined in the Colombian Amazon throughout the 20th century.

At the end of the 19th century, the state gave Catholic missionaries tutelage over Indigenous groups and their territories, but, in the case of the Colombian Amazon, this tutelage was challenged by evangelical missionaries that arrived in the region in the 1940s with different ideas of civilization and social change. Indigenous conversion to evangelical Christianity caused frictions with other actors, while Indigenous groups perceived conversion as way of leverage with settlers. This book shows how evangelical Christianity shaped new forms of indigeneity that did not coincide entirely with the ideas of civilization or development that Catholic missionaries and the state promoted in the region. Since the 1960s, the state adapted development policies and programs to Indigenous realities and practices, while Indigenous societies appropriated evangelical Christianity in order to navigate the changes brought on by colonization, modernity and state-formation.

This study demonstrates that not all projects of civilization were the same in Amazonia, nor was missionization of Indigenous groups always subordinate to the state or resource extraction.

Esteban Rozo is a Professor of Anthropology at Universidad Nacional de Colombia in Bogotá. His research focuses on how conversion to Christianity in the Colombian Amazon relates to processes of colonization, state-formation and the emergence of new forms of indigeneity.

Routledge Studies in the History of the Americas

30 **The New Pan-Americanism and the Structuring of Inter-American Relations**
   Edited by Juan Pablo Scarfi and David M. K. Sheinin

31 **The Middle Classes in Latin America**
   Subjectivities, Practices, and Genealogies
   Edited by Mario Barbosa Cruz, A. Ricardo López-Pedreros, and Claudia Stern

32 **Narratives against Enslavement from the Court Rooms of Nineteenth-Century Brazil**
   Fighting for Freedom
   Clara Lunow

33 **Recasting the Nation in Twentieth-Century Argentina**
   Edited by Benjamin Bryce and David M. K. Sheinin

34 **Social Struggle and Civil Society in Nineteenth Century Cuba**
   Edited by Richard E. Morris

35 **An International History of South America in the Era of Military Rule**
   Geared for War
   Sebastián Hurtado-Torres and Joaquín Fermandois

36 **A Plurilingual History of the Portuguese Language in the Luso-Brazilian Empire**
   Luciane Scarato

37 **Remaking Indigeneity in the Amazon**
   Christianity, Colonization and the State
   Esteban Rozo

For more information about this series, please visit: https://www.routledge.com/Routledge-Studies-in-the-History-of-the-Americas/book-series/RSHAM

Remaking Indigeneity in the Amazon
Christianity, Colonization and the State

Esteban Rozo

NEW YORK AND LONDON

First published 2024
by Routledge
605 Third Avenue, New York, NY 10158

and by Routledge
4 Park Square, Milton Park, Abingdon, Oxon, OX14 4RN

Routledge is an imprint of the Taylor & Francis Group, an informa business

© 2024 Esteban Rozo

The right of Esteban Rozo to be identified as author of this work has been asserted in accordance with sections 77 and 78 of the Copyright, Designs and Patents Act 1988.

All rights reserved. No part of this book may be reprinted or reproduced or utilised in any form or by any electronic, mechanical, or other means, now known or hereafter invented, including photocopying and recording, or in any information storage or retrieval system, without permission in writing from the publishers.

Trademark notice: Product or corporate names may be trademarks or registered trademarks, and are used only for identification and explanation without intent to infringe.

Library of Congress Cataloging-in-Publication Data
Names: Rozo, Esteban, author.
Title: Remaking indigeneity in the Amazon : Christianity, colonization and the state / Esteban Rozo.
Description: New York, NY : Routledge, 2024. | Series: Routledge studies in the history of the Americas ; 37 | Includes bibliographical references and index.
Identifiers: LCCN 2023022665 (print) | LCCN 2023022666 (ebook) | ISBN 9781032440583 (hardback) | ISBN 9781032440590 (paperback) | ISBN 9781003370215 (ebook) | ISBN 9781000963038 (adobe pdf) | ISBN 9781000963113 (epub)
Subjects: LCSH: Missions--Colombia--Social aspects. | Indigenous peoples--Colombia--Religion. | Catholic Church--Missions--Colombia. | New Tribes Mission. | Conversion--Christianity--Social aspects. | Church and state--Colombia--History--20th century. | Colombia--Religion. | Colombia--Social conditions.
Classification: LCC BV2853.C7 R69 2024 (print) | LCC BV2853.C7 (ebook) | DDC 266/.023861--dc23/eng/20230601
LC record available at https://lccn.loc.gov/2023022665
LC ebook record available at https://lccn.loc.gov/2023022666

ISBN: 978-1-032-44058-3 (hbk)
ISBN: 978-1-032-44059-0 (pbk)
ISBN: 978-1-003-37021-5 (ebk)

DOI: 10.4324/9781003370215

Typeset in Sabon
by KnowledgeWorks Global Ltd.

Contents

List of Figures and Maps	*viii*
Foreword	*ix*
Acknowledgements	*xi*
Introduction	1
1 The Making of an Amazonian Frontier	14
2 Conversion Under Dispute: Evangelical Christianity and the State	58
3 Between Rupture and Continuity: The Politics of Conversion	87
4 Christianity, Materiality and the Critique of Modernity	108
5 Indigeneity, Development and Extractivism	130
Conclusions	160
Index	*166*

List of Figures and Maps

Figures

1.1	Missionary Hubert Damoiseux, Mandú and his son, 1916.	23
1.2	Indigenous captains, 1928. Picture of Indigenous captains of the *reducciones* in Vaupés.	32
1.3	A boarding school in Vaupés, 1928. "How borders are defended: a school in Vaupés."	36
1.4	Missionary Pierre Kok and his students, 1919.	37
2.1	Functionaries of the national government in charge of establishing the *comisaría* of Guainía in 1965.	72
4.1	The Bible as milk and food, the Bible as mirror.	118
4.2	The Bible as brake and rudder. The Bible as sword of the spirit.	120
4.3	"Tied-up by business and pleasures."	122
5.1	Mining raft with dredges for extracting gold.	144

Maps

I.1	Region of the Upper Rio Negro and the provinces of Vaupés, Guaviare and Guainía.	2
1.1	Map of 1914 showing the location of Montfort (Papurí) in Vaupés.	20
1.2	First rough map of Montfort-Papurí made by missionaries in 1915. (Mandu's house is marked with an X.)	22
1.3	Map based on Pierre Kok's map of the Papurí River made in 1925 with its tributaries, mission towns and language groups.	28
1.4	Mission towns established by Montfort missionaries on the border with Brazil by 1949.	45
2.1	Map of the province of Guainía established in 1965.	62
5.1	Map of Guainía with the Indigenous Mining Zone and Indigenous Reservations.	142

Foreword

At a gathering of evangelical Christians on the banks of the Guainía River in rural Colombia, not far from the border with Brazil, an indigenous pastor stepped forward to criticize the behavior of his guest, whom he accused of violating one of the mission's strict taboos against "worldliness," which include materialism, drinking *chicha*, an alcoholic beverage made from fermented manioc, and dancing. Soon afterward, other members of the church began to make hand gestures miming someone smoking a cigarette while pointing at the visiting anthropologist. While the author of *Remaking Indigeneity* does not dwell on this collective reproach, the interaction provides a telling illustration of how the local community draws on its religious beliefs and commitments in unexpected ways.

As a student in the interdisciplinary doctoral program in anthropology and history at the University of Michigan, Esteban Rozo set out to research and write a historical ethnography of the frontier region of Vaupés and Guainía in the Colombian Amazon, working initially with Curripaco and Puinave groups on the Inirida River, and later with other indigenous communities from the Vaupés River region known for their linguistic exogamy. He was interested in how state formation and indigenous conversion to Christianity were connected. Our first conversations took place in a graduate seminar that I was teaching on indigenous political movements, in which we considered the relational character of indigeneity, in contrast to its status as an independent identity or claim.

In *Remaking Indigeneity*, Esteban Rozo offers a valuable corrective to contemporary political discourse about settler colonialism, which is usually framed in binary terms between states and indigenous peoples. Instead, he describes the importance of other institutions and dynamics that influence these interactions: churches with very different relationships to the state competing for indigenous converts; extractive economies that expropriate indigenous labor and resources; armed conflicts that endangered indigenous communities; and efforts by the state to secure its international boundaries by controlling the movement of the indigenous peoples living in the region. Most importantly, by productively and creatively integrating archival and ethnographic

x *Foreword*

research, Rozo shows how indigeneity in the Colombian Amazon emerged as a result of the choices made by indigenous peoples themselves, albeit in circumstances not entirely of their own making.

This recognition leads Rozo to treat Christianity as a form of cultural and political mediation. Even though the missionaries regularly trafficked in negative stereotypes about them, indigenous leaders decided that conversion was the best way was to push back against these misrepresentations. To be sure, the missionaries and members of indigenous churches viewed religious conversion very differently, as Rozo explains. Evangelists saw themselves as anticolonial because they offered indigenous converts emancipation through religion, whereas their critics saw them as a barrier to modernization because the missionaries limited indigenous mobility and autonomy. Similarly, missionaries viewed conversion as an individual choice, whereas indigenous converts experienced it as a collective process. Catholics and Protestants also disagreed as to whether certain practices should be regarded as cultural or religious, and consequently subject to acceptance or rebuke, such as the evangelical ban on smoking. In describing these doctrinal differences, Rozo foregrounds how the indigenous peoples with whom he worked treated conversion as a means to address the challenges posed to them by colonization and modernity. Establishing themselves as fellow Christians on an equal plane with white settlers was intended to reduce their exposure to uncertainty, exploitation and violence. Rozo persuasively argues that embracing Christianity allowed indigenous communities to become modern on their own terms, helping them achieve a viable way of living in this tumultuous region.

Stuart Kirsch
Professor of Anthropology
University of Michigan

Acknowledgements

Most of the research for this book was undertaken with funding from the Rackham Graduate School at University of Michigan. It was written between Ann Arbor, Buenos Aires and Bogotá. The initial ideas for Remaking Indigeneity in the Amazon came from my PhD dissertation at the graduate program in Anthropology and History at the University of Michigan. In Ann Arbor I want to thank my advisor Stuart Kirsch who gave me insightful and detailed comments on different parts of this book and pushed me to think in innovative ways about my research throughout graduate school. I also want to thank Paul C. Johnson who also read and commented on specific chapters and fostered my interest in the anthropology of Christianity. Julie Skurski, Fernando Coronil and David W. Cohen were always supportive when I was living in Ann Arbor and I greatly benefited from their generosity and commitment to the Anthropology and History graduate program at University of Michigan. I also want to thank Deidre de la Cruz in Ann Arbor for organizing a workshop where the first chapter was discussed. My friends Federico Helfgott, Dan Birchock, Daniel Hershenzon, Davide Orsini, Guillermo Salas, Bertrand Metton, Alejandro Quin, Randall Hicks, Federico Pous and Jennifer Bowles made it easier for me going through graduate school.

In Buenos Aires I want to thank César Ceriani, Pablo Wright and Nicolás Viotti for their interest in my work and for reading and commenting also on different parts of this book. In Buenos Aires I benefited from different workshops and events with the *Red de Estudios de la Diversidad Religiosa en Argentina* (Network for the Study of Religious Diversity in Argentina). Conversations with this wonderful group of colleagues were always useful for my work.

In Bogotá I would like to thank Carlos del Cairo who was generous enough to share with me some of the concepts and ideas I develop in Chapter 5. My colleagues at the School of Human Sciences in Universidad del Rosario were also supportive of this project, especially Thomas Ordoñez who helped me proofread most of the book manuscript. I also want to thank Franz Hensel, Pedro Velandia, Diana Bocarejo, Max Hering and Marisol Grisales who commented on different chapters. The staff at Biblioteca Nacional in

xii *Acknowledgments*

Bogotá was always very helpful. Gonzalo Castro helped me with the pictures that appear in the first chapter and Cristina Céspedes made all the maps that appear in the book.

In Inírida (Guainía) I am grateful to Cristina Ávila and Manuel Romero for their hospitality and support throughout my fieldwork. I would also like to thank Isael Díaz, Tiberio de Jesús Acevedo, Melvino Izquierdo, Mario Jiménez, Manuel and Venancio Tibidor. In Mitú (Vaupés) I am also grateful with Leonardo Caicedo, Monseñor Medardo Henao and Milciades Borrero.

My deepest gratitude goes to my family, to my mother Martha who is not here to read these pages, to my father Camilo and my siblings Juan Camilo and Javier for their continuous support. Ana Guglielmucci pushed me from the beginning to pursue this intellectual project and was always encouraging. Finally, I would like to thank Brill for their permission to use my article that appeared in the journal *Social Sciences and Missions* as Chapter 3 of this book. Part of Chapter 4 was also published in the book *Indigenous Churches. Anthropology of Christianity in Lowland Southamerica*, published by Palgrave Macmillan. I am in debt to the editors of the book César Ceriani, Minna Opas and Élise Capredon for their insightful and useful comments on my chapter.

Introduction

State-making, Missionaries and Indigeneity

This book is a historical ethnography of how indigeneity, Christianity and state-making became intertwined in the Colombian Amazon throughout the 20th century. In 1887 the Colombian government signed the Concordat with Pope Leo XII, reaffirming the ideal of making the country a Catholic nation and state. Indigenous residents of frontier regions, such as the Amazon, were considered underage, child-like subjects, incapable of self-government, and not yet ready to be ruled by the laws of the state.[1] The state thus assigned tutelage over indigenous populations to Catholic missionaries in 1890. During the 20th century, about three-quarters of the national territory in Colombia became "Mission territories" under the jurisdiction of the Catholic Church. Most of these territories were on the margins of the state. In this context, Indigenous groups in Amazonia became wards of the state, and their membership to the nation was shaped through the work of Catholic missionaries.[2]

While there are several historical works that address the role of Catholic missionaries in frontier regions in the Americas during the Colonial period, scholars have given less attention to the role religious missions played in post-colonial states in Latin America *vis-à-vis* frontier formation and the incorporation of Indigenous groups into the nation-state.[3] This study addresses the role of Catholic and evangelical missionaries in processes of state-making, focusing on how missionaries crafted representations of the Indigenous societies they encountered in Amazonia, as well as ideas and practices about how those groups were supposed to be governed or included into the body politic. Yet even though missionaries claimed to be "governing savages" and "reducing" them to civilized life, they had to rely on native Amazonians who already spoke Spanish and had some familiarity with foreigners for their work. Catholic and evangelical missionaries were crucial in producing ideas about native Amazonians, mediating the relationships between Indigenous communities and the state.

This study focuses on the frontier region of Vaupés and Guainía in the Colombian Amazon. During the Colonial period, both the Spanish and

DOI: 10.4324/9781003370215-1

2 Introduction

Portuguese empires claimed this area, and it was still under dispute between Colombia, Brazil and Venezuela in the 20th century. This region includes the contemporary Colombian provinces of Vaupés, Guaviare and Guainía, where the Upper Rio Negro and Upper Orinoco Basin coincide (see Map I.1).[4] Greater Vaupés has been historically inhabited by different Indigenous groups of Arawak, Maku and Tucano descent. To this day, there are no roads that connect the interior of the country to the capitals of these provinces, and it is only possible to get there by river or plane. This book explores how Catholic and evangelical missionaries in the Colombian Amazon were key in remaking indigeneity in the context of the expansion of national societies into "Indigenous lands that the nascent republics claimed as their jurisdictions."[5] Catholic missionaries were crucial in how state sovereignty was displayed in the province of Vaupés, where rubber extraction was already taking place using Indigenous labor and where the border was under dispute with Brazil.

Since the beginning of the 20th century, Catholic missionaries participated in the making and "nationalization" of frontier regions and their inhabitants in the Colombian Amazon. As part of this process, they resettled Indigenous populations in Vaupés and taught them about Colombia's history and culture. Catholic missionaries were crucial in expanding national

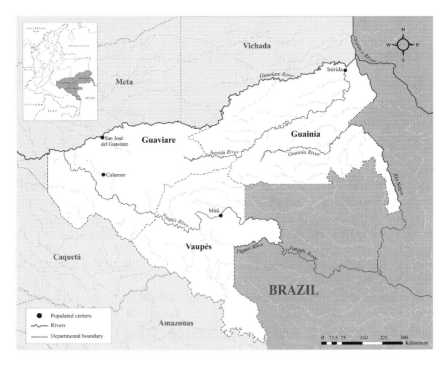

Map I.1 Region of the Upper Rio Negro and the provinces of Vaupés, Guaviare and Guainía.

Introduction 3

sovereignty in these territories to the extent that they disputed the location of the border with Brazilian authorities and fellow missionaries brought by the Brazilian government. The defense of state borders became associated with the establishment of boarding schools for Indigenous children. For most Indigenous groups in the Amazon region there was a thin line between embracing Catholicism and becoming Colombians. Catholic Missionaries developed a particular strand of patriotism that combined love for the country with Catholic devotion.

Starting in the 1940s, evangelical missionaries affiliated to New Tribes Mission (NTM) traveled to Vaupés and began to challenge the authority of Catholic missionaries, as well as the moral standards of settlers and state functionaries. Evangelical missionaries developed the first alphabets of Indigenous languages such as Curripaco and Puinave, translated the New Testament into these languages and unleashed a massive process of conversion to evangelical Christianity among different Indigenous groups. Unlike Catholic missionaries that built mission towns, evangelical missionaries lived in the Indigenous communities they wanted to convert and shared the idea that "going native" was part of their work as missionaries. New Tribes missionaries firmly believed that translating the New Testament into all unknown Indigenous languages was a necessary condition to bring about the second coming of Christ. This book shows how evangelical Christianity shaped new forms of indigeneity that were different from those Catholic missionaries disseminated and did not coincide entirely with the ideas of civilization or development that the state promoted in the region.

I attempt to historicize and problematize Indigenous conversion to Christianity, paying close attention to how its meaning and function has changed over time for missionaries, state agents, settlers and Indigenous evangelicals.[6] The book describes how evangelization can also be understood as a process of cultural and political mediation. In this case, Indigenous evangelists created a new kind of indigeneity associated with specific transformations in "traditional culture." They also tied these forms of indigeneity to changes in the relationship between their societies and settlers. I thus pay special attention to the role of local agents (such as "Indigenous evangelists" or native Christians) in processes of religious and social change.[7]

Specifically, this book analyzes what happens when Christianity is not always subordinated to colonization (state-led colonization, in this case). In the Colombian Amazon, the fact that evangelical missionaries were not part of the nation-state (whose official religion was Catholicism, since 1886) caused frictions with settlers and local state functionaries. Beginning in the 1960s, conflicts between Indigenous evangelicals and state officials transformed Indigenous conversion to evangelical Christianity into a political issue for the Colombian government. This fact raises questions about the relationships between colonization, Christianity and indigeneity. Christianity was crucial to how state power unfolded in the Colombian Amazon region but also informed emergent notions of indigeneity that challenged, to some extent,

4 *Introduction*

state authority. In this sense, I explore how Indigenous societies appropriated evangelical Christianity in order to navigate the changes brought on by colonization, state-formation and modernity.

The relationships that Indigenous evangelicals established with state officials and settlers were complex and ambivalent. While Indigenous evangelicals developed moral critiques regarding the behavior of state officials, they also started to incorporate the language of the state in terms of specific rights and demands to which state authorities were expected to respond. Evangelical missionaries and Indigenous evangelicals also developed a moral understanding of modernity through the idea of "worldliness" (*the mundane*), condemning specific practices such as the possession of material things or "vices" like smoking, drinking or dancing.

In the English speaking world, the word indigeneity is of recent appearance, specifically as a legal and juridical term during the Cold War era.[8] In Latin America, since "the wars of independence, the figure of the Indian was variously employed" in the construction of different states created after the end of Spanish rule.[9] Throughout the 20th-century *indigenismo* (indigenism) became a main concern for several intellectuals and politicians in Latin America. Debates about *indigenismo* were first about the incorporation of "Indian peoples into nation-states" and later about the defense of Indigenous cultures and rights within the context of multicultural reforms in different countries.[10] *Indigenismo* in Latin America made explicit the relationship between state-making and indigeneity in countries such as Mexico, Perú and Colombia. Since the 1920s, all these countries saw intense debates among intellectuals and politicians in the public sphere regarding the meaning of "Indigenousness" and how it related to national building and identity.

I draw here on the idea that indigeneity can be considered a relational category which acquires "its 'positive' meaning not from essential properties of its own, but through its relation to what it is not, to what it exceeds or lacks."[11] Without "natural boundaries" of any sort, the notion of indigeneity is related to the idea that "Indigenous cultural practices, institutions, and politics become such in articulation with what is not considered Indigenous within [a] particular social formation."[12] Who counts as Indigenous and what this means in Latin America varies according to specific historical and national contexts. In this regard, Argentinian anthropologist Rita Segato argues that each nation-state in Latin America developed specific "national formations of alterity."[13] Segato defines a national formation of alterity as a hegemonic "matrix of othering" that works through different discursive and material practices that define who counts as "other" or "indigenous."[14] These narratives of otherness, according to Segato, produced by the state become engrained in national culture, as well as appropriated from below by subaltern groups.

This book therefore emphasizes that indigeneity is forged through changing relationships between different actors who make different claims about its meaning. Recent scholarship shows that indigeneity "is not a new invention, with a clearly defined meaning and scope, and related to a well-crafted set

Introduction 5

of rights, but rather that it has been used in many different ways by various actors."[15] In the context of the Colombian Amazon, missionaries, rubber bosses, state officials, settlers, traders and teachers deployed specific ideas about who native Amazonians were and should be. Indigenous communities were also part of how indigeneity was constructed and practiced in Amazonia. In fact, this study analyzes how the meanings and nature of indigeneity in the Colombian Amazon were under dispute between different actors, including Indigenous communities. In this context, indigeneity was configured through the appropriation of Christianity and through the interactions of Indigenous societies with different projects of civilization and modernity embodied in specific actors and practices.

Frontiers and Colonization in the Amazon Region

Although some American historians have said that: "Latin American nations are 'frontier societies' lacking a frontier myth;"[16] this study furthers Margarita Serje's idea that a frontier myth in Colombia and Latin America exists but this does not fit idealized visions about the colonization of the American West. For Serje, the frontier myth in Latin America, crafted by political geographers and national elites since the 19th century, is associated with the chimeric and utopian visions projected upon frontier regions.[17] Simón Uribe also points out that frontiers are part of state-building discourses and practices in Latin America, and these are shaped by relationships of inclusive exclusion.[18] I address here processes of frontier formation in the Amazon region, analyzing the role that missionaries, settlers, indigenous communities and agents of the state played in them.

I question definitions of the state that only consider it a "rationalized administrative form of political organization that becomes weakened or less fully articulated along its territorial or social margins."[19] Veena Das and Deborah Poole point out how the state also constructs its own hegemony through the production of its own peripheries and margins.[20] In fact, frontiers, such as the Amazon region, can also be used as off-centered locations of analysis that enable us to track "vernacular" invocations and materializations of state power, no matter how mundane or transcendent these might be.[21] Frontiers are also places of "fractionated sovereignty" where there is a "dispersal of official state functions among various non-state actors" and different actors "perform as the state" and state power acquires unorthodox forms.[22] In the case of the Amazon region where this study takes place, different actors including Catholic missionaries, rubber bosses and settlers (*colonos*) on both sides of the border "performed as the state" and disputed the control over Indigenous populations, as well as the access to different resources that include rubber and, more recently, gold.

Colonización among Spanish speaking countries in Latin America usually refers to "the expansion of agricultural frontiers and the creation of settlements in previously uncultivated lands."[23] However, as historian Nancy

6 Introduction

Appelbaum has pointed out, translating *colonización* as "colonization" is somewhat misleading, because "the strictly agricultural definition of colonization is no longer the most common one used in English."[24] Frederick Cooper argues that the Greek and Roman origins of the word colonization, which is derived from the Latin word *colere*, meaning "to cultivate" or "to put to use," has retained significance into the 20th century, but the "principal meaning of colonization has come to involve people rather than land: coercive incorporation into an expansionist state and invidious distinction."[25]

I want to take advantage here of the different meanings of the word colonization in Spanish and English and associate the term with both the expansion of the "internal" agricultural frontier and state sovereignty through the incorporation of specific populations to the rule of the state. In Latin America, there is a close relationship between colonization and the expansion of state sovereignty into frontier regions and between colonization and the expansion of the "internal" agricultural frontier. In some cases, as historian Tamar Herzog points out, having the control of "external frontiers" was a way of having control over populations and territories that were internal to these frontiers.[26] While national elites had a blind faith on the *Uti possidetis iure principle* which entailed that the "newly born republics would preserve the colonial limits at the time of independence."[27] The *Uti possidetis de facto* (based on the actual control and occupation of territory) acquired importance throughout the 20th century as part of political and territorial conflicts between nations that claimed sovereignty upon different parts of the Amazon region.

In the case of Vaupés, the Colombian government combined or allowed different modes of colonization. In addition to the tutelage of Indigenous populations, since the Convention of Missions of 1902, signed with the Vatican, Catholic missionaries were given a new duty they did not have before: the defense of national borders. Missionaries established mission towns (*reducciones*) and boarding schools along the border, as a way of enacting state sovereignty on the territories under dispute with Brazil. This civilizing model of giving the governance and tutelage of Indigenous populations and the territories in which they lived to Catholic missionaries was combined, in the Amazon region, with a model of colonization based on granting concessions of huge amounts of land to companies or individuals that extracted rubber. The central government provided concessions to rubber entrepreneurs over large areas of land considered to be *terrenos baldíos* (or "empty land").[28] During the first rubber boom, Catholic missionaries had to compete with rubber bosses for Indigenous labor and loyalty. After evangelical missionaries arrived in the region in the 1940s, the state took the conversion of Indigenous communities to evangelical Christianity as an obstacle to the work of settlers or *colonos* who also depended on Indigenous labor to extract different natural resources. Protestantism was socially perceived as a risk to the authority of Catholic missionaries and a problem for the colonization of the region. Evangelical missionaries were accused of teaching converts not to work for white patrons and of limiting the capacity

Introduction 7

of Indigenous evangelicals to trade and accumulate commodities. During the 1960s, an indigenist bureaucracy replaced, to some extent, the Catholic missionaries as agents or intermediaries of the state in the Amazon region.[29] This bureaucracy tried to adapt development programs and policies to the cultural practices and realities of indigenous communities, producing a kind of developmental indigenism.

Frontiers in Amazonia were not only sites of conflict regarding the "use, rights, and definitions of territory and resources among distinct social groups,"[30] but also sites where competing claims to rule indigenous societies collided. In the midst of this conflictive process, Indigenous societies combined their own forms of government or political organization with those brought by missionaries and the state. The actors involved in conflicts about the government and civilization of native Amazonians changed their allegiances and position over time showing how there was no necessary correspondence or coherence between different projects of colonization and evangelization in the region. In fact, colonization should not be understood as a "monolithic and coherent process," it can include contradictory moments and frictions between different actors.[31] This book shows how the expansion of state power, the work of missionaries and the demand for raw materials or minerals (such as rubber and gold) shaped the lives and landscapes of those that live in the Colombian Amazon region.

Order of the Book

The first chapter of this book analyzes the role played by Catholic missionaries in the frontier-making process in the Upper Rio Negro, where knowledge of the region was scarce, and borders were contested with Brazil. Specifically, Montfort missionaries in Vaupés associated the control of Indigenous groups dwelling on the Papurí River with displaying state sovereignty on the border between Colombia and Brazil. This chapter shows how Montfort missionaries tried to consolidate tutelage (given to missionaries by Law 89 of 1890) over "not yet civilized" Indigenous populations, once again using the colonial practice of establishing *reducciones* (mission towns), but in a postcolonial context. The establishment of *reducciones* along the border was the easiest way –according to Montfort missionaries – to "civilize" and "nationalize" Indigenous groups. Despite this, missionaries had to rely on native Amazonians who already spoke Spanish and had some familiarity with foreigners for their work. These missionaries had to adapt their strategies of evangelization to local practices and realities in order to articulate the authority the state had granted them. For example, given that there were no centralized forms of political organization among Indigenous groups, Montfort missionaries had to establish several mission towns, each one with its own "chief." Finally, this chapter shows how trying to make Indigenous populations "Colombian" did not entail their cultural assimilation, but rather that processes of frontier making were entangled with the production of "new"

8 *Introduction*

forms of difference and specific representations of indigeneity. For instance, missionaries represented native Amazonians as "tribes" who had no history, no writing, and whose language and "features" were of Asian origin.

The second chapter of this book analyzes how the conversion to evangelical Christianity of Indigenous groups in the Colombian Amazon became a political problem for the state in the region. In Colombia during the Cold War, Protestantism was often regarded as a near relative of communism and was considered a threat to "national Colombian unity." The first part of the chapter describes the social milieu and ideas that gave birth to institutions such as the SIL and NTM. Both organizations were interested in getting to "unreached tribes" and translating the New Testament into unknown Indigenous languages to bring about the second coming of Christ. Through the establishment of Indigenous churches and the training of Indigenous pastors, NTM missionaries created new senses of community and indigeneity. Specifically, this chapter focuses on the work of American missionary Sophie Muller, affiliated to NTM, who traveled to Vaupés in the 1940s, and the frictions her work caused among different actors. The second part of the chapter shows how Catholic missionaries from Mitú (Vaupés) closely followed and tracked the work of evangelical missionaries such as Sophie Muller. Evangelical Christianity represented a challenge to the Catholic Church, whose authority over Indigenous groups came from the state. The state also considered the work of Sophie Muller a political threat to the point that the national intelligence agency carried out an investigation to verify the "activities" of both the SIL and Muller. State officials viewed the authority and control that Muller gained over Indigenous populations as a challenge to state authority in the region. Despite the moral critiques made by Indigenous evangelicals of the behavior of state officials, the former started to incorporate the language of the state that was associated with specific rights and demands.

The third chapter of the book explores the *politics of conversion* in Guainía, comparing missionary narratives of conversion with Indigenous accounts of the same process. It describes how, since the 1940s, conversion to Christianity has articulated new meanings and practices of indigeneity in the region. While academic explanations tend to view evangelical conversion as a rupture (and not just among Indigenous groups), this chapter shows that neither the missionaries nor the Indigenous populations in Guainía viewed conversion as rupture alone. Although they recognized the transformational process involved in conversion, they both emphasized cultural continuity, albeit for different reasons. This chapter explores how most accounts of the massive conversion of Indigenous communities to evangelical Christianity have explained it as a messianic phenomenon, suggesting that Indigenous communities viewed Sophie Muller, the first evangelical missionary to arrive to the region, as a messiah, echoing earlier messianic movements in the region during the mid-19th century. Little attention has been paid to Indigenous narratives of conversion and how they relate to missionaries' accounts of conversion and contemporary discourses of indigeneity. This chapter questions

Introduction 9

explanations of Indigenous conversion as a simple assimilation process ("becoming white"), revealing how ideas and practices of conversion articulated new forms of being and becoming "Indian" in Guainía. Finally, this chapter shows that a rupture-continuity dichotomy falls short of explaining the kinds of transformations involved in the emergence of what I call here Christian indigeneity. I analyze how Indigenous leaders and missionaries used and combined narratives of cultural change and continuity in strategic ways. These uses shape a specific *politics of* conversion which, in turn, postulate strong complementarities between Christianity and Indigenous values.

The fourth chapter of this book analyzes how different views of materiality reveal different understandings and relationships to modernity, closely associated with ideas about civilization (for Catholic missionaries) and/or "worldliness" (for Indigenous evangelicals). Specifically, this chapter describes how Indigenous evangelicals in the Colombian Amazon developed particular ideas about materiality and how these shaped their perception and use of different objects and commodities. It was common for evangelical missionaries to associate the use of certain objects or instruments among Indigenous communities with demon worship, while the possession of commodities was related to "worldliness." The evangelical critique of materiality was developed on two fronts: the destruction of objects that were used in shamanic practices or traditional rituals and the restriction of material possessions or the accumulation of commodities.

While Catholic missionaries in Vaupés relied heavily on commodities and material objects for their work, evangelical missionaries affiliated to NTM tried to restrict practices of object and commodity accumulation among Indigenous Christians, arguing that things or possessions would "tether them" and limit their agency. In a similar vein, Indigenous evangelicals and churches among the Curripaco and Puinave groups in Guainía developed an ongoing critique of materiality through the idea of "worldliness" (*lo mundano*), producing a selective appropriation of modernity. "Worldliness" is related to both material things (money, radios, etc.) and specific deeds, thoughts or desires. This chapter shows how Indigenous evangelicals were not so much concerned with the possessions of material things as such, but more so with the values and attitudes that certain objects or technologies might help to disseminate.

The last chapter of the book explores how the intermediary role of Catholic missionaries for the state in frontier regions such as Amazonia became less important and was ultimately replaced by an indigenist bureaucracy that formed part of the frontier state apparatus. Since the 1950s, this indigenist bureaucracy started to use the notion of "social integration" to design developmental policies aimed at simultaneously "protecting Indigenous culture" and promoting development projects among Indigenous communities. After the 1960s, state policies directed toward Indigenous communities in the Amazon became concerned with cultural difference and adapted to local realities, while Indigenous communities began to demand access to development plans, health

10 *Introduction*

services and lessons in the Spanish language. The notion of "developmental indigenism" entailed a new relationship between the state and Indigenous communities in which the former adapted its policies to "Indigenous customs" and the latter demanded access to development and material improvement.

The second part of this chapter looks at how, since the 1990s, small-scale gold mining has become a source of revenue for Indigenous communities and settlers who came with their families to the region from inland areas. More specifically, this last section analyzes recent transformations in how the state represents, names and controls informal mining in the region, as well as the social and environmental conflicts derived from gold mining. It also describes the relationships, agreements and interactions between miners and *indígenas* that make informal mining in Guainía possible, as well as the contradictions of formalization programs and state policies that render the former unviable. Finally, the chapter explores how gold mining and state policies designed to control gold extraction have reshaped the relationships and subjectivities of the miners and *indígenas* who partake in these activities.

Notes

1 Víctor D. Bonilla, *Siervos de Dios y amos de indios. El Estado y la Misión Capuchina en el Putumayo* (Cali: Editorial Universidad del Cauca, 1968).
2 In his critique of Benedict Anderson's theorization of nationalism, Claudio Lomnitz argues that bonds of dependence are equally important as fraternal ties in the making of an imagined community. Specifically, Lomnitz analyzes how subordinated groups such as women, children, slaves or ethnic communities shaped their membership to the nation through bonds of dependence with "full citizens" who become potential brokers between the national state and embryonic, weak or part citizens that are constructed as dependents. See Claudio Lomnitz, *Deep Mexico, Silent Mexico. An Anthropology of Nationalism* (Minneapolis: University of Minnesota Press, 2001), 11.
3 The role of Catholic missionaries in post-colonial Latin America has been addressed by different historians, see Víctor D. Bonilla, *Siervos de Dios y amos de indios. El Estado y la Misión Capuchina en el Putumayo* (Cali: Editorial Universidad del Cauca, 1968); Pilar García Jordán and Núria Sala i Vila, *La nacionalización de la Amazonía* (Barcelona: Universitat de Barcelona, 1998); Erick Langer, *Expecting Pears from an Elm Tree. Franciscan Missions on the Chiriguano Frontier in the Heart of South America, 1830–1949* (Durham: Duke University Press, 2009).
4 The *comisaria* (province) of Vaupés was created in 1910 by the Colombian government, it's capital was initially Calamar in what today is the province of Guaviare, but was later moved to Mitú in 1935 because it was closer to the border with Brazil. Before Vaupés was made a separate administrative unit of government, it was part of the territory of Caquetá since 1845. The Colombian Amazon includes six provinces or *departamentos*: Putumayo, Caquetá, Amazonas, Vaupés, Guaviare and Guainía. These provinces are located in the South and Southeastern parts of the country. The province of Guainía was separated from Vaupés in 1963 and the province of Guaviare in 1977. This work focuses on the area which comprises the provinces of Vaupés and Guainía today.
5 Erick Langer, *Expecting Pears from an Elm Tree. Franciscan Missions on the Chiriguano Frontier in the Heart of South America, 1830–1949* (Durham: Duke University Press, 2009), 1.

Introduction 11

6 The word used in Spanish when people refer to Protestant Christians is *evangélico* (evangelical). The term *evangélico* has a negative connotation in Latin American countries where most of the population is still Catholic.

7 Peggy Brock, ed. *Indigenous Peoples and Religious Change* (Leiden: Brill, 2005); Peggy Brock, Norman Etherington, Gareth Griffiths, Jacqueline Van Gent, eds. *Indigenous Evangelists and Questions of Authority in the British Empire 1750–1940* (Leiden: Brill, 2015); Aparecida Vilaça and Robin M. Wright, eds. *Native Christians. Modes and Effects of Christianity among Indigenous Peoples of the Americas* (Farnham: Ashgate, 2009).

8 Jean Jackson points out that the word indigeneity appeared recently, but the history of indianness and attempts to dramatize and appropriate it is long, see Jean Jackson, *Managing Multiculturalism. Indigeneity and the Struggle for Rights in Colombia* (Stanford: Stanford University Press, 2019), 22.

9 Rebecca Earle, *The Return of the Native. Indians and Myth-Making in Spanish America, 1810–1930* (Durham: Duke University Press, 2007), 2.

10 Andrés A. Fábregas Puig, *El Indigenismo en América Latina* (México: El Colegio de México, 2021).

11 Marisol de la Cadena and Orin Starn, eds., *Indigenous Experience Today* (Oxford: Berg, 2007).

12 Ibid,

13 Rita Laura Segato, *La nación y sus otros. Raza, etnicidad y diversidad religiosa en tiempos de Políticas de la Identidad* (Buenos Aires: Prometeo Libros, 2007).

14 Ibid, 29.

15 Eva Gerharz, Nasir Uddin and Pradeep Chakkarath, "Exploring Indigeneity: Introductory Remarks on a Contested Concept," in *Indigeneity on the Move. Varying Manifestations of a Contested Concept*, eds. Eva Gerharz, Nasir Uddin and Pradeep Chakkarath (New York: Berghahn, 2018), 3.

16 Alistair Hennessy, *The Frontier in Latin American History* (New Mexico: University of New Mexico Press, 1978), 3.

17 Margarita Serje, *El revés de la nación: territorios salvajes, fronteras y tierras de nadie* (Bogotá: Ed. Uniandes, 2005).

18 Uribe, Simón. *Frontier Road: Power, History, and the Everyday State in the Colombian Amazon* (Hoboken: John Wiley & Sons, 2017).

19 Veena Das and Deborah Poole, "State and Its Margins: Comparative Ethnographies," in *Anthropology in the Margins of the State*, eds. Veena Das and Deborah Poole (Santa Fe: School of American Research, 2004), 3.

20 Ibid.

21 Christopher Krupa and David Nugent, "Off-Centered States: Rethinking State Theory Through an Andean Lens," in *State Theory and Andean Politics. New Approaches to the Study of Rule*, eds. Christopher Krupa and David Nugent (Philadelphia: University of Pennsylvania Press, 2015), 5.

22 Ibid, 319–320.

23 Nancy Appelbaum, *Muddied Waters: Race, Region, and Local History in Colombia, 1846–1948* (Durham: Duke University Press, 2003 12).

24 Ibid.

25 Frederick Cooper, *Colonialism in Question. Theory, Knowledge and History* (Berkeley: University of California Press, 2005), 27.

26 Tamar Herzog, *Frontiers of Possession. Spain and Portugal in Europe and the Americas* (Cambridge: Harvard University Press, 2015).

27 Simón Uribe, *Frontier Road. Power, History, and the Everyday State in the Colombian Amazon* (Oxford: Wiley Blackwell, 2017), 33.

28 The notion of "empty territories" can be related to earlier notions that were common in international law such as the notion of *terra nullius* that circulated in the 18th century. According to Whatmore, the legal doctrine of *terra nullius*,

12 *Introduction*

which translates literally as "no one's land," legitimized the "annexation of 'uninhabited lands' by settlement as an acknowledged means, alongside conquest and secession, for the proper conduct of colonization by 'civilized' nations." In the case of Colombia, the national government established the existence *territorios baldíos* in frontier regions, and these "empty territories" were adjudicated to specific citizens under specific conditions, see Sarah Whatmore, *Hybrid Geographies, Natures, Cultures, Spaces* (London: Sage Publications, 2002), 63–64 and Catherine LeGrand, *Colonización y protesta campesina en Colombia 1850–1950* (Bogotá: Universidad Nacional de Colombia, 1988), 32–33.

29 Jean Jackson points out that in 1962 the Catholic Church lost its official monopoly over indigenous education with the signing of a contract between the Ministry of Government and the Summer Institute of Linguistics (SIL), see Jean Jackson, *Managing Multiculturalism. Indigeneity and the Struggle for Rights in Colombia* (Stanford: Stanford University Press), 31.

30 Seth Garfield, *In Search of the Amazon: Brazil, the United States, and the Nature of a Region* (Durham: Duke University Press, 2013), 1.

31 John L Comaroff, "Reflections on the Colonial State, in South Africa and Elsewhere: Factions, Fragments, Facts and Fictions," *Social Identities*, 4, no. 3 (1988): 321–361.

References

Appelbaum, Nancy. *Muddied Waters: Race, Region, and Local History in Colombia, 1846–1948*. Durham: Duke University Press, 2003.

Bonilla, Víctor D. *Siervos de Dios y amos de indios. el Estado y la Misión Capuchina en el Putumayo*. Cali: Editorial Universidad del Cauca, 1968.

Brock, Peggy, ed. *Indigenous Peoples and Religious Change*. Leiden: Brill, 2005.

Brock, Peggy, Norman Etherington, Gareth Griffiths, and Jacqueline Van Gent, eds. *Indigenous Evangelists and Questions of Authority in the British Empire 1750–1940*. Leiden: Brill, 2015.

Comaroff, John L. "Reflections on the Colonial State, in South Africa and Elsewhere: Factions, Fragments, Facts and Fictions." *Social Identities* 4, no. 3 (1988): 321–361.

Cooper, Frederick. *Colonialism in Question. Theory, Knowledge and History*. Berkeley: University of California Press, 2005.

Das, Veena, and Deborah Poole. "State and Its Margins: Comparative Ethnographies." In *Anthropology in the Margins of the State*, edited by Veena Das and Deborah Poole, 3–33. Santa Fe: School of American Research, 2004.

De la Cadena, Marisol, and Orin Starn, eds. *Indigenous Experience Today*. Oxford: Berg, 2007.

Earle, Rebecca. *The Return of the Native. Indians and Myth-Making in Spanish America, 1810–1930*. Durham: Duke University Press, 2007.

Fábregas Puig, Andrés A. *El Indigenismo en América Latina*. México: El Colegio de México, 2021.

García Jordán, Pilar, and Núria Sala i Vila, eds. *La nacionalización de la Amazonía*. Barcelona: Universitat de Barcelona, 1998.

Garfield, Seth. *In Search of the Amazon: Brazil, the United States, and the Nature of a Region*. Durham: Duke University Press, 2013.

Gerharz, Eva, Nasir Uddin, Pradeep Chakkarath, and Pradeep Chakkarath. "Exploring Indigeneity: Introductory Remarks on a Contested Concept." In *Indigeneity on the*

Move. Varying Manifestations of a Contested Concept, edited by Eva Gerharz and Nasir Uddin, 1–25. New York: Berghahn, 2018.

Hennessy, Alistair. *The Frontier in Latin American History*. New Mexico: University of New Mexico Press, 1978. 3.

Herzog, Tamar. *Frontiers of Possession. Spain and Portugal in Europe and the Americas*. Cambridge: Harvard University Press, 2015.

Jackson, Jean. *Managing Multiculturalism. Indigeneity and the Struggle for Rights in Colombia*. Stanford: Stanford University Press, 2019.

Krupa, Christopher, and David Nugent. "Off-Centered States: Rethinking State Theory Through an Andean Lens." In *State Theory and Andean Politics. New Approaches to the Study of Rule*, edited by Christopher Krupa and David Nugent, 1–31. Philadelphia: University of Pennsylvania Press, 2015.

Langer, Erick. *Expecting Pears from an Elm Tree. Franciscan Missions on the Chiriguano Frontier in the Heart of South America, 1830–1949*. Durham: Duke University Press, 2009.

LeGrand, Catherine. *Colonización y protesta campesina en Colombia 1850–1950*. Bogotá: Universidad Nacional de Colombia, 1988.

Lomnitz, Claudio. *Deep Mexico, Silent Mexico. An Anthropology of Nationalism*. Minneapolis: University of Minnesota Press, 2001.

Segato, Laura. *La nación y sus otros. Raza, etnicidad y diversidad religiosa en tiempos de Políticas de la Identidad*. Buenos Aires: Prometeo Libros, 2007.

Serje, Margarita. *El revés de la nación: territorios salvajes, fronteras y tierras de nadie*. Bogotá: Ediciones Uniandes, 2011.

Uribe, Simón. *Frontier Road: Power, History, and the Everyday State in the Colombian Amazon*. Hoboken: John Wiley & Sons, 2017.

Vilaça, Aparecida, and Robin M. Wright, eds. *Native Christians. Modes and Effects of Christianity among Indigenous Peoples of the Americas*. Farnham: Ashgate, 2009.

Whatmore, Sarah. *Hybrid Geographies, Natures, Cultures, Spaces*. London: Sage Publications, 2002.

1 The Making of an Amazonian Frontier

(…) the Indian, himself, doesn't have a fatherland. It is the fatherland who will adopt him and promote in his heart the love towards her.[1]

As happened before in the colonial period, during the 19th century in Latin America, "external frontiers vis-à-vis neighbors appeared before internal frontiers of occupation were possessed and integrated," making the control of "external frontiers" a way of having control over populations and territories that were internal to them, yet "hardly formed part of their polities."[2] In the case of Amazonia, at the beginning of the 20th century, there were still borders and regions in dispute between Colombia, Ecuador, Perú, Bolivia and Brazil. In fact, some of these disputes ended up in military confrontations as happened during the Acre war between Brazil and Bolivia (1899–1902) or the military conflict between Colombia and Perú in 1932.[3] At the beginning of the 20th century, Latin American countries were still defining the exact location of their borders in Amazonia.

This chapter analyzes the role played by Montfort missionaries in the process of frontier and boundary making in the region of the Upper Rio Negro where knowledge of this region was scarce and the borders were contested with Brazil. Since the Convention of Missions of 1902 signed with the Holy See, the Colombian government gave a new duty to Catholic missionaries that they had not had before: the defense of national borders. Here, I will show how Montfort missionaries in Vaupés associated the control of Indigenous groups that dwelled in the Papurí River with displaying state sovereignty on the border. Most of the Indigenous groups that lived there practiced linguistic exogamy, moved across national borders and lived dispersed in *malocas* (big houses).[4] Montfort missionaries tried to consolidate the sovereignty of the state and the tutelage over "not civilized yet" Indigenous populations (given to missionaries in law 89, 1890), once again using the colonial practice of establishing *reducciones* (mission towns), but in a postcolonial context. Indeed, the first *reducción* that Montfort missionaries established in Vaupés was compared by them, in 1922, with a small medieval town, with two monasteries of "manor appearance," one each side of the "house of God."[5]

DOI: 10.4324/9781003370215-2

The Making of an Amazonian Frontier   15

While the principle of *Uti possidetis iure* was based on jurisdictions and territorial possessions determined by law and treaties, the *Uti possidetis de facto* was based on the actual control and occupation of territory. During the 19th century, the principle of *Uti possidetis iure legal* entailed that the "newly born republics would preserve the colonial limits at the time of independence."[6] However, as it was described in the previous chapter, the boundaries between the former colonies were not clear in regions such as the Amazon. This facilitated the "*de facto* appropriation of territories in dispute."[7] Throughout the 19th century and part of the 20th century, the state and the elites in charge of it had a blind faith on the *Uti possidetis iure principle*.

Even if Montfort missionaries claimed to be "governing savages" and "reducing" them to civilized life, they had to rely on native Amazonians that already spoke Spanish and had some familiarity with foreigners for their work. Such foreigners included European and American expeditioners, as well as Brazilian traders, rubber bosses and officials. The success of Montfort missionaries hinged on previous experiences of colonization and evangelization. Catholic missionaries in Vaupés saw their work as a "moral defense" of the border [*frontera*] of Colombia and as part of an effort to bring the nation, "Christian civilization" and modernity to the far-reaching places of the Republic such as the Amazon jungle.

Reducción was a comprehensive project aimed at "coordinating transformations of space, conduct and language," keeping natives in a fixed place of residence in order to properly convert and civilize them.[8] As part of Convention of Missions signed in 1902, Dutch and French missionaries started to establish mission towns and boarding schools on the Papurí River, closer to Brazil than to the interior of the country. This river was located at two or three months of distance from Bogotá and marked part of the border under dispute with Brazil. Montfort missionaries thought that establishing *reducciones* along the border was the easiest way to "civilize" and "nationalize" Indigenous groups. In this sense, defending the national border implied resettling Indigenous populations that lived in the area, as well as transforming Indigenous housing patterns, kinship rules and supervising labor relation between rubber bosses and natives. The role of missionaries as Protectors of the Indians [*Protector de los Indios*], an official post created in Vaupés initially in 1916, mediated the authority of the state and the relationships between Indigenous communities and rubber bosses.[9] Missionaries could intervene in the "contracts" established between rubber bosses and Indigenous rubber tappers and could prevent "the *indígenas* from being taken to work in *caucheras* [rubber fields]."[10] This authority given to missionaries brought frictions and conflicts with rubber bosses on both sides of the border.

At the same time, Montfort missionaries had to adapt their strategies of evangelization to local practices and realities in order to articulate the authority the state had given them. Similar to rubber bosses, missionaries had to "seduce" and recruit natives giving them objects and commodities as gifts.

16   *The Making of an Amazonian Frontier*

Given that there were no centralized forms of political organization among Indigenous groups, Montfort missionaries also had to establish several mission towns, each one with its own "chief." Missionaries wanted each mission town or *reducción* to coincide with a specific "tribe," but this never happened, in part because of marriage rules based on linguistic exogamy. Different language groups could live in a single mission town. Missionaries also had to confront the burning of *malocas* and chapels by natives from Brazil, as happened in 1919 when a fire brought down the chapel in Montfort-Papurí (the first mission town established in 1914).

As part of the project of nationalizing regions and Indigenous groups on the margins of the nation, missionaries developed a kind of Catholic patriotism in which God and nation were synonyms, and sacrifice for the fatherland became a Christian virtue. God was defined as "the great provider and author of everything that existed," and the nation as "a novelty of God," whose independence had to be defended. Furthermore, missionaries' Catholic patriotism fostered the performance of public rituals that were simultaneously religious and civic. Spatial practices of sovereignty associated with the resettlement of Indigenous populations were complemented with the public performance of sovereign power. The performance of sovereignty included the renaming or baptism of places and planting a huge cross in each mission town established, as well as processions, public rituals, singing the national anthem and raising the flag. These public rituals were similar to the "ceremonies of possession" Europeans used during the Conquest of the New World as symbolic performances of their "right to rule."[11] However, Montfort missionaries' public rituals did not have a military counterpart, as did the early modern "ceremonies of possession" of the New World.

Sovereignty, in this context, needed to be "*performed* and reiterated on a daily basis in order to be effective."[12] Practices of evangelization also included the performance of everyday routines and repetition of several acts associated with praying, discipline and obedience to God and the nation. These repetitive acts were also documented in pictures that missionaries took of Indigenous children in which they appear dressed, working or raising the national flag. Native Amazonians that lived in mission towns participated actively in both public performances and everyday routines.

Finally, this chapter shows how trying to make Indigenous populations "Colombian" did not entail their cultural assimilation, even if missionaries thought they could be future soldiers of the nation. Missionaries not only translated parts of the Bible into languages such as Tucano and made Catechisms in Indigenous languages, but also framed indigeneity drawing upon evolutionary anthropological categories that circulated at the time. Missionaries represented native Amazonians as "tribes" who had no history, no writing and whose language and "factions" had an Asian origin.[13] Missionaries also deployed "religion" or the absence of it, as a comparative category used to describe and represent Indigenous "culture" and difference as inferior.[14]

The Making of an Amazonian Frontier   17

As Jonathan Z. Smith points out, in colonial encounters, religion, more than a theological category, works as an anthropological category.[15] This meant that religion serves as a comparative category to establish differences and hierarchies between Europeans and non-Europeans, including distinctions between true religion and false religion. Religion was used to recognize and classify different "nations" or "peoples." The distinction between "our religion/ their religion" became crucial in the encounter between Catholic missionaries and Amazonian Indigenous groups, with the latter "often expressed through generic terms such as 'heathenism,' 'paganism,' or 'idolatry.'"[16] Moreover, the writings of missionaries reveal how processes of frontier making were entangled with the production of "new" forms of difference and specific representations of indigeneity.[17]

The Convention of Missions of 1902

Relationships between Catholic orders and the state in what is today Colombia were not always friendly. Catholic orders, such as the Jesuits, were removed twice from the country. First, during the colonial period, the Society of Jesus was expelled from Spain and its colonies in 1767 by order of king Charles III, after they were expelled from Portugal in 1759 and France in 1762.[18] The second time the Society of Jesus was removed was in 1850, when the liberal government of José Hilario López promoted the separation of Church and State. Lopez' government was also interested in the disentailment of the real state and properties of the Society of Jesus. Since 1886, when the Conservative party ascended to power, as a reaction to liberal reformers of the mid-19th century, Catholicism and hispanism were crucial in how Conservatives imagined and governed the Republic. During the period known as the Regeneration in Colombia (1886–1902), the formal government of Indigenous peoples and their territories was given to different orders of Catholic missionaries.[19]

In order to develop further the Concordat of 1887, especially articles 25 and 31, the national government and the Holy See signed in 1902 the Convention of Missions.[20] The opening paragraph of the Convention of Missions of 1902 expressed that "it is widely known the interest that both the Holy See and the government of the Republic of Colombia have in increasing the missions for the reduction and evangelization of the tribes of Indians that are disseminated in the territory of this Republic."[21] In this sense, the establishment of Catholic missions in the frontier regions of the country was a project of both the Colombian state and the Holy See. Catholic missions should be simultaneously understood as a global and a national phenomenon. At the beginning of the 20th century, Catholic missions were also being established in other countries of Latin America, Africa and Asia. As I show in this chapter, the first generation of Montfort missionaries that worked in Vaupés were European, and they claimed to be serving both the Colombian nation and the Church.

18   *The Making of an Amazonian Frontier*

The Convention gave a new function to missionaries that they had not had before: the defense of national borders. The 4th article of the Convention established that the Apostolic Vicariate of Caquetá should establish outposts in places that were located on the border with Brazil, Perú and Ecuador, while the Oriental Intendancy should establish one outpost on the border with Venezuela. Missions were used as a way of expanding the sovereignty and authority of the state into frontier regions and national borders, given that some of these regions were under dispute with other neighboring nations. Some of the Catholic missions in Colombia also worked as "islands of occupation" surrounded by spaces deemed to be empty and officially called wastelands (*territorios baldíos*) or "no one's land." The notion of *territorios baldíos* refers to large extensions of land, "owned" by the nation and administered by the state, considered to be empty, uninhabited and uncultivated.[22] The idea of emptiness that underlies the notion of *territorio baldío* was also projected on to missionaries' representations of Indigenous societies as emptied of history, civilization and religion.

In this context, the control of external frontiers became a way of achieving control over populations and territories that were internal to these frontiers.[23] Missionaries also produced information for the state in terms of census, geography and national borders. Most of the places where religious orders operated were also called national territories (*territorios nacionales*) and were unknown for the state. Ironically, these territories which were located on the outskirts of the populated areas of the country were the least national of all.[24] Since the 19th century, elites in Colombia made several attempts to create special legal regimes and administrative policies for those territories and their inhabitants. *National Territories* were considered to be in need of special regimes and exceptional legislation, as their Indigenous residents were considered underage, child-like subjects, incapable of self-government, and not yet ready to be ruled by the laws of the state.[25] Therefore, Indigenous groups in Amazonia were considered to be wards of the state, and their membership to the nation was shaped through the "bond of dependence" between them and Catholic missionaries.[26]

The Convention of Missions of 1902 also gave the head of each mission the control over the schools that existed in the territorial jurisdiction of the mission.[27] A widespread practice of Catholic missionaries was the creation of orphanages and schools run by nuns. The 9th article of the Convention expressed a commitment of the national government to grant to the missions the amount of "empty territory" (*territorios baldíos*) needed for their work without exceeding 1,000 hectares. Each head of mission had to present a yearly report to the representative of the Holy See, regarding the state of the mission and how the money received from the national government was spent. The 12th article of the Convention stated that the national government would promote good relations between state officials and the heads of each mission, while public officers could be removed if the head of the mission complained about them. In exchange for all the support of the government,

The Making of an Amazonian Frontier   19

the missionaries had to promote the aggrupation of Indigenous groups into families, first, and then into *reducciones*, encouraging Christian civilization and the material prosperity of the territory, and therefore the "Indians" established themselves in these.[28] By 1968, after more than five conventions of missions signed between the Holy See and the Colombian government, about 72% of the national territory was part of one of the 11 vicariates or the 3 apostolic prefectures that existed in the country.

The resettlement of Indigenous populations in Vaupés became crucial in the "defense" of national borders and the incorporation of these groups into the body politic through the establishment of *reducciones* as well as religious and civic instruction. Moreover, the nationalization of native Amazonians also implied their incorporation to the nation as racially and humanly inferior. Missionaries represented Indigenous societies as "tribes with no history, written records or religion," yet missionaries' reports and correspondence were often contradictory, showing the flaws and drawbacks of their own work.

Despite the control that missionaries aspired to have over Indigenous populations that lived and moved across the border of Colombia and Brazil, their authority was contested by rubber bosses on both sides of the border. The sovereignty the national government had given to missionaries over frontier regions had to compete with other actors that were already there colonizing the region through the extraction of rubber and *balatá* (a local type of gum tree). The disputes with rubber bosses, especially Brazilian, were intermeshed with disputes regarding the exact location of the border. Therefore, Montfort missionaries were politically active in terms of where precisely to draw the line that separated Colombia from Brazil in this region.

Mission Towns, Resettlement and Sovereignty

The first Montfort missionaries traveled from Bogotá to Villavicencio in February 1904. Villavicencio was founded in the middle of the 19th century and was located in the eastern plains of the country (*Llanos Orientales*). In 1909, this small town became the capital of the *Intendencia* of Meta. The trip was made on horses or mules through muddy trails and paths, crossing over the *Cordillera Oriental*, the trip could take at least three days or more from Bogotá to Villavicencio. The presence of Montfort missionaries in Villavicencio became important for the configuration of this small town, establishing a bank, schools, a theater, a press, a blacksmith, carpentry and binding workshops, a hospital named Montfort and libraries. The first parish priest of Villavicencio between 1904 and 1908 was Hubert Damoiseaux, who was born in 1875 in Netherlands and later became the Superior of the Missions of Vaupés.

In 1909, Joseph-Marie-Désiré Guiot, the French priest who was appointed in 1908 Vicar of the *Llanos de San Martin*, assigned to priest Pierre Baron (also French) the realization of a few expeditions to explore the possibility

20   *The Making of an Amazonian Frontier*

of establishing a mission in Vaupés. These expeditions would allow the missionaries to have a better knowledge of the territory that corresponded to the central and southern sections of the Vicariate.[29] Baron arrived to Villavicencio in 1905 with other Montfort missionaries from France and Netherlands. The first trip Baron made was in 1909 to Calamar, capital of the *comisaría* of Vaupés, and from there went back to Villavicencio. In 1911, Pierre Baron reached the Vaupés River from Calamar, and from there continued to Manaos in Brazil, and found his way back to Bogotá navigating the Amazon and then the Atlantic. Two years later, in 1913, Joseph-Marie-Désiré Guiot appointed Hubert Damoiseaux as Superior of the missions of Vaupés, after he requested it.[30] Damoiseaux was later featured in in the newspaper called *Eco de Oriente* (Echo of the East), which was printed in Villavicencio in the press owned by the missionaries, as the "Apostol of Vaupés."

The final expedition to establish the mission in Vaupés was done in 1914 and both Baron and Damoiseaux were part of it. This time they chose to reach the place where the mission would possibly be established on the Papurí River rather than from the interior starting in Villavicencio, but once again using the Atlantic Ocean, from east to west, in the opposite direction that Baron had taken in 1911 (see Map 1.1). Certainly, the fact that Damoiseaux and Baron chose this route shows how far from the interior of

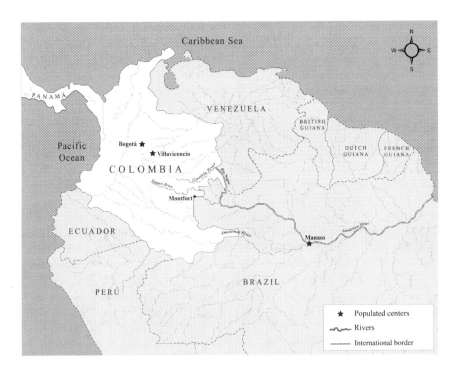

Map 1.1 Map of 1914 showing the location of Montfort (Papurí) in Vaupés.

The Making of an Amazonian Frontier   21

the country the Papurí River was located. In normal weather conditions, the trip from Bogotá to the Papurí River by land and water could take between two and three months. Montfort missionaries had chosen the Papurí River as the center of their "apostolic operations" in Vaupés because it was allegedly the "most populated" (7,500 people according to initial calculations) and this river marked the disputed border with Brazil.[31] Baron thought that the Indigenous groups in the Papurí River were "more docile" and easier to "reduce."[32] This region was closer to Brazil and the closest trading post was Manaos on the Rio Negro. The border was located both symbolically and geographically at the "outer-edge" of the sovereign state.

On June 1, 1914, Damoiseaux and Baron reached the confluence of the Macú and Papurí Rivers, and they established a provisional camp there. From there, Pierre Baron made a trip to the Upper Papurí in a small boat he rented from some natives and came back with the news that he had found an appropriate place to establish a mission, on a stream called *Cupín* (ant). Baron found a native family there that had lived in Venezuela before and understood Spanish very well.[33] This family was from a Tucano called Mandú, which is mentioned in several of the reports and chronicles about the mission published in the newspaper.

Mandú appears for the first time in a report sent by Damoiseaux to the Vicariate of the *Llanos de San Martín* written in June 1914 and published in *Eco de Oriente* on December 15, 1915. In most of the official histories of the mission, Mandú is featured as a "co-founder" of Montfort-Papurí. In the report about the foundation of the mission, Damoiseaux describes how on June 19, 1914, the day designated to celebrate the holiday of the Divine Heart of Jesus and the day of Montfort, the "region was Christianized giving it a rational name."[34] The stream called *Cupín*, where the first mission town was established, was renamed and baptized Montfort-Papurí. The mission was also conceived as a border town (*pueblo fronterizo*) that could enact the sovereignty of the state in the region. On this day, as had happened on many others, a strict program was followed which included a holy mass in the morning followed by a long session listening to a phonograph. In the afternoon, fireworks followed the triple ceremony of the "solemn erection of the cross of the mission, the baptism of the place and the beautiful and expressive statue of the patron saint [Montfort]."[35]

The godfathers (*padrinos*) of the baptism of the place and the statue were "the members of the colony we brought from San Martín, the Indian captain Mandú and his wife."[36] Years later, the missionaries administered to Mandú the sacrament of confirmation and blessed his marriage. In 1915, Mandú visited Villavicencio and Bogotá, with Hubert Damoiseux, as the "main chief of the 'tribes' of Vaupés and was received in a paternal way by the "highest authorities of the Republic." There was a place for Mandu's house in the first rough map of the mission published in *Eco de Oriente* in January 1915 (see Map 1.2).

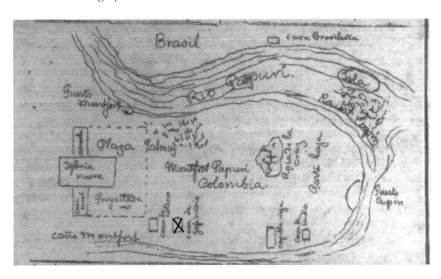

Map 1.2 First rough map of Montfort-Papurí made by missionaries in 1915. (Mandu's house is marked with an X.)

Source: Eco de Oriente, January 15, 1915. Colección Biblioteca Nacional de Colombia.

Mandú appears again in the first picture of the mission published on September 7, 1916 of *Eco de Oriente*. In the image (see Figure 1.1), Mandú and Damoiseux are both wearing hats, while Damoiseaux wears his traditional missionary garment, Mandú is wearing a complete dress and holding a long stick, and his son wears a traditional skirt and a plume of feathers on his head. Damoiseaux is wearing a crucifix on his chest. This picture of Mandú in full dress contrasts with other pictures in which natives appear naked in front of a *maloca* next to a missionary.

Moreover, Mandú is mentioned several times in the book *Jungle Paths and Inca Ruins* (1927), written by English explorer William Montgomery McGovern who traveled to the region in 1925. McGovern describes Mandú as his "Tukano companion," as a "Tukano chief," as someone "exceedingly shrewd," whose "occasional words of advice were always very much to the point."[37] McGovern also praises Mandú's abilities at hunting *pecarí* with a rifle. At the end of his trip, McGovern described how upon his recommendation, the "Interventor" in Manaos gave his two native chiefs (one of them was Mandú) the "titles and perquisites of captain in the Brazilian Army."[38] Each of the Indians that collaborated with McGovern also received a banknote.

Mandú's trajectory and his importance in the establishment of the first mission on the Papurí River show that despite missionaries claiming to be "reducing savages to civilized life," their work depended precisely on "natives" who were, to some extent, already "civilized." Montfort missionaries relied heavily for their work on the experience of go-betweens such as Mandú

Figure 1.1 Missionary Hubert Damoiseux, Mandú and his son, 1916.
Source: *Eco de Oriente*, September 7, 1916. Colección Biblioteca Nacional de Colombia.

who already spoke Spanish and was accustomed to interactions with *colonos* (settlers) and visitors such as McGovern.[39]

Montfort missionaries also learned Indigenous languages, such as Yeral and Tucano, and used them in their interactions with natives. Yeral or Nheengatú was introduced by the Jesuits in the Rio Negro during the 18th century and was transformed into a lingua franca in order to make colonization viable and exclude civil authorities from the control and access to Indigenous populations. According to Ardila, at the beginning of the 20th century, Yeral was also

24 *The Making of an Amazonian Frontier*

used in Vaupés as a lingua franca for the communication between settlers and *indígenas* during the first rubber boom.[40]

Pierre Kok, another Montfort missionary from the Netherlands, joined Damoiseaux and Baron in 1916. Kok would later be in charge of learning different Indigenous languages and making catechisms, translations of the Bible, dictionaries and grammars of languages such as Tucano, Yeral, Tupi, Piratapuyo, Desana and Macú. Some of these translations were published in Vienna. Kok soon understood that in order to "discipline, evangelize and Colombianize" the Indigenous groups that lived on the Papurí River, he had to learn Tucano, which was used as a lingua franca there.

The conflictive encounter between settlers and Indigenous groups made the work of missionaries harder, but they had to use similar strategies to those used by rubber bosses. Pierre Baron argued that their work became harder because they "were amongst savage Indians, predisposed to being against the white man, [whose] trust is only won with a great amount of patience and, above all, with gifts of all kinds."[41] Catholic missionaries, using strategies similar to those used by rubber bosses, had to seduce native Amazonians giving them commodities and objects as gifts. In fact, Damoiseux quoted a very old Spanish saying: "Strike with thy rod while thou dost beg to thy God" [*A Dios rogando y con el maso dando*]. While this saying refers to the combination of praying with human deeds or action in order to achieve specific things in the world, Damoiseux pointed out that in the case of Vaupés the rod would be replaced with gifts: "strike with the gift" [*el regalo dando*].[42] Missionaries were aware of how commodities and "gifts" were crucial in terms of what they could achieve in their interaction with Indigenous groups.

Missionaries, according to Stephen Hugh-Jones, will "often put a material bait on the hook of faith."[43] The value and significance of manufactured goods for native Amazonians, according to Hugh-Jones, lies in the "circumstances of acquisition from White people."[44] Missionaries reproduced the unequal relationships of exchange Indigenous groups had established with "white people," while natives increasingly depended upon "manufactured goods" whose acquisition altered the terms of Indigenous internal trade and status. Harry Walker shows how the Indigenous demand for foreign goods in Amazonia can be also understood as a "function of internal or intracommunity dynamics."[45] Objects or specific commodities were also important in terms of how interactions between visitors and natives were framed. For instance, English explorer Gordon MacCreagh claims they had to acquire specific objects in order to protect themselves and not be confused with rubber traders. MacCreagh visited a "witch-doctor" who told him: "For a piece of cloth and a machete and a mirror I will carve you a very good-speaking stick."[46] MacCreagh compared the stick with a "Bradstreet rating" that mediated his interactions with local residents and worked as a sort of "sealed letter of introduction."[47]

Montfort missionaries had brought with them a colony of settlers, who were different from the rubber bosses or traders that already lived there.

The Making of an Amazonian Frontier 25

Since the establishment of the mission, the Vicariate had the idea of adding a colony to the mission (an agricultural colony, specifically), given that "mission and colony" would soon bring "good for the Church and the fatherland (*la patria*)."[48] In 1917, three years after the establishment of the mission, Pierre Baron wrote to the *Junta de misiones* [mission board] that: "We thought at first about colonizing, and in order to do this we brought two families from the plains [*llaneras*], but as every beginning is harsh, they could not withstand the sufferings of the first days and so they returned. This was an expense entirely lost."[49] Despite the failure of this settler colony, mission towns entailed the resettlement of Indigenous groups as way of exercising control over the border and expanding the sovereignty of the state.

After the colony failed, two young men were left and with the help of some *indios* they were able to build a big and comfortable house. The missionaries later built the chapel and the house for the nuns. Doors, windows and tables were all made out of wood. As soon as they could, they opened a school with only six or seven children to start. Pierre Baron complained about the supposed laziness and inconstancy of the Indians, students "skipped school very often, some went out, others came in, with no apparent results."[50] But missionaries were sure that after the visit of Mandú to Bogotá and the warm welcome he received from the highest authorities of the Republic, captain Mandú would deploy his "effort, authority and recognized influence in pro of civilization, that is, instruction."[51] In 1914, two years after its establishment, the school had 20 young students attending.

According to Baron, with "effort, good treatment and gifts, the Indians started to arrive to Montfort-Papurí from everywhere and from Brazil."[52] The natives that were attracted to the mission in Montfort constructed their houses where missionaries told them to and they had a *caserío* [group of houses] of 14 houses. Those that lived a little far from the mission and could not come or build a house in Montfort-Papurí also "accepted congregating themselves in towns and asked where and how could they built their own chapel."[53] Following the model that dated back to the colonial period, Montfort missionaries tried to resettle Indigenous groups and establish several towns or *reducciones* where they could evangelize native Amazonians.

The second mission town that Montfort missionaries established was *Santa María del Cuduyarí*, on a tributary of the Vaupés River. Another cross was planted in this place as a "sign of redemption and civilization" for those who have lived "buried in the shadows of death."[54] According to Pierre Baron, the chief of this place was not as "collaborative" as Mandú. Most of the people brought to live here were Cubeo speakers. In order to get the "*indios* to work," the missionaries gave them "axes, *machetes*, cloth, music, etc." and then they built a small house.[55] By 1918, Catholic missionaries had established five new *reducciones* in Vaupés, trying to "reduce all the *indígenas* of this region at the feet of Montfort," once they abandoned their "customs incompatible with the law of God."[56] Missionaries considered the Indians'

26 *The Making of an Amazonian Frontier*

willingness to live concentrated in communities a "huge step" as it facilitated religious teaching and surveillance.[57]

Each of these mission towns was supposed to coincide with a specific "tribe." San José was two days upriver from Montfort and those who already lived there were known as the "dojka-puras" (today called Tuyucas) built a chapel. Damoiseux called them the "race of the trees" and there were around 30, who had moved to Colombia (from Brazil) a few months before and had "chosen" this place as a "promised land."[58] In San Bernando they were establishing an exclusively Desano town, and the later were undecided if they would reunite to live there or not, finally deciding to do it, apparently calling a missionary who could tell them where and how to build a chapel.[59] The place chosen to establish the mission was cleaned and 20 families moved there. San Javier was established one day down-river from San Bernando and was created for the "pira-tapuyas" to live there (the "race of the fishes" as Damoiseux called them).[60] However, only the chief of this group was on the Colombian side of the border, and Damoiseux expected the other members of the group to gather soon with his chief. In the contemporary ethnographic literature of the region, the language group Bará are known as the fish people.

Finally, San Pablo was established half a day up river from San José, and missionaries expected Tucanos to live there. Tucanos were hard to convince, according to Damoiseux. The Superior of the Missions of Vaupés wrote that *indígenas* obeyed the following axiom: "each one in his house with their loved ones."[61] In his report, Damoiseux explained that "each *capitán* rejects submitting to the authority of another peer, so therefore the multiplication of centers."[62] A visitor of Montfort-Papurí in 1918 pointed out that "the nomad tribes have not accepted living in one specific place and have relationships with the group of houses that have been established around Montfort-Papurí."[63] In this sense, Montfort missionaries had to adapt and negotiate their practices of evangelization with the political forms of organization of the Indigenous societies they were trying to transform.

Dutch missionary Alfonso Cuypers described the establishment of a mission town in the following terms: "At the beginning it is hard. You make a ranch in the forest, you look for some *indígenas* that can help you build the first houses. During the first months you suffer a lot."[64] Cuypers emphasized how "you can never put together two or more tribes. They should remain afar one from the other because they do not get along with each other, only between families."[65] However, the evidence presented by Pierre Kok and other missionaries seems to contradict the idea that "tribes" did not get along well with each other. Furthermore, linguistic exogamy is based on the "prohibition of getting married with members of the same group, considering each other as siblings."[66] Despite the attempt of building five new mission towns, naming a headman for each town, Damoiseux complained that their efforts were useless given the "versatile" character of *indígenas*. Therefore, the process of resettlement that Montfort missionaries were promoting entailed a new correlation

The Making of an Amazonian Frontier 27

between language, tribe and place that did not exist before as well as an attempt to incorporate Indigenous populations to the rule of the state.

Before Montfort missionaries came to the region most of the Indigenous groups lived in long houses, known in Spanish as *malocas*, and practiced linguistic exogamy. Each of these houses constituted a local kinship group with its own headman. Anthropologists have described this "cultural complex" or social system as Tukanoan (or East Tukanoan), and it includes between 16 and 24 patrilineal clans or sibs that correspond to language groups that intermarry with each other.[67] In 1925, Montfort missionary Pierre Kok reported that: "the Indians of the same group do not live in the same house, but each house contains between two and ten families, houses distant from each other sometimes more than half a day's walk."[68] In a chronicle published in May 1918 in *Eco de Oriente*, a visitor to Montfort-Papurí reported that the *indígenas* that lived there "spoke an infinity of dialects" and "each family has its own language," and there were also those "who understood Spanish."[69] Damoiseaux referred to Vaupés as a branch or reminiscent of Babel. Multilingualism was hard for missionaries to understand and classify. In spite of the frequency of intermarriage between different linguistic groups, most Tukanoans in Vaupés were (and still are) multilingual, speaking more than three or four Indigenous languages, besides Spanish and Portuguese. Multilingualism also led to a particular kind of Indigenous cosmopolitanism that was also fed up with "intertribal trade" and travel.[70]

According to Kok, Indigenous territoriality in Vaupés was, to some extent, discontinuous. Each "tribe did not have its own territory, but you could have, for example, Tucanos living between Desanas, and Piratapuyos living between Carapanas."[71] In an article published in *Anthropos* in 1925, Pierre Kok drew a rough map of the region where the names of the rivers and "tribes" were in Tupi (*Ñengatú*), showing how language groups were intermeshed with one another. Some of the mission towns also appear in this map (see Map 1.3). In addition, in an interview he gave in 1920, Pierre Kok pointed out that "the tribes have been scattered because of exactions, fear, etc ... (...) there is no homogenous group, we are in the presence of dislocated, dispersed, atrophied and exhausted members."[72] In that time, as Theodor Koch-Grünberg wrote in his travel accounts, it was a common practice among rubber bosses to destroy or burn the *malocas* where Tukanoans lived in order to make them work by force in the rubber fields.[73] Similarly, Montfort missionaries condemned the life in long houses and also promoted their abandonment. In 1925, Baron reported to the mission board that: "in those big barrels [*tambos*] lived up to seven or eight families, facilitating immorality and criminality (a lot died poisoned). Today everything has changed: those big houses have disappeared, most of the Indians abandoned the jungle and gathered on the shores of the river where they have established towns with different houses for each family."[74]

However, the project of establishing mission towns that corresponded with specific "tribes" was not entirely successful and was not developed as

28 *The Making of an Amazonian Frontier*

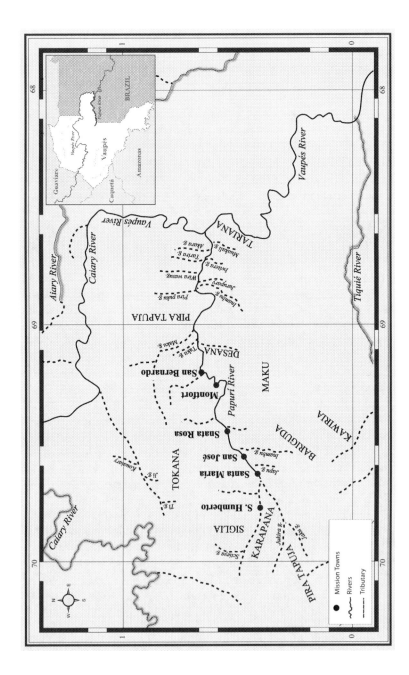

Map 1.3 Map based on Pierre Kok's map of the Papurí River made in 1925 with its tributaries, mission towns and language groups.
Source: Pierre Kok, "Quelques notices ethnographiques sur les Indiens du Rio Papuri," *Anthropos* 20, no. 3 (May–August 1925): 625. Courtesy of Anthropos Institute.

The Making of an Amazonian Frontier   29

it was initially planned. By 1924, according to Pierre Kok, there were 110 Desanos and 50 Tucanos living in San Bernando. In addition to this, San Bernando was moved several times and finally reestablished in the place known as Piracuara where it still exists today. Two of the first towns established by missionaries (Santa Rosa and Santa María) later disappeared. According to Manuel Barón, a Tucano born in 1939, brazilians caused the end of Santa María: "the Brazilians brought food: beans, rice … in order to catch people that could move to the other side of the border."[75] In 1934, Santa María was moved to the place where Acaricuara is located today on the upper Papurí River. Dutch missionary Andreas Linsenn established Acaricuara in order to defend the border of Colombia on the upper Papurí River, after he denounced, to one of the representatives of Colombia in the bilateral border commission of 1933, the "maneuvers of the Brazilians to make all the inhabitants of the upper Papurí River move to Brazil."[76]

In this context of political disputes and people moving across the border, by 1939 Montfort missionaries had established four *reducciones* on the Papurí River, and each *reducción* had its own priest and a semi-boarding school: Montfort, Switzerland, Teresita and Acaricuara.[77] Teresita was the biggest mission town, with almost 400 inhabitants.[78] Switzerland was one of the latest *reducciones*, Tucanos and Desanos lived there and numbered up to 350 individuals. Montfort was still the capital of the mission, the Superior of the mission had his residence in this place and 200 people lived there. Acaricuara was still in the process of being established, and it's population fluctuated between 200 and 300 individuals because of "fights and differences" between the Indians. According to father Limpens, Superior of the mission by then, these conflicts had to do with fishing, land and marriages. Because of these conflicts, between six and eight families had fled again to the forest.[79]

Although it is difficult to know how Tukanoans perceived and related to missionaries and their work, missionary practices and towns were also appropriated and mobilized in unexpected ways. For instance, missionary Alfonso Cuypers from Netherlands, who founded mission town of Teresita de Piramarí in 1929, recalled later in an interview published in the Journal of Missions in 1974 how:

> I had problems with the foundation of Santa Teresita with the *Capitán* of the first tribe that already lived there, who said: the land is ours, the father [missionary] is ours, the mission is ours and threatened to poison other tribes who wanted to live close to the mission. Because of that, it is better to establish [a mission town] where there are no Indians, then they come and nobody can complain.[80]

The new mission town and Cuypers were literally possessed by the people that already lived there, inverting the relationships between missionaries and neophytes. Another missionary recounts that "the chief of Piramarí" resisted and "was hostile to the mission because he was jealous of the authority of

30 *The Making of an Amazonian Frontier*

the priest."[81] Apparently, the chief tried to burn down the mission during the midnight mass on Christmas eve, but the attempt was deterred.

Regarding Indigenous perceptions of missionaries, explorer William Montgomery McGovern narrates in his book how, as an outcome of missionary activity on the Rio Negro many decades ago, the news had spread among Indians of a "magic rite which could be administered only by a white man, and which brought good luck, especially to children."[82] Piratapuyos on the Papurí River wanted McGovern to "perform the mysterious name-giving ceremony of the white men on the children in order to prevent further evil."[83] McGovern recalls that "brats" were brought forward to McGovern for their baptism and he wanted to "baptize the children with names originally given to them by their parents," but the "parents refused to reveal the native names of their offspring."[84] These names, according to McGovern, were considered "secret" and "sacred" and could be used, through other "magic rites" to bring disaster upon someone.

Montfort missionaries were dealing with Indigenous groups that moved across national borders and had no specific national affiliation or no particular concern about it. Missionaries had to "convince" Indigenous headmen and their families to live on the Colombian side of the border where they were establishing mission towns. In September 1917, Damoiseux received a complaint from an "official delegate" from Brazil saying that the *capitanes* (captains) under their jurisdiction made the Indians that were living on the Brazilian side of the border move to Colombia appealing to the authority of the priests [*los padres*] and threatening those who opposed with being taken to a penitentiary in Bogotá. The complaint also said that natives were detained in Colombia by the *capitanes* that worked for the Montfort Missionaries. Damoiseux replied that he had no knowledge of such "abuse."[85] Furthermore, he said that *racionales* [settlers] from Brazil made Montfort missionaries' parishioners move to the Brazilian side of the border. In his response, Damoiseux mentioned that he did know of the burning of a "Colombian *maloca*" perpetrated by Indians that were under the jurisdiction of the delegate from Brazil who signed the letter. Before this event, Indians from Brazil had attacked a *maloca* on the Colombian side of the border, as revenge for the murder of a relative of the delegate.[86]

Damoiseux considered these events a violation of national sovereignty. In fact, a brother-in-law of the delegate had spread rumors about Montfort missionaries among Indigenous families in order to make them flee from Colombia. His brother-in-law also tried, in Damoiseux's words, to "conquer captain Mandú offering him dances, parties and alcoholic beverages."[87] Another relative of the delegate had carried away an "India" [Indigenous woman] from Colombia. Damoiseux turned his reply into a formal complaint against the Brazilian delegate:

> (...) in the name of my superiors and Colombia [I protest] against your extreme boldness of calling the Indians of the *Cuyucuyu* and other

The Catholic missionary finished his reply recalling how during a census that was made in the region, Indians fled to the forest to avoid the delegate and later gave the list of the census to Damoiseux, as did other communities living on the border, apparently saying to him: "we don't want to be Brazilian nor from another nation, we want to be Colombian."[89] Montfort missionaries interacted with different types of actors that appeared as "Brazilians" in their writings: state officials (delegate), regular settlers, rubber bosses and Salesian missionaries, among others.

The conflicts with "Brazilians" led Damoiseux to ask the national government to give Montfort missionaries a formal "title" and authority as Protectors of the Indians [*Protector de los Indios*]. While the position of *Protector of Indígenas* [Protector de indígenas] existed in Vaupés since 1916 and was occupied by the M.R.P. [very reverend priest] Chief of the missions of the region, in April 1918 the government issued the decree 614 on the "governance and protection of non-civilized *indígenas* in the region of Vaupés."[90] The decree reiterated the principle of Law 89, 1890 that Indians "not civilized yet, but reduced to missions, are not subject to the common laws of the Republic and will be extraordinarily governed by the missionaries."[91] This decree was a response to the demand of giving the "missionary a title, above all, an authority through which he can remediate and prevent the abuses that *racionales* [settlers] committed and sometimes the *indígenas*."[92] This title was requested under the assumption that civil authorities "could not take action at such a long distance," and it could be more effective for the protection of the borders.[93]

The role of "protectors" of *indígenas* was to "protect *indígenas* against abuses from the civilized that go to the reductions or *poblaciones de los indios* and intervene in the contracts signed between one another in order to avoid that the former [natives] are tricked and deceived by the latter [the civilized]."[94] Missionaries were also in charge of "preventing the *indígenas* from being taken to work in *caucheras*, or from working outside the jurisdictional terms of the missionaries in charge of them."[95] In this sense, controlling the frontier entailed having control over Indigenous groups that lived on the Colombian side of the border, as well as regulating Indigenous labor. The "protection" of *indígenas* was clearly a practice of sovereignty that entered into conflict with the claims and practices of rubber bosses on both sides of the border.

The petition of having an official title as protectors of Indians, also included the power to name "chiefs" who would earn a small salary to be distributed among them and their people. They would also serve as couriers between the missionaries and the regional government. One year after decree 614 was made public by the missionaries. The same act included the appointment and possession of Indigenous policemen, after being instructed regarding their "duties and obligations," the missionaries "gave them the uniform that they had been given in Bogotá and we forwarded their appointment."[96] Damoiseux pointed out how: "from now on, with a hat from the government, our *Capitanes* [captains] will look, before their fellow men, covered with dignity and authority whose value, we the white men, fail to understand."[97] In fact, in April 26, 1928, a picture appeared in one of the pages of *Eco de Oriente* in which six Tukanoans appear with policemen hats, fully dressed and looking at the camera (see Figure 1.2). The picture is explained in the phrase: "the Indigenous captains of the different *reducciones* of the Montfort Mission of Vaupés."[98] In this sense, among the functions given to the protector of *indígenas* were, besides attracting *indígenas* to live in populated centers, designating among the *indígenas* the captains and policemen that would rule their fellow men. Certainly, the defense of the border and constituting

Figure 1.2 Indigenous captains, 1928. Picture of Indigenous captains of the *reducciones* in Vaupés.

Source: *Eco de Oriente*, April 26, 1928. Colección Biblioteca Nacional de Colombia.

The Making of an Amazonian Frontier   33

state sovereignty in the region went hand in hand with the government of Indigenous populations from within and without.

Catholic Patriotism, Evangelization and Indigeneity

After decree 614 was issued in 1918, missionaries became the main representatives of the state before native Amazonians. The "protector" of *indígenas* was also there to ensure that the natives knew, loved and respected the laws of Colombia. Montfort missionaries were agents of both nation and Church. Missionaries always conceived their work as part of a patriotic and civilizing mission described in terms of "conquering souls for God and citizens for the fatherland."[99] Montfort missionaries defined the "fatherland [*patria*]" as the "conscience and sentiment of the moral and historical community of which we are part."[100] Without that "conscience and sentiment," said the article, *no hay patria* [there is no fatherland]. Missionaries thought that childhood was the most appropriate age to infuse those "noble sentiments" associated with patriotism.

In some of the articles published in *Eco de Oriente*, patriotism was presented as an essential Catholic virtue, while nationalist Catholics were associated with a pragmatic ethos. In fact, an article about Catholicism and patriotism suggested that the most famous patriots of history had been "profoundly pragmatic" Catholics.[101]

Montfort missionaries also expressed in writing their deep love for Colombia, even if they had not lived in the country for too long. That was the case of Luis María Monplaisair, director of *Eco de Oriente*, who published an article in December 1916, after two years of residing in the country, saying that: "Colombian tricolor you are mine! Because you are the emblem of my life and my ideals. That's why I pay tribute to you, at the end of this first day at the shadow of your flagpole, I salute those whom I wanted to make more Christian, real patriots."[102] Montfort missionaries had to cultivate their own patriotism, which was expressed in their sacrifice and work in the frontiers of Colombia. The work of missionaries was often praised as a service to God and the fatherland. Catholic patriotism contrasted with how Tukanoans were represented as lacking any notion of what a nation could be, as well as having no written records and history. In this sense, nationalization and evangelization of Indigenous groups were closely intertwined and this became clear in the ways in which sovereignty was performed through celebrations that were simultaneously Catholic and national.

A clear example of how Catholic patriotism was displayed in Montfort-Papurí was the celebration of the 1st anniversary of the establishment of the mission which coincided with the first celebration of the patron saint (*fiesta patronal*) of the place: Saint Louis de Montfort. As is still usual in Colombia and other places of Latin America, each town had its own Catholic saint. The *fiesta patronal* celebrated the foundation of the town and the day of the saint. The account of the celebration starts describing how: "the national

34 *The Making of an Amazonian Frontier*

flag embellishes and protects the houses of the Indians. They do not fit in the chapel, 40 Indians take a monumental cross with faith and devotion."[103] The main event of the celebration was the procession and the carrying of the cross. A cross that was made out of wood and was 11 meters high. At the designated hour, after students of the school sang the Rosary, the procession took off from the church in the direction of the port and Mandú "directed it and ordered it all."[104] Half way to the port, on a small hill, the procession stopped and the cross was raised. After the cross was blessed, all the participants in the procession shouted:

Viva la cruz! Viva!	[Hail the cross! Hail!]
Viva el Beato de Montfort! Viva!	[Hail the Saint of Montfort! Hail!]
Viva Montfort Papurí! Viva!	[Hail Montfort Papurí! Hail!]
Viva Colombia! Viva! Viva!!	[Hail Colombia! Hail! Hail!]

According to Damoiseaux, this act marked the end of the "religious part" of the first *fiesta patronal* of the mission and was followed by the distribution of medals, Saints, refreshments and tobacco. Missionaries saw the Indians as feeble for tobacco. Big Rosaries were also given to those who had carried the cross and were put around their necks. Their wives had cooked some cookies called *Huntley Galman* for that day. This procession and the performance involved reveal how Montfort missionaries tried to sacralize the nation and bring together the reverence of Montfort with the reverence of Colombia. Nonetheless, two years later, in April 1917, the celebration of the day of Montfort had to "compete" with a *cachiri* (local festivity) organized by an "Indian neighbor" of the mission, which included traditional dances and drinking *chicha*. Hubert Damoiseaux said that "several of them stopped coming to the religious celebration in order to attend the profane [party]."[105]

The political meaning of religious and civic festivities displayed by missionaries in Montfort-Papurí and mission towns should not be overlooked. Missionaries' spatial practices of sovereignty (such as establishing mission towns on the border with Brazil) were complemented with the performance of sovereign power through public rituals that were simultaneously religious and national. Hansen and Stepputat show how the performance of sovereign power is crucial for understanding how the "sovereignty of the state as an aspiration" is created and legitimized in the face of "internally fragmented, unevenly distributed and unpredictable configurations of political authority."[106] Homi Bhabha also argues that the permanent identification of the people with the nation should not be taken for granted, but it has to be "continually signified, repeated and performed."[107] State power and national sovereignty also became real and tangible through practices that included singing the national anthem, hoisting the national flag and showing images of the president of the Republic.

The Making of an Amazonian Frontier   35

Montfort missionaries also performed sovereignty in their interactions with civil authorities. In May 1915, on their way to Montfort-Papurí, Damoiseux and Baron passed in front of the Colombian custom office raising the Colombian flag in their three ships and the flag was also raised in Yavaraté, where the government office was located. Damoiseux narrates how: "the authorities of [Yavaraté] saluted us with shots that R. P. Pedro Barón in his role of former Algerian *zouave* replied with ten gunshots, the only canon we had on board."[108] In an interview published in *Eco de Oriente* in October 1920, Pierre Kok was described by his interviewer as the type of "priest-soldier" from the Middle Ages. In a similar vein, the Inspector of Public Schools from the *Llanos de San Martín* signed a resolution in December 1914 that included military instruction in the schools under his jurisdiction assuming that Colombia needed a strong army to solve pending international problems and military instruction was more effective and easier to give in schools with young children. The idea of using native Amazonians as future soldiers for military confrontations went in tandem with the idea of establishing a system of military education in the boarding schools run by missionaries. Pierre Baron was grateful with those who contributed to their job of training soldiers for the fatherland. As is still remembered by local inhabitants, Montfort missionaries participated in disputes about the exact location of the border line that separated Colombia from Brazil on the Papurí River.

These performances of sovereign power were also combined with everyday performances of routines and repetitive acts that marked Tukanoans' experiences of evangelization. Sovereignty can also be understood as "a tentative and unstable project whose efficacy and legitimacy depend on repeated performances."[109] In February 1918, Damoiseux reported how in the mission, "school and religious instruction had a well determined schedule." The day started at 5:30 a.m. in the church with the first mass with a Rosary praying, continued at 6:00 a.m. with another mass with a morning prayer and singing. At 6:30 a.m. Christian doctrine was taught and another Rosary was prayed, as well as a night prayer with more teaching of doctrine and singing. On Fridays, instead of the Rosary prayer, an "exercise of the *via crucis*" was done in Tucano. On Sundays and holidays at 1:00 p.m. a Rosary was prayed and Christian doctrine was taught. Those sessions finished with a listening session of the phonograph. The last Sunday of Pentecost, Damoiseux gave the sacraments of baptism and confirmation to the first adults, while captain Mandú received a vigil.

Religious teaching was combined with school instruction, Damoiseux taught in the morning and Pierre Kok in the afternoon. In the school at Montfort they had 26 interns by 1918, this number was similar to other schools in the interior. According to Damoiseux: "in the church tucano is spoken, so everybody can understand, but in school the official language is Spanish, which we want our students to learn soon and well, because it is their maternal language."[110] In order to preach and teach in Tucano, Pierre Kok had made a catechism in Tucano and summaries of the Old and the New Testament in that language. Teaching of Spanish was combined with lessons of national history and geography.

Civic and religious instruction entailed, in Damoiseux' words, the "isolation" of Indigenous children, so they can "forget the customs of their elders."[111] Tukanoans homes were seen as a source of corruption and a "school of all vices."[112] Therefore, Damoiseux recommended complete isolation and continuous surveillance upon students, as well as combining the teaching of Christian morality with "fertile and moralizing physical work."[113] Historian Amada Carolina Pérez points out that missionary reports and pictures produced in Colombia at the beginning of the 20th century can be understood as a "performance of civilization" which consisted in a *mise en scène* of Indians doing physical activities or work in order to portray how civilization had transformed their lives.

According to Pérez, practices of evangelization also included "performative rituals" such as singing the national anthem, swearing allegiance to the flag or presenting public exams of national history and urbanity.[114] A special issue of *Eco de Oriente* in June 1926 featured pictures of Indigenous boys working on a carpentry workshop, a bookbinding workshop and a marine workshop. A visitor of Montfort-Papurí in 1918 narrated how the few Indigenous families that lived in Montfort spend their days devoted to agricultural chores. In 1933, missionaries decided to abandon orphanages as a "system of civilization" and decided to disseminate themselves throughout the Papurí River, establishing *reducciones* each one with its own priest and semi-boarding school. This change did not imply less surveillance, as the missionary kept on watching his students after school on the mission town.

Furthermore, in the June 1st edition of 1919 of *Eco de Oriente*, a picture of all the male and female students of the school at Montfort with missionaries on each side of the picture was presented with a short description on its right side: "How frontiers are defended: a school in Vaupés" (see Figure 1.3).

Figure 1.3 A boarding school in Vaupés, 1928. "How borders are defended: a school in Vaupés."

Source: *Eco de Oriente*, June 1, 1928. Colección Biblioteca Nacional de Colombia.

Through his kind of *montage*, missionaries established a relation between the defense of the national border with the evangelization of Indigenous groups and the control of Indigenous children. In May 22, 1919, pictures taken by Montfort missionaries were presented on the front page of the newspaper *Eco de Oriente* as real evidence of their work with native children on the frontier: "(…) they are not just names that could be invented by the priest, they are men of flesh and bone. I can count them: there are 29, they are boys, their features show this, and they are Indian, the color and the facial angle reveal it."[115] It was common that missionaries displayed pictures in their newspaper of "their" students all dressed and crossing their arms in front of the camera (see Figure 1.4).

Missionaries thought the arrangement and smiles of Indigenous children in their pictures were signs of discipline, education and civilization: "these boys are arranged with art, so they can be portrayed! There is discipline, many are smiling – smiling, not laughs and laughter is proper of the civilized men: there is advance."[116] Missionaries praised the composure observed by Indigenous children and how "each of them has their own simple, but correct dress, long pants and a sweater or flannel shirt: their parents give them clothes and do not let them go naked."[117] Nonetheless, Pierre Baron reported that interns were not used to discipline, order and work, and they frequently escaped. According to Baron, in July 1920 their parents "came to claim their kids, they did not want more school, nor Fathers [priests], or any white men."[118]

Figure 1.4 Missionary Pierre Kok and his students, 1919.

Source: *Eco de Oriente*, May 13, 1919. Colección Biblioteca Nacional de Colombia.

38 *The Making of an Amazonian Frontier*

Pictures, before the eyes of missionaries, were considered an index of "inner transformations," as well as evidence of changes in status and personhood: "in other pictures I see the same girls cultivating their garden. They are not the slaves we met; it is the worthy woman, the housekeeper that fixes 'her' yard."[119] In a similar vein, missionaries considered the agricultural work of Indigenous children as work done by "man that reasoned and deduced." Still, in September 1919, Damoiseux wrote a report saying that their influence among young Indians was insufficient given the "vicious" and "pagan" environment that surrounded them, as well as the "inveterate vices of adults and elders."[120] Missionaries saw *cachiris*, "traditional parties," that included dances and drinking of *chicha* for several days, as an obstacle to evangelization. An European anthropologist who traveled to the region in 1961 reported that "*kashiri* is drunk in huge quantities on every possible occasion and it is such an essential ingredient of the dance feast held fairly regularly that it is customary simply to speak of 'holding a *kashiri*.'"[121] Missionaries tried to ban *cachiris*, but they failed.

Representing and Translating Indigeneity

The nationalization of Indigenous groups through practices of evangelization did not imply cultural homogenization or simple assimilation into a recently invented "national culture" which was already contested, heterogeneous and spatially differentiated. Rather than just assimilating Indigenous peoples, nationalizing these groups through evangelization entailed specific ways of representing and translating Indigenous "customs" (including religious beliefs and practices). Racializing and othering were crucial in processes of nation-making in Latin America. Rita Segato coined the term "national formations of alterity" as way of referring to how the nation becomes a matrix for the production of differences that varies geographically and historically. The discourses produced by elites and dominant regional groups (such as Catholic missionaries) about "internal others" are part of theses national formations of alterity.[122]

Furthermore, the evolutionary notion of tribe denied the "coevalness" to the groups missionaries were interacting with, placing them in a different time-space.[123] Kok compared Indigenous groups of the region to "primitive hordes" that preceded the formation of peoples (*des peuples*), Indigenous groups were considered by missionaries to be "pre-political." Regarding the origins of Indigenous languages, Kok said that: "language is multiple but it shows irrefutably an Asian origin (…) just their face reveals in the *indígenas* of Vaupés a remarkable resemblance with the Japanese and Chinese race: small and slanted eyes, prominent cheekbones, are characteristics that leave no doubt."[124] Missionary narratives of Tukanoans as inhabiting a different time and having a different "origin" contributed to articulating what Partha Chaterjee calls the "heterogeneous time of the nation."[125] In 1924, Missionary Pierre Kok published an article in the journal *Anthropos* saying that the "tribes" they had contacted in Vaupés "have no national life, neither chiefs of the tribe," he also added that "our Indians have no history, they do not possess documents, they ignore writing, nor historical documents, nor traditions, their memories do not go back very far [in time]."[126] These representations of Indigenous societies as lacking historical consciousness reproduced the idea that they were "people without history," about to enter the "waiting room of history."[127]

Missionaries' translations and accounts of Indigenous "customs" were fundamental in how they represented indigeneity. As Paula Montero points out, the translation of "Indigenous customs" and languages constituted one of the main practices that mediated the "expected passage to civilization."[128] As had already happened during the early colonial expansion of Europe, "religion" became the main comparative category used to describe and articulate cultural difference.[129] David Chidester shows how "frontier comparative religion was a 'rhetoric of control,' a discourse about others that reinforced their colonial containment."[130] Montfort missionaries also drew on religion as a comparative category to explain why Indigenous were supposedly different, but also shared some similarities with Christians such as the idea of the "immortality of the soul."

In the interview of October 17, 1920, the interviewer asked about the "superstitions" that might exist among "our Indians," and Kok replied saying: "Superstition! Well sir, superstition is thoroughly their religion. Properly, they don't have gods, idols, or priests (...)."[131] Kok translated Indigenous practices and "beliefs" as "shadows of the big dogmas of our religion: immortality of the soul, contrition and confession."[132] Specifically, Kok used the example of the ashes Indians left on top of the tombs of dead people and how the "enemy" who had caused the death of the person through "witchcraft" or other means will come regretful to the place where his victim lies and leave his footprint on the ashes. Kok thought that the footprint of the "enemy" on the ashes of the victim was similar to the act of contrition and confession. Missionaries' representation of "Indigenous religion" made it look different but also similar to Christianity in one way or another.

Kok argued in the interview that those "same Indians," which did not have any "documents, writing, history or traditions," will tell you that "God had created their ancestors making them come out of a big hole dug in the water in a stone in the *cachuera* Ipanore, two days of distance from the mouth of the Papurí on the Vaupés."[133] Kok also describes the ancestors that each "tribe" recognized as their "patriarchs." In an interview published on October 17, 1920, Kok recognized that the word they used for God was taken from Yeral and they had "divinized" this word.[134] The word was used to designate a kind of "Romulus or Remus, founder of their race, the father of all of them, a superior being, etc."[135] Kok described their procedure as "rational and theological" because they had learned Yeral so they could "find" such "prehistoric being" in order to "canonize, sanctify and divinize him."[136] Certainly, the status of "Indigenous religion" was

40   *The Making of an Amazonian Frontier*

ambiguous as it served as the basis for introducing Christian theological concepts and notions.

In sum, missionaries' representations and translations of Indigenous "customs" and practices were often contradictory. Representations of Indigenous subjects oscillated between the "hyper-real" civilized Indian students that appeared in the pictures of the school of Montfort, and the "pagan," "drunk" and "irrational" primitive. Still in 1965, a member of the Xaverian Missionaries of Yarumal, who replaced the Montfort missionaries in 1949, declared that: "the religious problem of the Vaupés could be reduced to paganism. Thousands of *indígenas* have not been baptized, and the ones that have already been baptized practice very little in order to say that they are Christians."[137]

Missionaries, Rubber and the Border with Brazil

Missionaries disciplined natives, sometimes making the work of rubber bosses easier. For example, Pierre Baron quoted a *balatá* boss in a report saying that: "the boys that come out of our schools work more than the others and the entrepreneurs of *balata* have told us they behave better."[138] Nonetheless, frictions with rubber bosses were permanent and missionaries referred to the difficulties of "moralizing the *indios* among white men of worse customs than theirs."[139] Pierre Kok also complained about how their "work of civilization" was confronted by Colombians that came looking for rubber and told the Indians that what missionaries taught were "lies and pranks."[140] Even if some of the attempts of missionaries at establishing colonies of settlers failed, missionaries were confronted with practices of colonization and rubber extraction that were already taking place when they arrived to Vaupés.

In his "Explorations in the North-West Amazon Basin," American explorer Hamilton Rice, who traveled to the region between 1912 and 1913, described Calamar (capital of Vaupés) as the "receiving and distributing center for the *caucheros* or rubber gatherers working black rubber [in the] districts of the Upper Caquetá and Vaupés regions."[141] In his report published in 1914, Rice wrote:

> The *comisario* had the invaluable services of Gregorio Calderón, a Tolimense Colombian, whose name is known throughout the Republic. It was he who founded Calamar, cut paths through the great forest from the Guaviare to the Amazon, acquired both the Hiutoto and Carijona dialects, formed the Indians of both those nations into colonies, teaching them the value of co-operation and organized labor, and founded the great rubber *empresa* [company], only to have much of his work undone as a result of the so-called Putumayo atrocities.[142]

The close relationship between Calderón and the *comisario* [commissary] that Rice describes, corroborates that state-formation and rubber extraction

The Making of an Amazonian Frontier   41

were intertwined in the region. Calderón founded Calamar which later became the capital of the *comisaría* of Vaupés until 1936. The *comisario* depended on the rubber baron and, in a similar way, rubber extraction was possible and even promoted by the guarantees the state provided to rubber entrepreneurs. The central government provided concessions to rubber companies or specific individuals over large areas of land that were considered to be *terrenos baldíos* (empty land). The monopoly of huge extensions of "empty land" in the hands of rubber entrepreneurs supported by the government was common by then, usually as a "consequence of the ignorance of the territory over which it was forced to exercise sovereignty."[143]

Rubber bosses also claimed to civilize native Amazonians, sometimes drawing upon missionaries' techniques, such as learning Indigenous languages and resettling Indigenous populations. Hamilton Rice clearly describes with admiration the "civilizing" practices of Calderón, who organized the natives into permanent settlements and taught them the "value of co-operation and organized labor" while running his company. Although, Rice seems to ignore in his description the importance of debt peonage in the rubber industry, as well as the negative connotations this practice had among Indigenous communities.[144] Debt peonage used commodities, given in advance, as payment for work. In this sense, two competing projects of rule coexisted in the Colombian Amazon, both claimed to "civilize" native Amazonians and both were encouraged by the state. Rubber bosses and Catholic missionaries had to compete with each other for Indigenous labor and loyalty, but the former could interfere in the contracts and agreements established between natives under their jurisdiction and rubber bosses.

The extraction of rubber in Vaupés predated the arrival of Montfort missionaries to the region. Since the mid-19th century, Amazonia became the sole supplier of wild rubber in response to a growing international demand for this resource. This started to change in the first decades of the 20th century, after Henry Wickham smuggled more than 70,000 rubber seeds from the Brazilian Amazon to England in 1876, and 2,800 of these seeds germinated in Key Gardens were later planted in South East Asia where huge rubber plantations were established. In 1913, the rubber from these seeds smuggled from Brazil flooded the market, outselling the more expensive wild rubber that was produced in Amazonia. By 1928 the Amazon produced less than 3% of the world's rubber, but there was a second rubber boom in the 1940s after the Japanese took over the plantations of South East Asia, forcing the United States to rely on Amazonian wild rubber again. In a report written in July 10, 1921, from Montfort to the Board of Missions, Pierre Baron related that "the crisis of rubber was felt in all the region" and it had brought to the mission a "huge amount of [Indigenous] people asking for salt and clothes."[145] It was, according to Baron, a "delicate" problem because refusing them would "return them to a life wilder than before and they would become our enemies."[146] As an outcome of the rubber crisis, Baron wrote on October 25, 1921, the "Indians" came to the mission to ask for work and

42 The Making of an Amazonian Frontier

missionaries helped those who lived close to the mission but rejected "those who live afar."[147] Apparently, as vengeance, those rejected were upset and burned down the chapel in 1919.

The conflicts between Montfort missionaries and Brazilian rubber bosses started to take place soon after the mission on the Papurí River was established in 1914. Two years later, in 1916, Pierre Baron informed to the central government that:

> The lower Vaupés region has a population of between 7,000 and 8,000 Indians whose job is to attain *mañoco* for the white men and help them extract *seringa* (rubber). This product represents huge trade for Brazilians and its producers, taking between 50 and 100 *Indios* to Brazil each year, who consequently never return. In this same region there are also four Colombian companies. Two years ago, as Brazilians noticed that our mission represented a hindrance, they began to contest the current borders, claiming that up to Yuruparí belonged to them. That is, the region including 15 days north of here, which is the entire region inhabited by Indians.[148]

Missionaries described several times how "Indians", including women and children, were taken to Brazil. In 1921, Baron reported that it was known that "Brazilian greed and their claims to a huge part of Vaupés cause Brazilians to continually commit abuses on the Colombian side, taking people to work with them that never come back and stealing kids."[149] As is clear from the report, Brazilians also disputed the exact location of the border because this had direct implications regarding whether natives could be recruited or not as rubber tappers. Damoiseux pointed out in 1918 that if the *patron* that recruited the natives was Brazilian, there was a higher chance that the "chief nor his family will ever come back because the unpaid debts in this life won't let them go back to their fatherland."[150] In 1919, Antonio Nieto, who was *comisario* of Vaupés, wrote for the central government a report where he stated that:

> (...) in Brazil they force the Indians to call themselves Brazilians, to work in the *caucheras* [rubber fields] as slaves without wages and during extraction season they take *naturales* [natives] from the Republic, with-holding from Colombian *caucheros* [rubber bosses] those who help them and who in fact they pay.[151]

The *comisario* defended the work of Colombian *cacucheros* vis-à-vis Brazilian *caucheros*. Conflicts in this frontier moved across different lines and occurred between Catholic missionaries and rubber traders, as well as between rubber bosses of different nationalities. These conflicts between Colombian and Brazilian rubber bosses led the government to move, in 1936, the capital of the province of Vaupés from Calamar to Mitú, on the Vaupés River, where it is located today, far closer to the border with Brazil. The first *comisario* was Miguel Cuervo Aráoz, who visited Montfort-Papurí in 1936 and built the airstrip of Mitú with the help of missionaries.

In fact, in 1931 there was a border commission that visited the Papurí River for three months, in response to the "social problems already reported to the national government by the missionaries."[152] The idea of the border commission was to realize the exploratory work in order to reach a bilateral border agreement. Montfort missionaries collaborated with the Colombian representatives led by Dr. Burno facilitating buildings, personal and resources. Nonetheless, the border commission left a bitter impression regarding the treatment the Colombian government gave to its borders. July 20, 1931 corresponded to independence day and the superior of the mission invited Dr. Burno to give a speech to the students of the boarding schools. All expected to receive "a stimulus to their sense of belonging and national solidarity."[153] Surprisingly, Dr. Burno "rejected the honor of expressing his national identity," neither did he recognize the "generosity" of Dutch and French missionaries who "far from their own countries were fighting to promote culture, patriotism and the national borders of the people which they served with loyalty and devotion." The story, written by a Montfort missionary, of the visit of Dr. Burno to the Papurí River finishes suggesting that "Colombia was not interested in the Indians of Papurí."[154] Apparently, Dr. Burno said contemptuously before he left: "they'd better move to Brazil."[155]

There was a second bilateral commission in 1933 aimed at solving the border conflicts between Colombia and Brazil in the region. Unlike the first commission, the three members that represented Colombia were "models of patriotism," left a better impression upon the missionaries as they treated the *indígenas* better and showed interest in them. This commission inaugurated in January 1933, provided two milestones that were put on the confluence of the Papurí and the Vaupés River. In the report of the commission it reads that the two commissions were "unable to reach an agreement regarding the demarcation of the Papurí or Capurí River" and, therefore, decided to "submit the case to each of its government for its solution and continue with the non-controversial stretches."[156] Manuel Barón, from Acaricuara, recalls that "Montfort missionaries contributed to having the border located not on the river mouth of *caño Paca* but down [on the Papurí River] in Melo Franco. Where Colombians and Brazilians from the border commission arrived."[157] Manuel's father worked helping to pin down several milestones along the border for two years.

In 1933, Aurelio Acuña, the administrator of the Colombian customs post in Yavareté sent a report to the minister of government, in which he related that since 1928, the government of the Republic of Brazil had established several posts for the *protección* of *indígenas*, specially located on border points where the "majority of tribes are."[158] Acuña complained about the fact that Brazilian officials pressured Indians that lived on the Colombian side of the border to move and establish towns at the posts of "protection."[159] Therefore, Salesian missionaries had been starting to do something

44   *The Making of an Amazonian Frontier*

similar in the Vaupés and Tiquié Rivers in Brazil to what Montfort missionaries had been doing since 1914 on the Papurí River in Colombia. Despite the fact that in 1918 Salesian missionaries visited Montfort-Papurí and met Hubert Damoiseux personally, they became part of the actors that would challenge the authority the government had given to Montfort missionaries in Vaupés. According to father Limpens, the Salesian Mission in Brazil received 30,000 pesos every year, without including all the facilities it gave to "Indians in remedies, food and tools."[160] Salesian missionaries also contributed to the extensive propaganda that Brazil always carried out in order to win over the "Indians."

In a similar way, in 1925 Pierre Baron wrote a letter published in the *Revista de Misiones* [Journal of Missions] in which he recognized that:

> Brazilians exert a lot of pressure in order to attract our Indians to the other side of the river, where they provide authorities that may attend to the Indians' complaints about the white men. Colombia, it is shameful to say, does not boast such authorities, and God knows how many methods are used by the civilized in order to oppress the poor Indian! Given that the latter have nobody to appeal to here, they enter Brazil when they can, or even seek justice for themselves by killing the white men. This happened recently with one particular case, where the person in fact deserved it, though vengeance was such that the miserable was shattered.[161]

Despite the fact that Father Baron lamented how natives were leaving to enter Brazil because they had more "protection" there from Brazilian authorities, in another letter from September 7, 1929, he recognized that "in the area where we evangelize, all of them have come to Colombia, yet how much work and displeasure has it caused us to get a few things done!."[162] In February 28, 1934, Baron wrote a letter to the Government Minister remembering him that, after the disagreement of the bilateral border commission, "Colombians kept the right of the nation to maintain the actual limits, and the Brazilians pretended to locate the border milestones six more days upriver the Papurí River."[163] Baron clarified in his letter that while both governments reach an agreement, "Brazil occupies the contested territory" and it has tried all means (including promises, threats and the use of force) in order to make "Colombian Indians move to Brazilian territory."[164]

The fact that the job assigned to Montfort missionaries was not entirely successful, led the *comisario* of Vaupés in 1933 to write a proposal of reforming Decree 618 of 1918, under the basis that it had commissioned the missionaries with catechizing and protecting the *indígenas*, but the "outcome of such missions has been completely negative."[165] Other state officials such as Acuña disagreed with these kinds of judgements. Acuña insisted on the necessity of regulating Indigenous labor in order to avoid the exploitation of "Indians" by Colombians and Brazilians. For Acuña, regulating Indigenous labor required a more effective support of the mission at Montfort-Papurí in order to expand the range of action of missionaries to all the "tribes that live in the territory of Vaupés."[166] A few years later Montfort missionaries had to leave the region when a new prefecture was created.

In 1949, the Holy See decided to dismember the Apostolic Vicariate of the *Llanos de San Martin* and created the Apostolic Prefecture of Mitú in order to facilitate the administration and evangelization of the territory that was under the jurisdiction of the Vicariate. Montfort missionaries were replaced with the Xaverian Misionaries of Yarumal (Colombia), trained in the Seminary of Missions in Yarumal (Antioquia) established in 1927. Out of all the mission towns that Montfort missionaries tried to establish, there were four left: Acaricuara, Montfort, Teresita and Piracuara. The last three of these towns are located on the Papurí River and still today mark the border with Brazil (see Map 1.4). On the other hand, the rubber industry went through a second boom, since the 1940s, as an outcome of the effects of World War II when the Japanese took over rubber plantations in Southeast Asia, producing a global shortage. Frictions between Colombian missionaries and rubber bosses continued until the end of the 1960s when missionaries publicly denounced the sale and purchase of the debts of Indigenous rubber tappers with the bosses, under the complicity of state officials.[167]

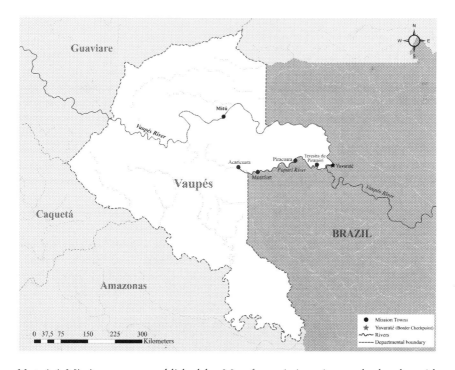

Map 1.4 Mission towns established by Montfort missionaries on the border with Brazil by 1949.

46   *The Making of an Amazonian Frontier*

At the same time, during the 1940s evangelical missionaries started to develop their work on the northern sections of the Vicariate, with Indigenous groups unreached by Montfort missionaries. Evangelical missionaries and Indigenous evangelicals began to challenge the authority of Catholic missionaries, as well as the moral standards of settlers and state functionaries. New ideals of civilization and modernity were introduced to the region through evangelical Christianity.

Conclusions

This chapter analyzed the role played by Catholic missionaries in the frontier-making process in the Vaupés region of the Upper Rio Negro, where knowledge of the region was limited and the border with Brazil was disputed. In 1916, Montfort missionaries were appointed as "protectors" of *indígenas* as a way of controlling the relationships between Indigenous communities and rubber industry bosses. Missionaries also had to ensure that the natives knew, loved and respected the laws of Colombia. Missionaries had to compete with rubber bosses on both sides of the border for the allegiance and labor of Indigenous groups. In Vaupés, Montfort missionaries became agents of both nation and Church, while evangelization went hand in hand with nation building. Boarding school education served the purpose of turning natives into Colombian citizens.

Specifically, Montfort missionaries in Vaupés associated control over Indigenous groups dwelling on the Papurí River with displaying state sovereignty on the border between Colombia and Brazil. This chapter shows how Montfort missionaries tried to consolidate tutelage (given to missionaries by Law 89 of 1890) over "not yet civilized" Indigenous populations thus once again, using the colonial practice of establishing *reducciones* (mission towns), but in a postcolonial context. The establishment of *reducciones* along the border was the easiest way – according to Montfort missionaries – to "civilize" and "nationalize" Indigenous groups. Spatial practices of sovereignty associated with the resettlement of Indigenous populations were complemented by the public and everyday performance of sovereign power.

Furthermore, Montfort missionaries adapted their strategies of evangelization to local practices and realities in order to articulate the authority the state had granted them. Montfort missionaries had to establish several mission towns, each one with its own "chief," because there were no centralized forms of political organization among Indigenous groups. Missionaries failed in their attempt to establish an isomorphism in which each mission corresponded to a specific "tribe." Missionaries' translations and accounts of Indigenous "customs" were crucial in how they represented indigeneity. Missionaries' representations of Indigenous subjects oscillated between the "hyper-real" civilized Indian students that appeared in the pictures published in their newspaper, and the "pagan," "drunk" and "irrational" primitive version. Above all, Indigenous groups were represented as "primitive hordes"

The Making of an Amazonian Frontier   47

without history, writing or documents. Still today, most of the Indigenous elders who attended boarding schools administered by Catholic missionaries emphasize that evangelization was advanced through strict disciplinary practices. Among elder Tukanoans, becoming Catholic is associated with following strict bodily routines and "religious" practices.

Notes

1 "La misión Montfortiana en el Vaupés. Breve informe sobre el estado actual de la misión. Sus dificultades y sus necesidades," July 13, 1939, Archivo General de la Nación, Ministerio de Gobierno, División de Asuntos Indígenas, Correspondencia Recibida Comisaría del Vaupés, fol. 4.

2 Tamar Herzog, *Frontiers of Possession. Spain and Portugal in Europe and the Americas* (Cambridge: Harvard University Press, 2015), 4.

3 Between 1932 and 1933, Colombia and Perú waged a war after 300 armed Peruvians took over the Amazon city of Leticia as a reaction to the frontier Treaty Lozano-Salomón originally signed in 1922 between Colombia and Peru. This treaty gave sovereignty to Colombia over a portion of land north of the Amazon River that some Peruvians considered being part of the province of Loreto. The war did not last more than three months and Colombia won it, after Peru withdrew its military forces from the region. This war started as a confrontation between rubber barons and companies that dates back to 1899, when the Arana brothers (owners of the well-known Arana House) made incursions into the upper Putumayo River expanding the rubber industry they had started in the Peruvian Amazon.

4 In the ethnographic literature, they are known as Eastern Tukanoan, including between 16 and 24 patrilineal clans or sibs that correspond with language groups that intermarry among themselves. See Jean Jackson, *The Fish People. Linguistic Exogamy and Tukanoan Identity in Northwest Amazonia* (Cambridge: Cambridge University Press, 1983).

5 "De la Cartera del límo Sr. VC Ap. De los Llanos S. M. sus impresiones de viaje sobre el Vaupés," *Eco de Oriente*, October 1, 1922, 289.

6 Simón Uribe, *Frontier Road. Power, History, and the Everyday State in the Colombian Amazon* (Oxford: Wiley Blackwell, 2017), 33.

7 Ibid.

8 The idea of "reducing" the natives to civilized life and/or Christianity was a part of a broader project of colonization summarized through the term *reducción* coined during the Colonial Period. Willian F. Hanks glosses *reducción* as "pacification, conversion, ordering," depending on the context. The project of *reducción*, according to Hanks, was organized in three interrelated spheres that included *"pueblos reducidos* 'ordered towns', *indios reducidos* 'ordered Indians' acting in accordance with *policía cristiana* 'Christian civility', and *lengua reducida*, the new version of the native language attuned to proper civility and religion." *Converting Words*, William Hanks (Berkley: University of California Press, 2010), xiv–xv. American historian Herbert Bolton also points out that Spanish authorities soon discovered that: "in order properly to convert, instruct and exploit the Indian, he must be kept in a fixed place of residence (...)", and notes "it soon became a law that Indians [had to] be congregated in pueblos, and made to stay there, by force if necessary." These "pueblos were modeled on Spanish towns and were designed not alone as a means of control, but as schools in self-control as well as well." See Herbert Bolton, "The Mission as a Frontier Institution," *The Hispanic American Historical Review* 23, no. 1, October 2017: 44.

48   *The Making of an Amazonian Frontier*

9 Both terms *indio* and *indígena* appear in the documents I use here, although they have different historical connotations. The term *indio* has a negative connotation, and it is usually used as a discriminatory and derogatory term, while Indigenous social movements use the term *indígena* as an affirmation of cultural difference. In this article I translate the term *indígena* as native and I leave it untranslated when it appears as such in the documents or testimonies I quote. See Joanne Rappaport, *Intercultural Utopias. Public Intellectuals, Cultural Experimentation and Ethnic Pluralism in Colombia* (Durham: Duke University Press, 2005), 48.

10 "Decreto No. 614 (13 de Abril de 1918)," *Eco de Oriente*, April 30, 1918, 707.

11 Patricia Seed, *Ceremonies of Possession in Europe's Conquest of the New World, 1492–1640* (Cambridge: Cambridge University Press, 1995), 2.

12 Thomas Blom Hansen and Finn Stepputat, "Introduction," in *Sovereign Bodies. Citizens, Migrants, and States in the Postcolonial World*, eds. Thomas Blom Hansen and Finn Stepputat (Princeton: Princeton University Press, 2005), 7.

13 The notion of tribe was also used by anthropologists such as Irving Goldman in *The Cubeos*, who did fieldwork later in the region during the 1940s, and defined the term as: "a common identity of language, descent, and custom." See Irving Goldman, *The Cubeo. Indians of the Northwest Amazon* (Urbana: University of Illinois Press, 1963), 26.

14 The historical and colonial use of religion as a comparative category has been developed by several authors. See David Chidester, *Colonialism and Comparative Religion in Southern Africa* (Charlottesville: University Press of Virginia, 1996).

15 Jay Z. Smith, *Relating Religion: Essays in the Study of Religion* (Chicago: University of Chicago Press, 2004), 180.

16 Ibid, 187.

17 The "knowledge" produced by Montfort missionaries circulated in specialized anthropological journals and was recognized by famous ethnologists such as French ethnologist Paul Rivet.

18 The Jesuits were expelled from Spain and its colonies because they were considered a threat and menace to the authority of the King. Charles III feared the rise of the Company of Jesus and the growing "control the order had reached in all the domains of social life, especially education." See Guillermo Wilde, *Religión y poder en las misiones de guaraníes* (Buenos Aires: Editorial Sb, 2009), 184.

19 Since 1874, liberal governments promoted indigenist policies that included the protection of Indigenous lands, banning the sale of alcohol for them, fair prices for their products and punishment for acts of violence against them. Since 1886, the conservative regime had to reconcile those policies with the commitments it had agreed upon with the Holy See in the Concordat of 1887. Consequently, the government issued Law 89 of 1890 that gave to Catholic missionaries the tutelage and government of "tribes" that were "not reduced yet to civilization." See Victor Daniel Bonilla, *Siervos de Dios y amos de Indios: el Estado y la misión capuchina en el Putumayo* (Cali: Editorial Universidad del Cauca, 1968), 60.

20 Article 25 of the Concordat established that the Colombian government would give to the Church an annual amount of money (100,000 pesos by then), and, after mutual agreement, this money could be used to fund dioceses, seminars, missions and other works that were part of the "civilizing action of the Church." While Article 31 of the Concordat stated that any convention signed between the Holy See and the government of Colombia for the promotion of "Catholic missions among barbarian tribes" will not require further approbation of the national congress. See Bernardo Rueda Vargas, *Intendencias y comisarías: organización política, organización administrativa, organización fiscal, contratos, contraloría, jurisprudencia administrativa, baldíos, régimen de tierras, colonización, convenio sobre misiones, protección de indígenas* (Bogotá: Imprenta Nacional, 1937).

21 Ibid.

The Making of an Amazonian Frontier 49

22 *Territorios baldíos* may be translated as "waste lands" or "empty territories." Since the Republic was established in the early 19th century, the national government had been in charge of adjudicating *territorios baldíos* to specific citizens under specific conditions. According to historian Catherine Legrand, the national policies regarding *territorios baldíos* show two contradictory tendencies that originate in the "attitude of the colonial regime towards land." On the one hand, land policy has been used to promote colonization and the development of rural economies, distributing land at low prices among peasants willing to cultivate this land. Those who cultivated land were supposed to have legal access to it. On the other hand, in the case of the second tendency *territorios baldíos* are considered to be a source of revenue for the state, and, therefore, lands have been sold or given in concession to the highest bidder. In both cases, the notion of *territorios baldíos* constituted a strategy of dispossession, given that most of the lands considered to be "empty" were actually occupied by Indigenous communities, afro-descendant groups or regular peasants. Therefore, the notion of "empty territories" can be related to earlier notions that were common in international law such as the notion of *terra nullius* that circulated in the 18th century. According to Whatmore, the legal doctrine of *terra nullius*, which translates literally as "no one's land," legitimized the "annexation of 'uninhabited lands' by settlement as an acknowledged means, alongside conquest and secession, for the proper conduct of colonization by 'civilized' nations." See Catherine LeGrand, *Colonización y protesta campesina en Colombia 1850–1950* (Bogotá: Universidad Nacional de Colombia, 1988), 32–33 and Sarah Whatmore, *Hybrid Geographies, Natures, Cultures, Spaces* (London: Sage Publications, 2002), 63–64.
23 Herzog, *Frontiers of Possession*, 4.
24 See Margarita Rosa Serje de la Ossa, *El revés de la nación: territorios salvajes, fronteras y tierras de nadie* (Bogotá: Ediciones Uniandes, 2011), 17.
25 Ibid, 16–17.
26 Claudio Lomnitz points out that the "fraternal bond" was critical in Benedict Anderson understanding of nationalism, but equally important were the "bonds of dependence" and how they mediated the access to citizenship and nationhood. According to Lomnitz, "the national community is not strictly about equality and fraternity, but rather about an idiom for articulating ties of dependence to the state through citizenship (fraternity)." See Claudio Lomnitz "Nationalism as Practical System: Benedict Anderson's Theory of Nationalism from the Vantage Point of Spanish America," in *Deep Mexico, Silent Mexico. An Anthropology of Nationalism* (Minneapolis: University of Minnesota Press, 2001), 12.
27 The Convention of Missions also included the creation, by the Holy See, of the *Prefectura Oriental* (Oriental Prefecture) in the south-eastern plains of the country. The jurisdiction of this new Prefecture coincided with the Oriental Intendancy and the administration of this new Prefecture was given to the Montfort Missionaries. In 1908, the Oriental Prefecture was merged with the Prefecture of the *Llanos de San Martin*, which already existed, in order to create the Apostolic Vicariate of the *Llanos de San Martin*. Part of the jurisdiction of this new Vicariate overlapped with the jurisdiction of the *Comisaría* of Vaupés which was created in 1910. According to canonical right, the Apostolic Prefecture is a "determinate portion of the people of God, which due to particular circumstances has not been constituted as a diocese, and it is entrusted to a prelate which rules it as its pastor." The vicariate is defined in the same way but it is run by an apostolic vicar.
28 Vargas, *Intendencias y comisarías*, 193–194.
29 "Nuestras misiones s.m.m. Vicariato Apostólico de San Martín," *Eco de Oriente*, November 15, 1913.
30 "Gobierno Eclesiástico- Decreto de Octubre de 1913," *Eco de Oriente*, November 15, 1913.
31 "Informe," *Eco de Oriente*, September 7, 1916.

50   *The Making of an Amazonian Frontier*

32   "Misión del Vaupés," *Eco de Oriente*, September 1, 1915.
33   Andreas Linssen, "Los orígenes de la Misión del Vaupés," *Revista de misiones*, no. 559 (May–June 1974): 127.
34   "Informes del M.R.P. Superior de la misión del Vaupés," *Eco de Oriente*, December 15, 1915.
35   Ibid.
36   Ibid.
37   William Montgomery McGovern, *Jungle Paths and Inca Ruins. The Record of an Expedition* (London: Hutchinson & Co, 1927), 201.
38   Ibid, 278.
39   Since the 18th century, the Jesuits had established posts on the Rio Negro and since mid-19th century the Portuguese crown promoted the work of Capuchin missionaries who created the mission of the Vaupés and Isana Rivers in 1852. In fact, Damoiseux reported in January 1915 that an old chapel made out of bare existed already in Montfort-Papurí.
40   Olga Ardila, "Diversidad linguistica y multilinguismo en los grupos Tucano del Vaupés," *Forma y función*, no. 4 (1989): 23.
41   Pedro Barón, "Datos sobre la Misión indígena del Vaupés, suministrados por el Reverendo Padre Pedro Barón a la honorable Junta de la Misiones," in *Informes sobre las Misiones del Caquetá, Putumayo, Goajira, Casanare, Meta, Vichada, Vaupés y Arauca* (Bogotá: Imprenta Nacional, 1917), 168.
42   "Las misiones de la Compañía de María," 593.
43   Stephen Hugh-Jones, "Yesterday's Luxuries, Tomorrow's Necessities: Business and Barter in Northwest Amazonia," in *Barter, Exchange and Value. An Anthropological Approach*, eds. Caroline Humphrey and Stephen Hugh-Jones (Cambridge: Cambridge University Press, 1992), 46.
44   Ibid.
45   Harry Walker, "Demonic trade: debt, materiality, and agency in Amazonia," *The Journal of the Royal Anthropological Institute*, 18, no. 1 (2012): 146.
46   McGovern, *Jungle Paths and Inca Ruins*, 253.
47   Ibid.
48   "Nuestras misiones s.m.m. Vicariato Apostólico de San Martín," *Eco de Oriente*, November 15, 1913.
49   Pedro Barón, "Datos sobre la Misión indígena del Vaupés, suministrados por el Reverendo Padre Pedro Barón a la honorable Junta de la Misiones," in *Informes sobre las Misiones del Caquetá, Putumayo, Goajira, Casanare, Meta, Vichada, Vaupés y Arauca* (Bogotá: Imprenta Nacional, 1917), 168.
50   Pedro Barón, "Datos sobre la Misión indígena del Vaupés, suministrados por el Reverendo Padre Pedro Barón a las honorable Junta de las Misiones," *Eco de Oriente*, January 28, 1917, 157.
51   "3a Escuela Indígenas a Comisaría y Misión del Vaupés, Montfort Papurí," *Eco de Oriente*, January 1, 1916.
52   Pedro Barón, "Datos sobre la Misión indígena del Vaupés, suministrados por el Reverendo Padre Pedro Barón a la honorable Junta de la Misiones," in *Informes sobre las Misiones del Caquetá, Putumayo, Goajira, Casanare, Meta, Vichada, Vaupés y Arauca* (Bogotá: Imprenta Nacional, 1917), 169.
53   Ibid, 168.
54   Pedro Barón, "Datos sobre la Misión indígena del Vaupés, suministrados por el Reverendo Padre Pedro Barón a las honorable Junta de las Misiones," *Eco de Oriente*, January 28, 1917, 158.
55   Ibid.
56   "Las misiones de la Compañía de María. Informe que sobre la reducción de Montfort Papuri remite el R. Padre Huberto Damoiseux S. M. M. Superior," *Eco de Oriente*, February 26, 1918, 599.

The Making of an Amazonian Frontier 51

57 Ibid.
58 Ibid.
59 Ibid.
60 Ibid.
61 Ibid.
62 Ibid.
63 Luis Martínez Delgado, "Vicariato Apostólico de los Llanos de San Martín. Montfort-Papurí," *Eco de Oriente*, April 30, 1918, 705.
64 Miguel Patiño, "45 años con los tucano y guahibos," *Revista de Misiones*, mayo-junio (1974): 132.
65 Ibid.
66 Olga Ardila, "Diversidad linguistica y multilinguismo en los grupos Tucano del Vaupés," *Forma y función*, no. 4 (1989): 23.
67 According to Irving Goldman "except for the Cubeo and the Makuna of the Pirá-Paraná River, all Tukanoans of the Vaupés follow a rule of language exogamy and look upon mating with a speaker of one's own language as equivalent to brother-sister incest." See Irving Goldman, *Cubeo Hehénewa Religious Thought: Metaphysics of a Northwestern Amazonian People*, ed. Peter J. Wilson (New York: Columbia University Press, 2004), 57–58.
68 Pierre Kok, "Quelques notices ethnographiques sur les Indiens du Rio Papuri," *Anthropos*, no. 20 (1925): 627.
69 Luis Martínez Delgado, "Vicariato Apostólico de los Llanos de San Martín. Montfort-Papurí," *Eco de Oriente*, April 30, 1918, 705.
70 In his classic ethnography about the Cubeo in Vaupés, Irving Goldman points out that the Northwest amazon exhibits a high degree of cultural cosmopolitism, given that "many Indians are multilingual because of the frequency of intermarriage with other linguistic groups and the love of the Indians for travel and intertribal trade," see Irving Goldman, *The Cubeo. Indians of the Northwest Amazon* (Chicago: University of Illinois Press), 15.
71 Kok, "Quelques notices," 627.
72 "Interesante entrevista con un Misionero del Vaupés, el R. P. Pedro Kok," *Eco de Oriente*, October 3, 1920, 426.
73 Michael Kraus, "Testigos de la época del caucho: experiencias de Theodor Koch-Grünberg y Hermann Schmidt en el alto río Negro," in *Objetos como testigos del contacto cultural. Perspectivas interculturales de la historia y del presente de las poblaciones indígenas del alto río Negro (Brasil/Colombia)*, eds. Michael Kraus, Ernest Halbmayer and Ingrid Kummels (Berlin: Gebr. Mann Verlag, 2018), 97.
74 Pedro Barón, "Informe que rinde a los Honorables Miembros de la Junta Arquidiocesana de las Misiones Católicas en Colombia, el Superior de los Misioneros Montfortianos establecidos en el Vaupés," *Revista de Misiones*, no. 7 (December 1925): 292.
75 Juan Manuel Cruz Cifuentes, *La historia del Vaupés contada por nuestros mayores. Biografías e Historias* (Medellín: Instituto Misionero de Antropología, 2016), 57.
76 Bernardo J. Calle, *Caminos de esperanza* (Vicariato Apostólico de Mitú, 2014), 32.
77 Humberto Limpens, "La misión Montfortiana en el Vaupés ...," fol. 12.
78 This mission town had three neighborhoods: Teresita, Africa and Estrella. Piratapuyos lived in Teresita and Africa, while Desanos lived in Estrella.
79 Ibid.
80 Miguel Patiño, "45 años con los Tucanos y Guahibos," *Revista de Misiones*, no. 559 (1974): 100.
81 Calle, *Caminos*, 30.
82 Ibid.

52 The Making of an Amazonian Frontier

83 McGovern, *Jungle Paths*, 121.
84 Ibid.
85 Huberto Damoiseux, "La Compañía de María y la integridad de Colombia," *Eco de Oriente*, January 31, 1918.
86 Ibid.
87 Ibid.
88 Ibid.
89 Ibid.
90 "Decreto No. 614," *Eco de Oriente*, April 30, 1918.
91 Ibid.
92 Huberto Damoiseaux, "Desiderata de los misioneros," *Eco de Oriente*, March 5, 1918.
93 Huberto Damoiseaux, "Desiderata de los misioneros," *Eco de Oriente*, March 5, 1918.
94 "Decreto No. 614."
95 Ibid.
96 "Informe que sobre la marcha y adelanto del Vicariato Apostólico de los Llanos de San Martín e Inspección Escolar del territorio del mismo nombre rinde a sus superiores eclesiásticos y civiles el secretario de las citadas entitades," *Eco de Oriente*, May 11, 1919.
97 Ibid.
98 *Eco de Oriente*, April 26, 1928, 128.
99 Huberto Damoiseaux, "Correo de las misiones. Misión Montfort," *Eco de Oriente*, June 1, 1914. A letter written in November 1914 by two visitors to the "Apostolic Provincial Father" suggested that first sentiment to be instilled upon children was the love of God and the Fatherland. God was defined as "the great provider and author of everything that existed," and the nation as "a novelty of God," whose independence had to be defended. See "Al Muy Reverendo Padre Provincial Apostólico, Inspector de Instrucciones," *Eco de Oriente*, January 1, 1915.
100 "Noción de Patria," *Eco de Oriente*, September 18, 1924, 232.
101 A clear historical example of this phenomenon, according to some missionaries, was French general Ferdinand Fuche who participated in World War I. Fuche went to church and had a brother that was a priest. "La Religión Católica y el patriotismo," *Eco de Oriente*, April 6, 1920.
102 Luis María Mauricio Dieres Monplaisair, "¡Oh Tricolor Colombiano eres mio!," *Eco de Oriente*, December 14, 1916, 141.
103 "Primera fiesta Patronal," *Eco de Oriente*, August 15, 1915.
104 Ibid.
105 "Informe sobre los adelantos espirituales y materiales de la Misión indígena del Vaupés (Frontera brasilera), dirigida por los PP de la Compañía de María," *Eco de Oriente*, August 23, 1917, 391.
106 Hansen and Stepputat, "Introduction," 3.
107 Homi Bhabha, "DissemiNation," in *Nation and Narration*, ed. Homi Bhabha (London: Routledge, 1990), 291–322.
108 "Informes del M.R.P. Superior de la misión del Vaupés," *Eco de Oriente*, December 15, 1915.
109 Hansen and Stepputat, "Introduction," 3.
110 "Las misiones de la Compañía de María. Informe que sobre la reducción de Montfort Papurí remite el R. Padre Huberto Damoiseaux S.M.M Superior," *Eco de Oriente*, February 24, 1918, 594.
111 Ibid, 593.
112 "Lo que en este año han hecho en Montfort Papurí los RR.PP. Montfortianos (Cía. de María)," *Eco de Oriente*, October 12, 1919, 377.

The Making of an Amazonian Frontier 53

113 Ibid.
114 Amada Carolina Pérez, "Fotografía y misiones: los informes de misión como *performance civilizatorio*," *Maguaré* 30, no. 1 (2016): 126.
115 "Informe gráfico importantísimo sobre la Instrucción pública en las misiones del Vaupés (Cía. de María)," *Eco de Oriente*, May 22, 1919, 185.
116 Ibid, 186.
117 Ibid.
118 Pedro Barón, "Informe de la Misión del Vaupés a los honorables miembros de la Junta Arquidiocesana de las Misiones de Colombia. Octubre de 1920 a julio de 1921," in *Las Misiones Católicas en Colombia, Informes años de 1922 y 1923* (Bogotá: Imprenta Nacional), 1922, 22.
119 "Informe gráfico importantísimo ...," 185.
120 "Lo que en este año han hecho ...," 373.
121 P. Van Emst, "Indians and Misssionaries on the Rio Tiquié Brazil-Colombia," *Internationales Archiv für Ethnographie*, 50, no. 2, 163.
122 Rita Laura Segato, *La nación y sus otros. Raza, etnicidad y diversidad religiosa en tiempos de Políticas de la Identidad* (Buenos Aires: Prometeo Libros, 2007).
123 Johannes Fabian, *Time and the Other: How Anthropology Makes Its Object* (New York: Columbia University Press, 2002).
124 "Interesante entrevista con un Misionero del Vaupés, el R. P. P. Pedro Kok," *Eco de Oriente*, October 3, 1920, 425.
125 Partha Chaterjee, *The Politics of the Governed. Reflections on Popular Politics in Most of the World* (New York: Columbia University Press, 2004), 8.
126 Pierre Kok, "Quelques notices ethnographiques sur les Indiens du Rio Papuri," *Anthropos* 20, no. 3-4 (May–August 1925): 627. The trope of the absence of writing and history in the representation of Indigenous peoples was widely used in colonial discourse as an index of savagery. In post-colonial contexts, the absence of writing and history came to signify a marginal position within the national community, not limited to Indigenous groups, but to all those who didn't know how to read and write and were excluded from citizenship. This explains the importance that Catholic missionaries gave to literacy (and education, in general) in their practices of evangelization.
127 Dipesh Chakrabarty, *Provincializing Europe. Postcolonial Thought and Historical Difference* (Princeton: Princeton University Press, 2000).
128 Paula Montero, "Introdução. Missionários, Índios e Mediação Cultural," in Deus Na Aldeia. Missionários, índios e mediação cultural, ed. Paula Montero (Sao Paulo: Editora Globo, 2006), 20.
129 Ibid, 18.
130 David Chidester, *Colonialism and Comparative Religion*, 2.
131 "Costumbres indígenas ...," 449.
132 Ibid.
133 Ibid, 628.
134 "Costumbres indígenas; supersticiones en el Vaupés.-2ª Entrevista con el R.P. Kok," *Eco de Oriente*, October 17, 1920, 449.
135 Ibid.
136 Ibid.
137 Diego Villa m.x.y, "Datos y fechas," in *Misiones del Vaupés 1914–1964* (Vicariato Apostólico de Mitú,1965), 11.
138 Pedro Barón, "Informe que rinde a los Honorables Miembros ...," 292.
139 Pedro Barón, "Misión indígena del Vaupés," *Revista de misiones*, no. 61 (1930): 259.
140 Pierre Kok, "Quelques notices ethnographiques sur les Indiens du Rio Papuri," *Anthropos*, no. 21 (1965): 935.
141 Hamilton Rice, "Further Explorations in the North-West Amazon Basin," *The Geographical Journal* 44, no. 2 (1914): 148.

54   *The Making of an Amazonian Frontier*

142 Ibid.

143 Camilo Domínguez, *Amazonía colombiana economía y poblamiento* (Bogotá: Universidad Externado de Colombia, 2005), 182.

144 Among the material practices implemented by rubber bosses were debt-peonage, coerced labor, and physical violence. According to Michael Taussig, debt-peonage in rubber extraction had the "appearance of trade in which the debtor is neither slave nor wage laborer but a trader with an ironclad obligation to pay back the advance." See Michael Taussig, *Shamanism, Colonialism and the Wild Man* (Chicago: Chicago University Press, 1986), 65.

145 Pedro Barón, "Informe de la Misión del Vaupés ...," 22.

146 Ibid.

147 Pedro Barón, "Informe de la Misión del Vaupés," in *Las Misiones Católicas en Colombia, Informes años de 1922 y 1923* (Bogotá: Imprenta Nacional), 1922, 34.

148 "Datos sobre la región del Vaupés suministrados por R. P. de la Misión Indígena," 1916, Archivo General de la Nación (AGN), Sección República, Ministerio de Gobierno, Tomo 768, fol. 67.

149 Pedro Barón, "Misión del Vaupés ...," 23.

150 Huberto Damoiseux, "Desiderata de los misioneros," *Eco de Oriente*, March 5, 1918.

151 Dominguez, *Amazonia colombiana*, 182.

152 Bernardo J. Calle, *Caminos de esperanza* ...

153 Ibid.

154 Ibid.

155 Ibid.

156 Ministerio de Relaciones Exteriores, *Arreglo de límites entre la República de Colombia y la República de los Estados Unidos del Brasil* (Bogotá: Imprenta Nacional de Colombia, 1982).

157 Juan Manuel Cruz Cifuentes, *La historia del Vaupés contada por nuestros mayores. Biografías e Historias* (Medellín: Instituto Misionero de Antropología, 2016), 57.

158 Aurelio Acuña, "Carta dirigida al ministro de gobierno," Archivo General de la Nación, Ministerio de Gobierno, Sección Intendencias y Comisarías, Caja 2, Carpeta 3, 23 December 1939, f. 80.

159 Ibid.

160 Humberto Limpens, "La misión Montfortiana en el Vaupés ...," fol. 10.

161 Pedro Barón, "Misión indígena del Vaupés," *Revista de misiones*, no. 61, 1925, 260.

162 Pedro Barón "Carta de un misionero del Vaupés," *Revista de misiones*, no. 57, 1930, 59.

163 Pedro Barón "Carta dirigida al señor Ministro de Gobierno," f. 80.

164 Ibid.

165 Aurelio Acuña, "Carta dirigida al ministro de gobierno," Archivo General de la Nación, Ministerio de Gobierno, Sección Intendencias y Comisarías, Caja 2, Carpeta 3, 23 December 1939, f. 80.

166 Aurelio Acuña, "Carta dirigida al ministro ...," f. 80.

167 In 1969, the missionaries in charge of the Vicariate, and other poor *colonos* (who also extracted rubber), made a public announcement in which they denounced the commerce (*compraventa*) of *indígenas* transferring debts between *patronos*. Missionaries also denounced that state officials established alliances with rubber bosses and worked for them. This public announcement led to the end of the rubber industry at the beginning of the 1970s. Rubber was replaced with coca crops and this change is also associated with the arrival of armed guerrillas (such as FARC) to the region.

The Making of an Amazonian Frontier 55

References

Ardila, Olga. "Diversidad linguistica y multilinguismo en los grupos Tucano del Vaupés." *Forma y función*, no. 4 (1989): 23–34.

Baron, Pedro. "Carta de un misionero del Vaupés." *Revista de misiones*, no. 57 (February 1930): 59.

Baron, Pedro. "Datos sobre la Misión indígena del Vaupés, suministrados por el Reverendo Padre Pedro Barón a la honorable Junta de la Misiones." In *Informes sobre las Misiones del Caquetá, Putumayo, Goajira, Casanare, Meta, Vichada, Vaupés y Arauca*, 167–170. Bogotá: Imprenta Nacional, 1917.

Baron, Pedro. "Datos sobre la Misión indígena del Vaupés, suministrados por el Reverendo Padre Pedro Barón a las honorable Junta de las Misiones." *Eco de Oriente* (January 28, 1917): 157–158.

Barón, Pedro. "Informe de la Misión del Vaupés." In *Las Misiones Católicas en Colombia, Informes años de 1922 y 1923*, 33–35 Bogotá: Imprenta Nacional,1922.

Baron, Pedro. "Informe de la Misión del Vaupés a los honorables miembros de la Junta Arquidiocesana de las Misiones de Colombia. Octubre de 1920 a julio de 1921." In *Las Misiones Católicas en Colombia, Informes años de 1922 y 1923*, 21–24. Bogotá: Imprenta Nacional, 1922.

Baron, Pedro. "Informe que rinde a los Honorables Miembros de la Junta Arquidiocesana de las Misiones Católicas en Colombia, el Superior de los Misioneros Montfortianos establecidos en el Vaupés." *Revista de Misiones*, no. 7 (December 1925): 292–295.

Baron, Pedro. "Informe que rinde a los Honorables Miembros de la Junta Arquidiocesana de las Misiones Católicas en Colombia, el Superior de los Misioneros Montfortianos establecidos en el Vaupés." *Revista de Misiones*, no. 7 (December 1925): 292–295.

Baron, Pedro. "Misión indígena del Vaupés." *Revista de misiones*, no. 61 (June 1930): 259–261.

Bhabha, Homi. "DissemiNation." In *Nation and Narration*, edited by Homi Bhabha, 291–322. London: Routledge, 1990.

Bolton, Herbert. "The Mission as a Frontier Institution." *The Hispanic American Historical Review* 23, no. 1 (October 2017): 42–61.

Bonilla, Victor Daniel. *Siervos de Dios y amos de Indios: el Estado y la misión capuchina en el Putumayo*. Cali: Editorial Universidad del Cauca, 1968.

Calle, Bernardo J. *Caminos de esperanza*. Mitú: Vicariato Apostólico de Mitú, 2014.

Chakrabarty, Dipesh. *Provincializing Europe. Postcolonial Thought and Historical. Difference*. Princeton: Princeton University Press, 2000.

Chaterjee, Partha. *The Politics of the Governed. Reflections on Popular Politics in Most of the World*. New York: Columbia University Press, 2004.

Chidester, David. *Colonialism and Comparative Religion in Southern Africa*. Charlottesville: University Press of Virginia, 1996.

Cruz Cifuentes, Juan Manuel. *La historia del Vaupés contada por nuestros mayores. Biografías e*. Historias, Medellín: Instituto Misionero de Antropología, 2016.

Damoiseaux, Huberto. "Informes del M.R.P. Superior de la misión del Vaupés." *Eco de Oriente* (December 15, 1915): 3–8.

Delgado, Luis Martínez. "Vicariato Apostólico de los Llanos de San Martín. Montfort-Papurí." *Eco de Oriente* (April 30, 1918): 705–706.

56 The Making of an Amazonian Frontier

Domínguez, Camilo. *Amazonía colombiana economía y poblamiento*. Bogotá: Universidad Externado de Colombia, 2005.

Fabian, Johannes. *Time and the Other: How Anthropology Makes Its Object*. New York: Columbia University Press, 2002.

Goldman, Irving. *Cubeo Hehénewa Religious Thought: Metaphysics of a Northwestern Amazonian People*, edited by Peter J. Wilson. New York: Columbia University Press, 2004.

Goldman, Irving. *The Cubeo. Indians of the Northwest Amazon*. Urbana: University of Illinois Press, 1963.

Hansen, Thomas Blom, and Finn Stepputat. "Introduction." In *Sovereign Bodies. Citizens, Migrants, and States in the Postcolonial World*, edited by Thomas Blom Hansen and Finn Stepputat, 1–36. Princeton: Princeton University Press, 2005.

Herzog, Tamar. *Frontiers of Possession. Spain and Portugal in Europe and the Americas*. Cambridge: Harvard University Press, 2015.

Hugh-Jones, Stephen. "Yesterday's Luxuries, Tomorrow's Necessities: Business and Barter in Northwest Amazonia." In *Barter, Exchange and Value. An Anthropological Approach*, edited by Caroline Humphrey and Stephen Hugh-Jones, 42–74. Cambridge: Cambridge University Press, 1992.

Jackson, Jean. *The Fish People. Linguistic Exogamy and Tukanoan Identity in Northwest Amazonia*. Cambridge: Cambridge University Press, 1983.

Kok, Pierre. "Quelques notices ethnographiques sur les Indiens du Rio Papuri." *Anthropos* 20, no. 3-4 (1925): 624–637.

Kraus, Michael. "Testigos de La época del caucho: experiencias de Theodor Koch – Grünberg y Hermann Schmidt en el alto río Negro." In *Objetos como testigos del contacto cultural. Perspectivas interculturales de la historia y del presente de las poblaciones indígenas del alto río Negro (Brasil/Colombia)*, edited by Michael Kraus, Ernest Halbmayer and Ingrid Kummels, 97–134. Berlin: Gebr. Mann Verlag, 2018.

LeGrand, Catherine. *Colonización y protesta campesina en Colombia 1850–1950*. Bogotá: Universidad Nacional de Colombia, 1988.

Linssen, Andreas, "Los orígenes de la Misión del Vaupés." *Revista de misiones*, no. 559 (1974): 26–127.

Lomnitz, Claudio. *Deep Mexico, Silent Mexico. An Anthropology of Nationalism*. Minneapolis: University of Minnesota Press, 2001.

McGovern, William Montgomery. *Jungle Paths and Inca Ruins. The Record of an Expedition*. London: Hutchinson & Co, 1927.

Montero, Paula. "Introdução. Missionários, Índios e Mediação Cultural." In *Deus Na Aldeia. Missionários, índios e Mediação Cultural*, edited by Paula Montero, 9–29. Sao Paulo: Editora Globo, 2006.

Patiño, Miguel. "45 años con los Tucano y Guahibos." *Revista De Misiones*, mayo-junio (1974): 130–136.

Pérez, Amada Carolina. "Fotografía y misiones: los informes de misión como *performance civilizatorio*." *Maguaré* 30, no. 1 (2016): 103–139.

Rappaport, Joanne. *Intercultural Utopias. Public Intellectuals, Cultural Experimentation and Ethnic Pluralism in Colombia*. Durham: Duke University Press, 2005.

Rice, Hamilton. "Further Explorations in the North-West Amazon Basin." *The Geographical Journal* 44, no. 2 (1914): 137–164.

Rueda Vargas, Bernardo. *Intendencias y comisarías: organización política, organización administrativa, organización fiscal, contratos, contraloría, jurisprudencia*

The Making of an Amazonian Frontier 57

administrativa, baldíos, régimen de tierras, colonización, convenio sobre misiones, protección de indígenas. Bogotá: Imprenta Nacional, 1937.

Seed, Patricia. *Ceremonies of Possession in Europe's Conquest of the New World, 1492–1640.* Cambridge: Cambridge University Press, 1995.

Segato, Rita Laura. *La nación y sus otros. Raza, etnicidad y diversidad religiosa en tiempos de Políticas de la Identidad.* Buenos Aires: Prometeo Libros, 2007.

Serje, Margarita. *El revés de la nación: territorios salvajes, rronteras y tierras de nadie.* Bogotá: Ediciones Uniandes, 2011.

Smith, Jay Z. *Relating Religion: Essays in the Study of Religion.* Chicago: University of Chicago Press, 2004.

Taussig, Michael. *Shamanism, Colonialism and the Wild Man.* Chicago: Chicago University Press, 1986.

Uribe, Simón. *Frontier Road. Power, History, and the Everyday State in the Colombian Amazon.* Oxford: Wiley Blackwell, 2017.

Van Emst, P. "Indians and Misssionaries on the Rio Tiquié Brazil-Colombia." *Internationales Archiv für Ethnographie* 50, no. 2 (1966): 145–197.

Villa, Diego. "Datos y fechas." In *Misiones del Vaupés 1914–1964,* edited by Vicariato Apostólico de Mitú, 11–13. Mitú: Vicariato Apostólico de Mitú, 1965.

Walker, Harry. "Demonic trade: Debt, Materiality, and Agency in Amazonia." *The Journal of the Royal Anthropological Institute* 18, no. 1 (2012): 140–159. https://doi.org/10.1111/j.1467-9655.2011.01735.x.

Whatmore, Sarah. *Hybrid Geographies, Natures, Cultures, Spaces.* London: Sage Publications, 2002.

Wilde, Guillermo. *Religión y poder en las misiones de guaraníes.* Buenos Aires: Editorial Sb, 2009.

2 Conversion Under Dispute
Evangelical Christianity and the State

The term *evangélico* has historically been used in Latin America to refer to any kind of Christian who is non-Catholic. *Evangélico* refers to a wide range of different Christian denominations that include traditional protestants (Lutherans, Baptists, Anglicans, Methodists and Presbyterians, among others), as well as more contemporary varieties of Christianity encompassed under the term Pentecostalism.[1] In Colombia, during the Cold War, Protestantism was "often regarded as a near-relation to communism" to the extent that military president Gustavo Rojas Pinilla declared in 1956 that "the Protestants are united with the Communists to destroy Colombian national unity."[2] It was not until the 1960s that Protestantism became a "significant pastoral challenge" for the Catholic Church in different countries of Latin America, as an outcome of the rapid expansion of Pentecostalism in rural areas and among working classes of industrial and urban centers.[3]

In Latin America, Protestantism was perceived as a risk to the "link that once tied the theologico-political authority" of the Catholic state to a "social body determined by a certain geographic territory and national sovereignty."[4] Similar to what happened in 17th-century France, the close relationship between Catholicism and absolutism made the obedience to the king synonymous with the obedience to God. Protestants were considered to be suspicious, political dissidents or opponents. In fact, in France, protestants were reintegrated to the broader national and Catholic society through the conversion to Catholicism. In this sense, as Peter van der Veer points out, disputes about the authenticity or meaning of Protestant conversion should be understood within broader tensions and historical conflicts between Protestants and Catholics.[5] In Europe, Catholics saw Luther as the Antichrist, while Luther saw the Antichrist in possession of the "holy throne."[6]

Years before the Pentecostal boom of the 1950s and 1960s in Latin American, non-denominational missionary organizations such as the Summer Institute of Linguistics (SIL) (1932) and New Tribes Mission (NTM) (1942) had already sent missionaries to different countries of South America. These missionary organizations were specialized in what they called "unreached tribes;" that is, Indigenous groups whose languages were not written and had no knowledge of the New Testament. At the same time, anthropologists

DOI: 10.4324/9781003370215-3

Conversion Under Dispute   59

started to describe the work of US protestant missionaries among Indigenous groups in Latin America as "cultural imperialism" and thought they were part of a larger "imperialist plot."[7] On the other hand, members of the SIL, for example, saw their "missiological models as anticolonial, in that they provided local peoples with spiritual tools of emancipation and critique."[8] Søren Hvalkof and Peter Aaby point out that as a response to anti-Americanism, SIL missionaries performed a dual-identity, playing missionaries at home and linguists abroad. In this sense, the importance of native language evangelism should be understood within the "linguistic economy of power and prestige of the nation-state" and the "sacralization" of specific ethnolinguistic groups through the translations of the New Testament.[9]

This chapter analyzes how the conversion of Indigenous groups in Vaupés to evangelical Christianity became a political problem for the state in this region. Since the 1940s, evangelical missionaries and Indigenous groups unreached by Montfort missionaries began to challenge the authority of Catholic missionaries, as well as the moral standards of settlers and state functionaries. Different ideas of civilization were at play in these interactions between Catholic missionaries, Indigenous evangelicals and settlers. The first part of the chapter describes the *milieu* and ideas that gave birth to institutions such as the SIL and NTM. Both organizations were interested in reaching "unreached tribes" and translating the New Testament into unknown Indigenous languages in order to bring about the second coming of Christ. The first section describes and analyzes the work of Sophie Muller, one of the first missionaries from NTM that traveled to Vaupés in the 1940s and translated the Bible into different Indigenous languages. Unlike predominant approaches to the work of Sophie Muller that render her "encounter" with Indigenous groups in terms of a messianic phenomenon, I show how Muller's project was framed as an indigenist project aimed at creating new senses of community and indigeneity. Muller's work also depended upon Indigenous translators, missionaries and pastors.

The second part of the chapter shows how the conversion of Curripacos and Puinaves to evangelical Christianity represented a challenge to the Catholic Church, whose authority over Indigenous groups came from the state. Using their authority and sovereign power in the region, Catholic missionaries from Mitú followed closely and tracked down the work of evangelical missionaries such as Sophie Muller that worked in the northern part of the province with different Indigenous communities. However, Catholic missionaries were confronted with the strong anti-Catholicism of evangelical Indigenous communities who saw them as the Devil. Anti-Catholicism went so far among Indigenous evangelicals that they refused to establish any kind of exchange or trade with Catholic missionaries.

The third part of the chapter analyzes the frictions between Indigenous evangelicals and state officials that were sent to establish the regional government of the province of Guainía. Despite the moral critiques that Indigenous evangelicals had of the behavior of state officials, the former started to incorporate the

60   *Conversion Under Dispute*

language of the state (associated with specific rights and demands) in tandem with specific forms of interaction with state authorities through written letters and formal petitions, among others. The last section of the chapter explores how evangelical missionaries such as Sophie Muller demonized both *colonos* and teachers that worked in boarding schools established by the regional government. Conflicts between teachers that worked for the state and evangelical missionaries became prominent when Muller was officially accused and investigated for obstructing public education. Furthermore, Muller's work was targeted in the 1970s by military officials and treated not just as a "religious problem," but as a political issue, a problem of "sovereignty and borders" and a risk for the consolidation of the authority of the state in the region.

In this sense, Indigenous evangelical conversion was transformed into a field of political disputes and frictions between different social actors, including Catholic and evangelical missionaries, Indigenous evangelicals, *colonos* and other agents of the regional state (such as teachers and state officials). These disputes were informed by anti-Catholicism, as well as moral critiques of the practices and habits of settlers and state officials that worked in the regional government. The disputes between Indigenous evangelicals, Catholic missionaries and state officials reveal how different notions of civilization and colonization were at play, as well as different views of indigeneity. These disputes were also about how better to incorporate Indigenous communities to the nation-state.

New Tribes Mission, Sophie Muller and the Making of Indigenous Churches

Like other institutions such as the SIL, NTM was a product of American evangelicalism and "its project of bearing the Good News to the last unreached people in the uttermost parts of the earth."[10] Paul Fleming and Bob Williams created NTM in 1942 in Los Angeles, after being "uprooted by the war from their work with tribes living in remote parts of South East Asia."[11] NTM was conceived of as a project that was global in scope, renewing the "world-building aspect" of Christianity, as well as the emphasis of North American Christianity on evangelization and missions.

All the missionaries affiliated to NTM thought the Bible had to be translated into all existing languages as a necessary condition to the second coming of Christ.[12] Translations of the New Testament into Indigenous languages were crucial in how New Tribes missionaries developed their project with strong millenarian undertones. The chairman of NTM in 1960 calculated that there existed, in the "jungle areas of the world," more than 2,000 "unreached tribes." Saving the last soul, probably "some tribesman out in the jungle somewhere," was needed to complete the Church (the body of Christ), and then "the Lord will come back for His own with a shout."[13] Once in Heaven, "all tongues, tribes, nations, and peoples will be represented around the Throne, singing that new song to our wonderful Saviour and Lord."[14] The project of "reaching the unreached" became the *leitmotiv* of NTM and was part of broader practices of mapping the globe in terms of "reached" and "unreached" territories. Reaching so-called "unreached tribes" entailed learning their languages, translating the Bible, training Indigenous missionaries and pastors, as well as founding "tribal" or "Indigenous churches."

While Catholic missionaries were concerned with the performativity of faith and the repetition of acts, evangelical missionaries were more interested in provoking "authentic" conversions, a "change of heart," interior transformations associated with the idea of being "born again" and starting a new life in Christ. Courtney Handman points out that for SIL and other American evangelical movements that focused on the global south, conversions had to be "created outside of the coercive forces of the state," because "imposed" conversions tended to "keep people un-Christian, turn them into syncretists, or make them susceptible to other malignant forces in global politics (communism and violent nationalism, in particular)."[15] In *Jungle Methods*, Sophie Muller pointed out that "'God hath made of one blood all nations', with the same capacity to accept or reject," and saw her work as an opportunity for making the word accessible to "those who have had no chance as yet to accept or reject."[16] This notion of conversion as the outcome of a "personal decision" was later actualized by evangelical missionaries in terms of a dichotomy between religion as something personal and culture as something collective associated with external traits. This topic will be addressed in the next chapter.

In her account of how she came to be a missionary, Sophie Muller tells of a transformative event. An invitation to accept Christ as Savior was extended to her by Jack Wyrzten,[17] leader of the original Word of Life group, on a street of New York in 1941. Muller was 31 years by then, and this invitation awoke in her, she relates, the "the desire to be active for God like Jack and his young group."[18] She renounced "all ambition to be a renowned artist," and while she was taking a course at the National Bible Institute she asked God, in prayer, to show her "what He would have me to do with my life."[19] God answered "with a burden to go to a tribe that had never heard the Gospel."[20] This answer turned out to be her "call," and she joined NTM in 1944. During the orientation to the Mission, she "asked God which country [she] should enter to work with that unreached tribe."[21] After a short period of prayer she "just knew it was Colombia."[22]

Sophie Muller made a first trip to Puerto Leguízamo in the Putumayo region with a medical missionary whose name was Catherine Morgan. The trip failed because there were no "tribes" in the area who were beyond the reach of the mission that was operated by Catherine's friends. After another failed trip to Leticia on the Amazon River, Muller followed the advice of Pat Symes, who lived in Bogotá and helped her get a permanent visa. Muller studied Spanish in Bogotá for six months and then traveled to Mitú in the Vaupés River. Muller describes how she was set to "search for a tribe whose language had never been reduced to writing – a tribe without one ray of spiritual light."[23] As an outcome of her work, Muller published three books in which all the writing and illustrations were done by herself.

62   *Conversion Under Dispute*

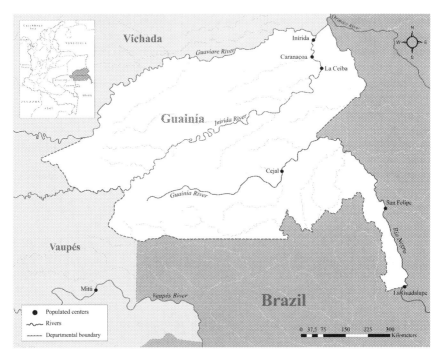

Map 2.1 Map of the province of Guainía established in 1965.

After a few weeks in Mitú, she decided to travel to the Curripaco community of Cejal on the Guainía River (see Map 2.1). As part of her work, Muller relied on key "tribesman" who "lived near to civilization."[24] This practice would allow her to gain access to Indigenous languages through the knowledge "informants" had of the trade language (Spanish). This was the case of Chicho, one of her first Curripaco informants. Practices of evangelization relied heavily on literacy, teaching people to read and write their own language in order to make the "Word of God accessible to the natives."[25] One of the first rumors about Muller's work was that she "taught people to read in a short time, in all the villages on the Guainía River."[26] The emphasis on literacy was also common in other missions that were protestant, where it was "believed that, by teaching the natives to read, they would [be] set on the path of self-improvement and salvation, revelation and refinement, civilization and, finally, conversion."[27]

Muller deployed in her work techniques that already existed, such as the Laubach method, which allowed her to teach the natives to read without using books, using a chart with syllables in specific Indigenous languages (she started with Curripaco).[28] But these techniques were combined with practices that included the training of Indigenous pastors that would later take charge of their own churches, as well as of Indigenous missionaries that would preach to other Indigenous groups. Finding audiences willing to hear

Conversion Under Dispute   63

the Word might require the help of former pupils that "will help you teach the new ones at the next village, and most important of all, you'll find eager ears and open hearts for the entrance of the Word of Life, if you go with a tribal escort."[29] In *Jungle Methods*, Muller asks herself what human help she had for the "evangelization of those other tribes" and answers herself saying: "The Indians themselves – that is, the Curipacos – became the missionaries to the Puinavis, and the Puinavis to the Piapocos, and right now the Curipacos are making trips to the Cubeos and the Guayaveros, while the Puinavis and Piapocos are making trips to the Guajivos, Cuivas and Salivas."[30] Muller thought initially the establishment of local Indigenous churches as an Indigenous "people's movement" that transcended "tribal boundaries," a "pan-tribal" movement of conversion in which "Curripacos, Puinaves and Piapocos would take a united stand against sin and the devil."[31]

Until recently, predominant interpretations of Sophie Muller's work and "success" establish a direct connection between her work and Indigenous messianic movements of the late 19th century in the Upper Rio Negro. For instance, Robin Wright argues that Muller's message was couched "in almost the exact same terms as the early messiahs," provoking "a movement with strongly messianic and millennial overtones."[32] However, Muller was not always received by Indigenous communities as a "messiah" or as someone important. In her first book, Muller narrates how as she came near a village called *Matijáipan*, "Indians ran into their houses."[33] When she reached the first house where all the men were congregated: "I told them I had come to teach them about God and to read. It was a rather tense five minutes. They looked at me and laughed."[34] Muller's own writings show that the massive conversion to evangelical Christianity was only made possible through Indigenous translators and literacy campaigns. This required the training Indigenous pastors and missionaries that would teach their fellows how to read their own language and understand parts of the New Testament.

In 1960, the chairman of NTM, Keneth J. Johnston, praised Muller's work as "one of the most truly Indigenous works that has come to my attention."[35] While Johnston suggested there are "many shades" to the word "Indigenous," this word in Muller's own work acquired a positive value and "meant a great deal."[36] Johnston thought the churches that Muller helped to establish followed "Indigenous principles" because they were built "without funds from the United States" and functioned without any support from abroad. Local churches were built by "Indian Christians" themselves and each church had "pastors from among those of their own village."[37] In a similar vein, the superior of the Xaverian Missionaries of Yarumal, who was in charge of the Vicariate of Vaupés since 1949, pointed out in 1961 that:

> It is unexplainable the almost magic spell that this woman exercises upon the Indigenous soul. Responding to the spell of her voice the tribes travel through the rivers in humble *curiaras* (small canoes) from incredibly faraway places to the evangelical conferences. All reunited – up to

64   Conversion Under Dispute

600 – in big *malocas* that work as a temple. Above, emblems such as the flame, the book, painted over black walls, upfront was the table of the pastor crammed with notebooks that contain parts of the Bible in Indigenous languages. In the back, as in the bleachers of a theater, the elders were sitting on beams that were across the humble compound. They spend time – up to 8 days – between tiring *salmodia* [chanting salms] and explanations of the Bible. They call themselves "brothers" and all of them eat the agape, like the primitive Christians.[38]

In this sense, evangelization and conversion entailed the creation of a new kind of Indigenous Christian community. Indigenous evangelicals would be neither like their "pagan" ancestors, nor like the *colonos* that settled in the region and had, according to evangelical missionaries, lax moral standards. During my fieldwork in the Guainía River in 2009, I could see how communal practices and events were part of everyday life, mostly in rural Indigenous communities and not so much in those that were close to urban centers. In most of these communities, adults and elders get together twice a day in the communal hall, located next to the church. Early in the morning around 6 a.m. they get together and share *mingao* (a hot beverage made out of *mañoco* – bitter manioc powder) and in the afternoon, around 4 p.m., they do the same and share *yucuta* (cold water with *mañoco*). Once a week, usually on Fridays, they have the communal workday, in which all the male members of the community work together in specific tasks. Every Sunday at noon, all the members of the community get together to share an *ajicero* (a soup with peppers and fish or meat from animals that are hunted in the forest). Prayers and thanking the Lord for providing food precede all the communal and family meals. Members of the church watch over each other in their everyday life and at collective gatherings. Indigenous evangelical communities are also articulated through different practices of surveillance and public confessions (called *testimonios* in Spanish), in addition to other communal practices.

Nonetheless, Indigenous conversion to evangelical Christianity also had its own problems and drawbacks. For instance, in *Jungle Methods*, Muller noticed that "with their mouths they said, 'we all believe', but there was no real evidence of new life except for a faint flicker in some."[39] Most of the Indigenous evangelicals that I met during my fieldwork would have stories to tell about "failed" conversions or people who were "led astray" (*descarriarse*) and returned to a worldly life. In a similar vein, younger generations of Indigenous evangelicals tend to be less strict in following the moral prohibitions associated with evangelical Christianity, such as not smoking tobacco, drinking alcohol or dancing.

In 1965, a report of an inter-ministerial commission that visited the region of Guainía compared the methods of evangelization of Catholic and evangelical missionaries. The report suggested that evangelical missionaries lived with *indígenas*, learned their dialect and customs, developed intimate relationships with them and gained their confidence (no matter if they were

Conversion Under Dispute   65

children or adults). In contrast, Catholic missionaries were "solely devoted to childhood training, locked inside the mission, without interacting too much with Indigenous adults or the parents of the children."[40] In 1958, Catholic missionaries from Vaupés established, in a place known as La Ceiba on the Inírida River, a mission with a boarding school (see Map 2.1). This mission received the support of "white" settlers who sent their children to the boarding school, despite the fact that, according to missionaries, they didn't live an exemplary life. While settlers supported the mission, Indigenous groups, "under the direction" of Sophie Muller, were not only indifferent, but "reluctant and opposed to Catholic missionaries."[41] By 1965, the boarding school had 20 boys and 20 girls, and it was run by nuns (Sisters of Mother Laura), most of the children were sons of *colonos*.

Catholic Missionaries Encounter Evangelical Christianity

In April and May, 1961, more than 15 years after Muller's arrival to the Guainía river, Manuel Elorza and Luis Noel Rivera, priests of the Apostolic Prefecture of Mitú (since 1949 administered by the missionaries of Yarumal) carried out a missionary trip (*correría misional*) through the Guaviare, Inírida, Atabapo, Guainía, Isana and Querarí rivers. The missionaries describe the Guainía River, where Sophie Muller had settled down, as the "stronghold of Protestantism" in the region. The people along this river, according to the report, were in the hands of Indigenous catechists who were called *elders* "by the sect." Some of these elders, said the report, were taken to schools or establishments to Bogotá where they received training. Catholic missionaries perceived evangelical Christianity as a "sect" which isolated Indigenous groups from Catholicism, the state and colonization.[42] The missionaries complained because Muller was planting a "germ of division, and even opposition between white men or *colonos* and the natives in the region."[43]

Specifically, Elorza and Rivera reported that the "preachers of the sect attempt by all means to prevent natives from getting too involved in jobs aside from tending to their parcel of land [*conuco*] and building with great effort their houses and the village temple. Any other work or activity would impede the natives' religious practices and contribute to the disintegration of families, according to the protestant missionaries."[44] Before the eyes of Catholic missionaries, evangelical Christianity distanced Indigenous communities from *colonos*.

At the beginning of one of the reports they wrote, Elorza and Rivera refer to the "religious problem, given the proselytism of the evangelical protestants, based on the discredit of the Catholic religion and hatred towards Catholic priests."[45] Catholic missionaries identified a "religious problem" in Sophie Muller's evangelical work in some of the places they visited. The work of Muller and the conversion of native Amazonians to evangelical Christianity constituted a challenge to the authority of the state in the region, represented by Catholic missionaries: "Sophie doesn't let them have any kind of contact

66 *Conversion Under Dispute*

with anyone or nothing that has the seal of Catholicism."[46] This rejection of Catholicism also entailed a rejection of the Colombian nation and its institutions: "Not only they [natives] don't know anything about Colombia, it's history, it's government, etc. But they don't want to know it: they told us they didn't want official schools in their towns because they already knew a lot."[47] Rivera complained about the kind of education that Muller imparted to the natives, saying that "even if it's true that the *indígena* is taught to read, usually in his native tongue, these teachings only prepare them for using the book of religious chants and for the reading of the books of the Bible."[48] In practice, said Rivera, "teachings are reduced to reading and singing."[49]

Catholic missionaries accused the government of breaching the Convention of Missions of 1902, given that the Convention established that only the "Catholic religion could be catechized in the territories of missions."[50] According to Elorza, Muller instilled upon Indigenous communities the hatred toward Catholic priests, distorting the "Sacred Scriptures in order to explain to them that our antecessors, the Princes of the Jewish Priests, gave death to Jesus, that we are the same as them, even more, that we are the devil itself."[51] However, in the Querarí River, missionaries reported that some Indigenous groups declared themselves Catholics, before any previous contact with Catholic missionaries, and started to congregate in "*reducciones* in order to defend themselves from the protestant infiltration."[52]

Muller's work and presence in the region, according to Catholic missionaries, was a threat to their project of civilizing and nationalizing native Amazonians, which was led by them and *colonos* alike, although through different means. Catholic missionaries argued that "evangelical religion" reinforced the natives' "tendency towards laziness," deterring them from productive activities as well as trading activities with *colonos*. If an *indígena* was going to work for a white man, it was necessary to count with Muller's authorization. They also objected to the way evangelical missionaries taught *indígenas* to conceive of material improvement as sinful. Elorza and Rivera complained about the fact that "natives [were] very lazy; and now added to their innate laziness [was] what the evangelical religion [ingrained] in them: the idea that there is no need to rush to attain many possessions, and even the idea that those who have more than 3 dresses live in sin."[53] Both *colonos* and Catholic missionaries often deployed interpretations of Indigenous conversion to evangelical Christianity (i.e. makes them more lazy than what they already were) that reinscribe racist stereotypes.

Catholic missionaries thought that conversion to evangelical Christianity made natives unproductive and restricted material accumulation among them: "they limit the native's power to possess."[54] Father Rivera argued that, for example, none of the evangelical *indígenas* were permitted to own an outboard motor because this supposedly did not allow them to sing. The underlying assumption here is that material possessions (such as outboard motors) become an obstacle for Christian practices (such as singing in the cult), limiting their agency and autonomy. Most of the times, commodities given in advance to Indigenous "workers" had to be payed off with work for white patrons. In fact, Rivera claimed to have seen Muller scold an *indígena* who had received an outboard engine as payment for his work and apparently ordered the native to return it. According to Elorza and Rivera "the evangelical Indian [had] to escape civilization and material improvement as sinful things [*cosas de pecado*]."[55] With such an "orientation," according to Catholic missionaries, "it cannot be said that natives catechized into Protestantism are being civilized."[56] Unlike Catholicism, evangelical Christianity had a negative view of materiality and possessions.

In fact, Catholic missionaries perceived the work of Sophie Muller as an obstacle to the colonization and economic development of the region given that natives "can't, don't even want to work for any white boss."[57] Missionaries said that under the influence of Protestantism *indígenas* had "retracted" from the white man and concentrated in their "places of origin." In this regard, Rivera mentioned that in a place named *La Estación* on the Guaviare River there was a *colono* established there whose name was Abelardo Rivera. One day there was a problem between Abelardo and an *indígena* that worked for him. The news about this problem came to Sophie and she went to Abelardo's house: "in a seigniorial and authoritative tone she warned him [Abelardo] to abandon the place and leave the region, (...) arguing that the cocoa plantations he exploited and the lands he was cultivating belonged to the *Indios*."[58] Father Rivera saw this kind of situation as proof of the "supreme mastery" [*supremo dominio*] that Muller exercised over the "land and its *indígenas*," to the extent that she pushed the natives to ignore the "authorities of their own country and practically removes their notion of fatherland [*Patria*] and nationality."[59]

Not only did Catholic and evangelical missionaries promote, among Indigenous groups, different notions of civilization, but they also had different views of commodities and materiality. While Catholic missionaries relied heavily on commodities and material objects as part of their work, Indigenous evangelicals and churches developed an ongoing critique of materiality, commodities and money through the idea of "worldliness" (*lo mundano*), producing an ambiguous relationship with modernity. The critiques evangelicals made to material accumulation contradicted the values and rationalities that underwrote different projects of colonization and extractivism in the region.

Elorza and Rivera accused Muller of setting the natives against *colonos* and Catholic priests: "evangelical Indians refuse to say greet a priest, and cannot receive anything from them under any title."[60] The missionaries complained about "the atmosphere of indifference towards the arrival of a priest [in most the villages], this on the part of men, because women and children can't greet a priest. As soon as they see one, they hide or run into the forest."[61] Elorza and Rivera repeated in their report that "Sophie instills upon them a hatred against white men, as she points them out as allies of the devil, and so therefore working with them constitutes a sin."[62] Ironically, the image of the white man or the Catholic priest as the Devil could play against Muller herself.

68 *Conversion Under Dispute*

In *Beyond Civilization*, Muller confesses to be "scared of these people" and afraid "they'll turn and think I'm a devil one of these days."[63]

Muller also used the figure of the Devil to describe Indigenous rituals and religious practices in her written accounts. As it happened before with Catholic missionaries, Indigenous religious traditions were perceived to be tantamount to "demon worship."[64] Birgit Meyer shows how the "image of the Devil" was a product of the encounter between Indigenous groups and Western missionaries and became a "hybrid form which helped to constitute the reality in which both parties came to terms with each other."[65] In the case of Amazonia, Michael Taussig points out that with Christianity, the "missionaries also introduced magic, or *magia* as it is called in the Putumayo today, in reference to power that stems from a pact with the devil. The missionaries believed firmly in the efficacy of sorcery, which they supposed Indians to be especially prone to practice on account of their having been seduced by the devil."[66]

Elorza and Rivera argued that Muller pointed to the squalid lives of some *colonos* that were said to be Catholics in order to "show the natives how Catholics [were] friends of the devil, even going so far as to say that we the priests [were] the demon in itself."[67] All of these tensions with Indigenous evangelicals made the missionary trip of Elorza and Rivera harder than they imagined. When they arrived at the Isana River the missionaries decided to get rid of their garments and travel from "now on as civilians" trying to reduce the tensions with local communities.[68] The Indigenous evangelical community of Caño Colorado, in the upper Guainía River, refused the missionaries lodging, but they were able to sleep there after they "imposed themselves upon them talking to them strongly and invoking [their] nationality as Colombians."[69]

Despite the "religious problem" the Catholic missionaries referred to when they addressed Muller's work, it seems clear the issue was not about doctrinary or theological differences between Catholicism and evangelical Christianity. Rather, the problem was really the political consequences of her massive conversion of Indigenous communities for the state and the Catholic missionaries. In the report, father Rivera argues that,

> The obvious fact in all of our journey is that Sofía Muller, an American protestant missionary who has worked for several years in the region doing proselytizing activities, practically rules [*domina*] the North and North-Eastern areas of Vaupés: she exercises a real authority over the *indígenas*, that offer her complete submission and respect and, in fact do not recognize another authority different from her, not just in religious issues, but also regarding civil, economic, and social issues. It is not exaggerated to say that they obey her blindly and execute without repairs whatever she orders.[70]

In what sense did Muller's apparent rule in the northern Vaupés represent a threat for the state? Why was the Indian's "complete submission and

Conversion Under Dispute 69

respect" to Muller a problem for the state? Furthermore, in what ways does religion or religious conversion become a political issue or a problem for the state? While Catholicism constituted the civic and public religion *par excellence* in Colombia until the end of the 20th century, evangelical Christianity seemed to interrupt the "link" that tied the theologico-political authority of the state to a social body.[71] In this sense, questioning Catholicism as civic religion entailed questioning the foundations of the nation-state as well as the loyalty that citizens expressed through their membership to the Catholic Church. The adoption of evangelical Christianity implied, to some extent, pertaining to a different type of political and moral community *vis-á-vis* the Catholic nation-state. In fact, Elorza noted that "this problem of religious character has created another one of sovereignty and borders, because natives lead us to understand that they are willing today to leave Colombian territory and move to Venezuela or Brazil in case they fall under the tutelage of Catholic missionaries for their evangelization."[72]

On the Colombian side of the border, according to Elorza and Rivera, there were no public schools or Catholic chapels, instead every "village" (*caserío*) had its evangelical temple with its own catechistic school. What surprised Catholic missionaries the most was how *indígenas* infused with Protestantism "could not give us nor sell us anything, and they can't receive anything from us, not even the candies that please children and adults in other places so much."[73] In this sense, Indigenous evangelicals interrupted the practices of gift-giving, barter and exchange with Catholic missionaries. These practices were crucial in how Catholic missionaries developed their work among Indigenous communities in Vaupés. The refusal of Indigenous evangelicals to exchange with Catholic missionaries, to sell or receive objects from them, should be understood as a way of rejecting the possibility of establishing any kind of social relationship or bond with them. This rejection of transactions with Catholic missionaries should lead us to think about the implications of "unsuccessful transactions" or failed exchange. Anthropologists have usually emphasized the "constructive accomplishments of exchange rather than the consequences of its failure."[74]

The main reason for refusing any material exchange with Catholic missionaries was because they were associated with the Devil. Furthermore, objects of different kinds have historically been "building blocks" in Amazonian sociability to the extent that "artifacts were believed to be people or parts of people that were later transformed into other beings."[75] In addition, for several Indigenous groups in Amazonia, "histories of relations with other people are experienced in material forms" and "gifts received from outsiders have been sources of both agency and anxiety."[76]

In a similar vein, there were also frictions between evangelicals and other agents of the Colombian state, not just Catholic missionaries, throughout the 1960s and 1970s in Vaupés. As I will show in the next section, when state officials arrived in 1965 on the Inírida River to establish the capital of the new province (called *Guainía* in Spanish), most Indigenous communities were

70 Conversion Under Dispute

already evangelical. The new province was created as a way of expanding the sovereignty of the Colombian state into a region that was under dispute with Venezuela since the 1920s.

Indigenous Evangelicals and the State

Unlike other towns and provinces in the Colombian Amazon, Guainía and its capital (Puerto Inírida) were established in the 1960s as part of a state-led project of colonization and sovereignty in the region. Since the 1920s, visitors to the region of what is today Guainía complained about the fact that no state authorities, neither civil nor military, had any kind of presence in the region. In 1923, famous Colombian writer Jose Eustasio Rivera, author of *The Vortex* (1924), traveled to the region as part of a border commission and recounted how Venezuelan authorities send commissions to the area in order to "pick up" the "Indians from the Colombian zone and incorporate them into Venezuela through threats and tricks."[77] Rivera complained that since "immemorial times no other authority is exercised on both shores of these rivers other than the authority of Venezuela."[78] One of the first requests to create the *comisaría* of Guainía was done by a *colono* called Marco Acuña in 1925. In a letter directed to the central government that year, Acuña argued that it was necessary to create the *comisaría* of Guainía in order to "defend the lives, families and interests of the many *indígenas* that are constantly robbed, raped and forcibly recruited by Venezuelan elements that take them as slaves to work in the Venezuelan territory of San Fernando de Atabapo."[79]

In the report written in 1961, Father Manuel María Elorza dedicated a section to the "absence of authorities and the ineffectiveness of the existing ones." Elorza complained in the report about the "abandonment" of the border, as well as the lack of official authorities and military garrisons. While border posts in Brazil or Venezuela were well organized, with ships, radio communications, good salaries for their employees, Colombia's border towns only had a "poor and helpless *corregidor*, underpaid, with no official seals and paper for his communications and ordinances."[80] In addition, Elorza pointed out that state agents lacked the physical means to "impose" their authority among people (especially those considered civilized) who "were always armed and take a revolver wherever they go."[81] *Colonos* (especially those that lived in the lower Guaviare Region) carried of "justice among themselves," while state authorities did not count with the help of police officers. State offices were usually in a ranch where officials lived with their wife, sometimes an Indigenous woman, and their children.

The lack of state presence on the border encouraged abuses and hostilities toward Colombians that moved across it by the Venezuelan National Guard (stationed on the town of San Fernando de Atabapo). Catholic missionaries recounted that Colombians in this region were forced to travel to Venezuela for everything, especially for postal and telegraph services, and they had to accept the *Bolívar* as their currency. Father Elorza also complained about the

Conversion Under Dispute 71

absence of transportation available for state officials in a region where "every *colono* and trader had to look for his own medium of transportation."[82] State officials, according to Elorza, did not even have access to paper with which to write reports or letters for official purposes.

The creation of the *comisaría* of Guainía in 1963 was carried out in the context of disputes between Catholic and evangelical missionaries described in the previous section, but also responded to the precarious condition of state offices and institutions in the region. For example, in 1963 the National Police saw the establishment of the new province as a way of asserting "national sovereignty" in faraway regions of the country. The 100th edition of the magazine of the National Police in 1963 mentioned the juridical principle of the *Uti possidetis de facto* as the rationale behind the creation of new provinces and politico-administrative units. State institutions in Colombia such as the National Police established a close relationship between *de facto* possession of the territory and the exercise of national sovereignty in the region.

While the principle of *Uti possidetis iure* was based on jurisdictions and territorial possessions determined by law and treaties, the *Uti possidetis de facto* was based on the actual control and occupation of territory. During the 19th century, the principle of *Uti possidetis iure legal* entailed that the "newly born republics would preserve the colonial limits at the time of independence."[83] However, as it was described in the previous chapter, the boundaries between the former colonies were not clear in regions such as the Amazon. This facilitated the "*de facto* appropriation of territories in dispute."[84] Throughout the 19th century and part of the 20th century, the state and the elites in charge of it had a blind faith on the *Uti possidetis iure principle*.

One of the first strategies of the national government to put the principle of *Uti possidetis de facto* in the region into practice was to establish the capital for the province of Guainía, from which it could be governed, populated and administrated. Compared to other processes of colonization in Amazonia that were associated with the extraction of resources such as rubber, the creation of the province of Guainía was part of a project of state-led colonization which included the visit to the region of a technical commission in 1965 composed of naturalists, military engineers and geographers of the National University, as well as representatives of the ministries of government, war, agriculture and public works. This commission decided the capital of the province would be established on the Inírida River, on a small Indigenous village called *Las Brujas* (The Witches). One of the main reasons for choosing this place was the natural savanna located close to *Las Brujas*, that would make the construction of an airport cheaper and easier.

The regional government led by recently named *comisario* Hernando Ríos was inaugurated on February 7, 1965, in La Ceiba, where the Catholic missionaries had established their mission seven years before (see Figure 2.1). One month later, functionaries and members of the regional government moved from La Ceiba to Puerto Inírida. The office of the regional government operated first in the house of an *indígena* called Ramón Castillo. Several

Figure 2.1 Functionaries of the national government in charge of establishing the *comisaría* of Guainía in 1965.

Source: Museo Comunitario del Guainía. Courtesy of Museo Comunitario del Guainía and Carlos Ríos (https://www.facebook.com/media/set/?set=a.504660666409850&type=3).

properties of *indígenas* were "destroyed in order to organize the town."[85] Before the establishment of the new province, *indígenas* already had a subordinated position *vis-á-vis colonos*, working for them in the extraction of *balatá* and fiber. When the *comisaría* was created some of the *indígenas* that already lived there started to work for the regional government in basic tasks. One of the decrees issued by the regional government established that the adjudication of parcels in the "Indigenous urban sector" will be made "without concessions for natives," giving them support and assistance so they could "modernize their houses" with "hygiene and aesthetics."[86]

A local historian, Tiberio Acevedo, asserts that Hernan Ríos González, the head of the new regional government, "recognized" the authority of existing Indigenous authorities: *capitán* Delfín Acosta in Las Brujas and *capitán* Agapito Sandoval in Caranacoa.[87] The first *comisario* had apparently reached an agreement with Indigenous authorities in order to have access to their land, where the capital of the new province was going to be established. According to Acevedo, the "agreement" with Indigenous authorities included the official recognition of Agapito and Delfín: "in order to gain their affect [*congraciar*] the *capitanes* were taken by the *comisario* to Bogotá and invited to the National Congress where they were honored."[88] Agapito told Acevedo

Conversion Under Dispute 73

in a personal conversation how the *comisario* said to him: "Agapito, I name you *capitán* of the Puinaves and Delfín Acosta [*capitán*] of the Curripacos, so there won't be any problems."[89] In this sense, the official appointment of Indigenous authorities went hand in hand with processes of dispossession and expropriation of Indigenous land. Most of the Indigenous authorities appointed by the state would later become brokers between the state and Indigenous communities.

In May 5, 1965, some Indigenous leaders and evangelicals that lived in "Las Brujas" wrote and signed a letter directed to Gregorio Hernández de Alba, who was in charge of the Division of Indigenous Affairs at the Ministry of Government in Bogotá. Delfín Acosta also signed the letter and the signatories spoke in the name of "*indígenas* of the Puinave tribe." In the letter, the Indigenous evangelicals told Hernández de Alba they were very concerned about the "events that happened with the inauguration of the regional government."[90] The signatories considered those "events" as being "out of their customs." Specifically, Indigenous evangelicals said in the letter:

> (...) when the *comisario* and his people arrived here we thought the moment of our entrance to civilization had begun with all it can offer to people like us, abandoned. But it didn't happen, in Caranacoa, they started to make parties with huge amounts of *aguardiente* [liquor] they had brought, almost forcing, a lot of us to drink it, something we don't do following the teaching of our pastors, who have told us this vice is bad. In addition, they have not offered us alcohol out of courtesy, but in order to get us drunk and bother our women and daughters.[91]

This letter discloses the deceptive encounter Indigenous evangelicals had with the Colombian state. The description of how the practices of state officials, sent to create the new province of Guainía, were perceived by Indigenous evangelicals as "evil," makes explicit the different notions of civilization and morality that were at play in this region. Clearly, Indigenous evangelicals did not find anything good or civilized about the consumption of alcohol. White settlers in Amazonia and other peripheries of Latin America have historically used alcohol in their transactions and interactions with Indigenous societies. Since colonial times, drunkenness and the consumption of alcohol were considered by the *creole* elite essential traits of "Indigenous culture."[92]

Members of the regional government reproduced practices, such as getting natives drunk and abusing of Indigenous woman, that were previously deployed by rubber bosses and other *colonos*. Furthermore, signatories of the letter complained about being evicted from their own houses, because these were given to employees of the *comisaría*. Ramón Castilla (who also signed the letter) denounced that his house was used as the office of the regional government and that the *comisario* hadn't paid him the 1,200 pesos he offered for the house.

74   *Conversion Under Dispute*

Parts of the letter were about specific demands to the national government:

we are still "indebted" by those who exploit us. This means they give us things in advance, little money and we all have to work for a lot of time and never can pay back the entire debt. The government does not take action. Gum extractors [*chicleros*] force us to go into the mountain without anyone protecting us. We ask you to send a *visitador* to talk with us and know our situation.[93]

Despite these demands from the Indigenous inhabitants of Las Brujas, the arrival of the state did not entail the end of debt peonage and other forms of forced or coerced labor. As it happened before in Vaupés, in Guainía state authorities, be it missionaries or state officials would serve again as intermediaries between *indígenas* and *colonos*. For instance, in April 16, 1968, a state official (*Corregidor*) issued and signed a certification of a "debt-transfer" of nine *indígenas* from Mr. Romero to the Angarita Castilla and Bernal Company. In this sense, the claim directed to the state for protection from the gum extractors should be understood as a demand for a stronger state that could effectively protect their rights as both Colombians and Indigenous peoples.

The signatories' description of their situation to Hernández de Alba as "abandoned" by the Colombian state reveals how these people had started to incorporate the "language of the state," which included the idea of having rights and being able to demand specific things from the state (i.e. protection, attention, etc.). In the letter, they say they need "drugs for sick people, because in San Fernando, Venezuela, they don't give us assistance anymore, given that we are Colombians it is our government that should give them to us."[94] State attention was thus also demanded by the Indigenous population that lived where the capital of the new province was to be established. The ways in which these demands were framed implied the Indigenous appropriation of new languages of the state (associated with specific rights and demands) in tandem with specific forms of interaction and communication with state authorities through written letters and formal petitions, among others. The signatories finished the letter saying to Hernández de Alba: "*We are your friends. Sincerely.*" It was common to find, in the 1960s and 1970s, letters of Indigenous leaders written directed to regional state officials or to the President of the Republic with specific demands. Some of these letters included demands for better health conditions or access to land through reservations.

Boarding Schools, Evangelical Missionaries and the State

Relationships between evangelical missionaries and the Colombian state were always ambiguous and controversial. As I mentioned at the beginning of the chapter, military president Gustavo Rojas Pinilla had declared in 1956

Conversion Under Dispute   75

that "the Protestants are united with the Communists to destroy Colombian national unity."[95] Nonetheless, NTM obtained its legal status in Colombia on May 23, 1967, while six years earlier, the SIL had reached an agreement with anthropologist Gregorio Hernández de Alba (who was organizing Colombia's first Department of Indigenous Affairs) in order to "start an indigenist-oriented, government-controlled integration program and train national linguists."[96] Before the central government, evangelical missionaries presented their work as a civilizing enterprise that helped transform Indigenous subjects into national citizens. On June 22, 1970, the secretary and legal representative of the NTM sent a report to the chief of Indigenous affairs at the national government. The report expressed how the New Tribes missionaries had "helped in the transformation of Indigenous customs, in the responsibilities they [had] before other men, but especially before God and the Colombian Nation."[97] In a similar vein, the section of the report devoted to "culture" began by stating that missionaries "fix nomadic and semi-nomadic people in favorable sites or in farms in order to raise their quality of life. They are taught to respect the laws and other civic duties of society, the nation, and the family."[98]

On September 6, 1965, the *comisario* received a letter from Secretary of Interior with a new decree, issued five days earlier, attached. The decree was issued to promote what the central government called "popular integration." It began recognizing the existence of "a huge amount of Colombians from the city and the countryside facing difficult conditions, prey to diseases, unemployment, ignorance, civic inertia, lacking housing, recreations and opportunities of human progress."[99] According to the decree, such "fellow countrymen" found it impossible to participate in the "economic, cultural, spiritual and civic life of the country," as a result of their "condition of marginalization from social life, isolation and incapacity to resolve their own problems."[100] Popular integration was understood, then, as the way of overcoming the marginality of that huge mass of Colombians that lived in the poorer areas of the cities and the peripheral regions of the country. Popular integration was designed to promote the "integral development" and "real incorporation to national life" of the marginal sectors of society.[101]

One of the main strategies used by the regional and central government in order to reach the "real incorporation to national life" of marginal populations was to establish boarding schools in the Indigenous communities dispersed throughout the rivers of the region. In September 1968, the *comisario* wrote a report to the central government with an "inventory of the services and needs of the *Comisaría Especial del Guainía.*" The report referred to education, saying that,

> I think that this problem, along with public health [*salubridad*], is the most important to address in the inventory of accomplishments and needs that are being requested. The first one [education], besides the indispensable literacy campaign, is closely related to the rational exploitation of

76 *Conversion Under Dispute*

natural resources in order to defend the fauna and flora, given that in these regions hunting and fishing are misused and, as it happens in all of the national territory, logging destroys more than what it uses.[102]

Education of Indigenous communities was directly associated with the "rational exploitation" of natural resources. The *comisario* gave detailed information in the inventory about the schools that existed in the region with the costs of building each of them and what remained to be built. For instance, regarding the school of Guadalupe (which is far from Inírida and close to the border with Brazil in the Upper Rio Negro), the report says: "it operates in a locale ceded by a *colono*, with 25 students of both sexes, and is served by a [male] professor. Regarding the premises, it has materials that were randomly put together and will be arranged in the next visit to the region of the *comisario* and the secretary engineer of public works."[103] Most of the first schools were precarious and used buildings that were ceded by *colonos* or buildings that belonged to a police inspection, as it happened with the school in *El Coco*. The idea was that most of the schools built would become boarding schools in the future, given that the "population is very dispersed throughout this extensive territory and it will not be possible to have a school in every small nucleus [of population]."[104]

In this simultaneous process of nation and school building, teachers, some of whom were former *colonos*, became a sort of "secular missionaries" of the state. In a letter written to the *comisario* in February 1966, the head of one of the first schools that existed in Inírida expressed his interest in the creation of a literacy center for adults that would open at nights. The head of the school said in the letter that the support they received from the regional government would be a "reason for the pride for each of the Colombians that participate in this arduous labor of establishing [*implantar*] sovereignty and bringing to these remote national regions a piece of culture that will eco for the rest of eternity."[105]

Clearly, colonization and state-formation were carried out through the establishment of boarding schools and this process was challenged by evangelical missionaries when they established their own "schools" or questioned the moral standards and adequacy of teachers that worked at boarding schools. Conflicts between teachers (some of which had come to the region as *colonos*) and Sophie Muller were common. This was the case of Fernando Carrillo, who came to the region with his father when he was a young man, in the early 1970s, to *colonizar* (colonize/settle). After the *comisario* in charge convinced him to work for the regional government, Fernando started to establish (*fundar*) boarding schools. During the 1970s, Fernando established five boarding schools in different Indigenous communities throughout the Guaviare River. Fernando explained to me how, when he established his first school among Piapoco people in a community called Guaco, he had to look for the acceptance of the members of the community, including the *capitán*. The later accepted his presence and told Fernando that he could start

Conversion Under Dispute 77

teaching at the church, while they built the school. It was around 1973 that Fernando had his first encounter with Sophie Muller in Guaco. Fernando recalled his encounter with Muller at the place where he was staying,

> Teacher you're a devil, you're a devil! (…) she was upset, she turned red, and why am I a devil Sofía? I replied to her (…) that is a devil [pointing to a calendar poster with a woman in blue jeans], that radio is a devil, that is a devil! More devil are you Sofía! You have pants, she [woman in the poster] also has pants, then where is the nudity? You are more devil! When I replied to her like that she started tapping the floor with her shoes (…) I talked to her like that because I was upset, me a Colombian, constructing nation [*haciendo patria*] around here, creating schools, teaching to the people and all that, and then a foreigner comes here, I hadn't drunk my coffee that day, I was about to make one, to insult me!

The idea that New Tribes missionaries were simple instillers of civic and national virtues among Indigenous communities was challenged by conflicts arising on the ground between state authorities and Sophie Muller. On October 30, 1973, Cleomedes Caballero Bueno, the *comisario* of the recently created *Comisaría* of Guainía, started a formal investigation against Sophie Muller for damaging the success of public education. Muller was accused of obstructing public education in Barrancominas, a town located on the lower Guaviare River. In her last book *His Voice Shakes the Wilderness* (1988), Muller argues that teachers chosen by the government to "do the teaching did not contribute to the Indians' new moral standards. Most were young, atheistic men, fresh out of college, and full of Karl Marx."[106] As part of the investigation, several teachers from public schools who were educating *indígenas* were interrogated. One of them, whose name was Jorge Eliécer Gutierrez, stated in the interrogation that:

> (…) in my presence she told the natives that because I had long hair and a beard I was an individual with communist, socialist tendencies, (…) that I was the devil and in each cult she presented a movie and always said that socialists and communists were evil. This psychologically influenced the natives and that's why they showed signs of aggression towards me, speaking in their own language they demonstrated gestures of contempt.[107]

Muller demonized preachers and teachers working for the state, as it happened before with Catholic missionaries and *colonos*.[108] Orlando Espitia, another of the teachers interrogated, said that natives weren't attending school anymore because Muller had told them that white teachers were "evil," that they were the devil and drank *aguardiente*. In his declaration, Orlando expressed the concern that if "this *señorita* [lady] [was] not expelled from Colombian territory, the education and prosperity of the *indígenas* [would]

78 *Conversion Under Dispute*

never advance."[109] *Indígenas* were also interrogated as part of the investigation. One of such *indígenas*, Juan Gaitán, stated that he had known Muller for 29 years and that "she is always around teaching us the word of the Lord. She is a close friend of ours and she is our pastor."[110] Juan also stated in his declaration that Muller had told them that they should work and that if a "white man calls us to work we should work in order to avoid discrepancies of any kind."[111] Regarding the accusation made by the regional government, Juan said that Muller "didn't talk about white teachers," but continued: "we need an evangelical pastor, because white teachers don't teach that much (...) We want our kids to learn a lot."[112] In this sense, the differences between the testimonies of Indigenous evangelicals and teachers that worked for the state reveal different perceptions and meanings regarding Muller's work among Indigenous communities in Guainía.

Militaries Follow Evangelical Missionaries

Whereas regional state officials considered Muller a threat to their authority over Indigenous populations, placing in jeopardy the "civilization" and integration of these groups to the body politic, in 1976 the central government the Ministry of Defense opened a formal investigation against the SIL who were doing missionary work among Indigenous populations in the eastern plains of the country. Under the coordination of General José Matallana, director of the national intelligence agency at the time, the Ministry of Defense carried out an investigation to "verify the activities of the Summer Institute of Linguistics, get to know the situation of the region, [and] verify the facts that [had fed] rumors regarding foreign activities that [injured] national sovereignty in the east of the country."[113]

Besides the activities of the SIL, the commission of the Ministry of Defense also revised the work of other foreign institutions such as the NTM. General Matallana's commission pointed out that foreign religious institutions had carried out "actions of indoctrination and authority upon Colombian *indígenas*, [these institutions] [had] assumed in practice their control and orientation in this region and in the rest of the country."[114] The commission produced a report and part of it was dedicated to the NTM. Regarding the work of Muller, the report stated that "*señorita* Sofía Muller has been evangelizing the *indígena* for three decades in these vast territories and has won to a large extent their control, authority, and confidence."[115] According to the report, Muller represented the "most fanatic and intransigent sector of the evangelical church."[116] Among the main characteristics of Muller's work the report mentions the following: Muller (a) "tactically remains continuously among the tribes," (b) convinces the *indígenas* that "any kind of contact or transaction they have with the white man will doom their souls because the devil will penetrate their spirits and they will become evil beings, condemned to divine punishment," (c) wants the "*indígena* to be kept in a primitive state of isolation from the rest of their fellow countrymen while arguing that Indigenous life, as strongly communitarian, is what God wants and any issue that breaks this principle deserves condemnation."[117]

In a similar way to Catholic missionaries, militaries perceived the presence and work of Sophie Muller as a threat to national sovereignty and the authority of the state in the region. General Matallana suggested that Muller was keeping natives isolated from fellow citizens, condemning them to social and economic backwardness, and making them "reluctant to progress" as they couldn't work or trade with white men. The report for the Ministry of Defense concluded its reflection on Sophie Muller stating:

> In summary, the work of *señorita* Sophie Muller has had an extremely negative effect and has had severe consequences for the economic, social and cultural development of the several Indigenous communities that she has controlled for thirty years without any intervention on the part of the Colombian state. In consequence, and as a matter of vital importance for the defense of Indigenous culture, national sovereignty and the integration of Indigenous populations to the rest of the nation, the conclusion is drawn that putting an end to [her] activities is required.[118]

In this way, different agents of the state such as Catholic missionaries, teachers and militaries held a negative perception of Muller's work and influence upon Indigenous communities. These critiques of Muller's endeavor also demonstrate how evangelical missionaries were seen as an obstacle to state-formation and authority in the region, preventing the effective incorporation of Indigenous populations to the nation-state.

However, the interpretations of both local and national state officials regarding Muller's work contradicted Indigenous accounts of their own process of conversion to Christianity. As I will show in the next chapter, Indigenous communities in Guainía associate conversion to Christianity with the arrival of civilization and becoming "modern" in their own terms, among other things. It is common to hear among elder Indigenous evangelicals that since they became Christians, *colonos* cannot treat them any more as if they were savages. Indigenous evangelicals perceived the adoption of Christianity as a form of leverage with *colonos* that marked a break with the past in all realms of life.

Conclusions

This chapter explored how the conversion of Indigenous groups in the Colombian Amazon to evangelical Christianity became a political problem for the state in the region. In Colombia during the Cold War, Protestantism was often regarded as a near relative of communism and was considered a threat to "national Colombian unity." Through the establishment of Indigenous churches and the training of Indigenous pastors, NTM missionaries created new forms of community and indigeneity. Some of these forms clashed with state-led projects of colonization that were enacted by *colonos*, most of them

80 *Conversion Under Dispute*

were Catholic and had different moral standards. Despite that Indigenous evangelicals developed moral critiques of the behavior of state officials, they started to incorporate languages of the state (associated with specific rights and demands), sending letters and formal petitions to state authorities. These letters included complaints to the central government about regional state official and specific demands. The appropriation of these "languages of stateness" is crucial to understand how Indigenous communities become subjects of the state and part of different practices of governance.

The second part of the chapter shows how Catholic missionaries from Mitú (Vaupés) followed closely and tracked the work of evangelical missionaries such as Sophie Muller. Evangelical Christianity represented a challenge to the Catholic Church, whose authority over Indigenous groups in this region came from the state. State authorities also considered the work of Sophie Muller a political threat to the point that the national intelligence agency carried out an investigation to verify her "activities." The report made by military agency officials suggested that Muller was a problem for the incorporation of Indigenous communities to the body politic, isolating them from *colonos* and the national society. In fact, Muller was also followed and persecuted by FARC (Revolutionary Armed Forces of Colombia). In the last chapter of *His Voice Shakes the Wilderness*, Muller remembers that once a leader of FARC "entered a village at the end of a church conference. He was accompanied by a dozen heavily armed men and was asking for me. The Indians knew what he would do if he found me – either kidnap or kill."[119] After this episode, Sophie Muller had to spend the rest of her life living in the same region but on the other side of the border in Venezuela. Military intelligence officers and Catholic authorities in Colombia wanted the national government to deport Muller as she was considered a hindrance to national sovereignty in the Colombian Amazon.

Notes

1 Right after the wars of independence at the beginning of the 19th century, the first Protestant missionaries and envoys started to visit and travel to different countries of Latin America, establishing the first Biblical Societies in the region. One of the first protestant missionaries to travel to South America was the Scottish Baptist pastor James Thompson, member of the British and Foreign Bible Society, who arrived in Buenos Aires in August 1819 and then traveled to Chile, Peru, Ecuador and Colombia. In Bogotá, Thompson established the first Biblical Society in 1825 and two years later traveled to Mexico. Different authors have pointed out the historical and elective affinities between liberal governments or parties and Protantism in Latin America throughout the 19th century. Despite the attempts of liberal elites in trying to implement secular reforms, the cultural and political hegemony of the Catholic Church went unfettered in most countries of Latin America well into the 20th century. As a response to the political violence experienced after 1948, 19 different protestant denominations founded the Evangelical Confederation of Colombia (CEDEC) in Bogotá in June, 1950. In 1953, CEDEC reported that since 1948 (when liberal *caudillo* Jorge Eliécer Gaitán was killed in Bogotá), 42 churches

Conversion Under Dispute 81

were destroyed, 110 evangelical schools closed, 51 evangelicals killed and 28 of them murdered by the national police and government officials. See William Mauricio Beltrán, *Del monopolio católico a la explosión pentecostal: pluralización religiosa, secularización y cambio social en Colombia* (Bogotá: Lecturas CES, 2013), 70.

2 Paul Freston, *Evangelicals and Politics in Asia, Africa and Latin America* (New York: Cambridge University Press, 2001), 229.

3 Anthony Gill, *Rendering unto Cesar: The Catholic Church and the State in Latin America* (Chicago: University of Chicago Press, 1998), 79.

4 Hent de Vries, "Introduction. Before Around, and Beyond the Theologico-Political," in *Political Theologies. Public Religions in a Post-Secular World*, eds. Hent de Vries and Lawrence E. Sullivan (New York: Fordham University Press, 2006), 2.

5 Peter van der Veer, ed. "Introduction," in *Conversion to Modernities: The Globalization of Christianity* (New York: Routledge, 1996), 2–21.

6 Reinhart Koselleck, *Futures Past, On the Semantics of Historical Time* (New York: Columbia University Press, 1985), 12.

7 Søren Hvalkof and Peter Aaby, "Introducing God in the Devil's Paradise," in *Is God an American? An Anthropological Perspective on the Missionary Work of the Summer Institute of Linguistics*, eds. Søren Hvalkof and Peter Aaby (Copenhaguen: IWGIA and Survival International, 1981), 14.

8 Courtney Handman, *Critical Christianity. Translation and Denominational Conflict in Papua New Guinea* (Oakland: University of California Press, 2015), 61.

9 Ibid.

10 Peter Gow, "Forgetting Conversion. The Summer Institute of Linguistics Mission in the Piro Lived World," in *The Anthropology of Christianity*, Fenella Canell, ed. (Durham: Duke University Press, 2006), 216.

11 Joel Carpenter, *Revive Us Again. The Reawakening of American Fundamentalism* (Oxford: Oxford University Press, 1997), 180.

12 Aparecida Vilaça points out that it was not enough to simply reach "unreached tribes" with the word of God as a condition for the second coming of Christ, it was also necessary to provoke the conversion of all those "unreached tribes" to Christianity. See Aparecida Vilaça, "Indivíduos celestes. Cristianismo e parentesco em um grupo nativo da Amazônia," *Religao e Sociedade* 27, no. 1 (2007): 16.

13 Kenneth Johnston, *The Story of New Tribes Mission* (Sanford: New Tribes Mission, 1985), 283.

14 Ibid.

15 Courtney Handman, *Critical Christianity*, 64

16 Sophie Muller, *Jungle Methods* (Woodworth: Brown Gold Publications, 1960), 2.

17 Word of Life was created 1940 by Wyrzten and is a ministry committed to reaching youth with the Gospel. He wrote in 1988 the Introduction for Muller's book *His Voice Shakes the Wilderness*, where he recalls when Sophie Muller came for the first time one Saturday night to the open-air meetings the group held in Woodhaven, New York. See Sophie Muller, *His Voice Shakes the Wilderness*, 1988: IX.

18 Sophie Muller, *His Voice Shakes the Wilderness* (Sanford: New Tribes Mission, 1988), 5–6.

19 Ibid, 6.

20 Ibid.

21 Ibid.

22 Ibid.

23 Sophie Muller, *Jungle Methods* (Woodworth: Brown Gold Publications, 1960), 3.

24 Ibid, 13.

25 Ibid.

26 Sophie Muller, *Beyond Civilization* (Woodworth: New Tribes Mission, 1952), 18.

27 Comaroff and Comaroff, *Of Revelation and Revolution*, 63–64.

82 Conversion Under Dispute

28 The Laubach method was created in the 1930s by Frank C. Laubach while working in the Philippines. The method originated was a way of teaching adults to read and write in their own language. The Laubach method emphasizes learning through association rather than through memory. Letters and sound are introduced associating pictures with keywords.

29 Sophie Muller, *Jungle Methods*, 30.

30 Sophie Muller, *Jungle Methods* (Woodworth: Brown Gold Publications, 1960), 3–4.

31 Sophie Muller, *Jungle Methods*, 21.

32 Stephen Hugh-Jones, "Shamans, Prophets, Priests, and Pastors," in *Shamanism, History and the State*, eds. Nicholas Thomas and Caroline Humprey (Ann Arbor: The University of Michigan Press, 1996), 58.

33 Sophie Muller, *Beyond Civilization* (Woodworth: New Tribes Mission, 1952), 16.

34 Ibid.

35 Sophie Mulller, *Jungle Methods*, 1.

36 Ibid.

37 Ibid.

38 Bernardo J. Calle, *Caminos de Esperanza* (Mitú: Vicariato Apostólico de Mitú, 2014).

39 Sophie Muller, *Jungle Methods*, 5.

40 Informe Comisión Interministerial Comisaría del Guainía, Leguísamo, Marzo 22 de 1965.

41 Ibid.

42 "Informe sobre una correría misional por los ríos Guaviare, Inírida, Atabapo, Guainía, Isana y Querari," June 16, 1961, AGN, Ministerio de Gobierno, División de Asuntos Indígenas, Caja 190, Carpeta 1609, fol. 73.

43 Ibid, fol. 66.

44 Ibid.

45 Ibid, fol. 66.

46 Ibid, fol. 68.

47 Ibid, fol. 75.

48 Ibid.

49 Ibid.

50 Ibid.

51 Ibid.

52 Ibid, fol. 69.

53 Ibid, fol. 66.

54 Ibid. fol. 74.

55 Ibid.

56 Ibid.

57 Ibid.

58 Ibid.

59 Ibid.

60 Ibid.

61 Ibid, fol. 67.

62 Ibid, fol. 74.

63 Sophie Muller, *Beyond Civilization* (Woodsworth: Brown Gold Publications, 1952), 53.

64 R. L. Green, *Tropical Idolatry. A Theological History of Catholic Colonialism in the Pacific World, 1568–1700* (Lanham: Lexington Books, 2018), 1.

65 Birgit Meyer, *Translating the Devil: Religion and Modernity among the Ewe in Ghana* (Edinburgh: Edinburgh University Press, 1999), xxiii.

Conversion Under Dispute 83

66 Michael Taussig, *Shamanism, Colonialism, and the Wild Man: A Study in Terror and Healing* (Chicago: University of Chicago Press, 1986), 142–143.

67 "Informe sobre una correría misional ...," fol. 72.

68 Ibid, fol. 69

69 Ibid, fol. 75.

70 Informe sobre actividades de Sofía Muller. Prefectura Apostólica de Mitu. Mitú, Junio de 1961. Archivo General de la Nación. Fondo Comisarias, fol. 15.

71 Hent de Vries, "Introduction. Before Around, and Beyond the Theologico-Political," in *Political Theologies. Public Religions in a Post-Secular World*, eds. Hent de Vries and Lawrence E. Sullivan (New York: Fordham University Press, 2006), 2.

72 Ibid, fol. 16.

73 Informe sobre una correría misional por los ríos Guaviare, Inírida, Atabapo, Guainía, Isana y Querari," June 16, 1961, AGN, Ministerio de Gobierno, División de Asuntos Indígenas, Caja 190, Carpeta 1609, fol. 8.

74 Stuart Kirsch, *Reverse Anthropology. Indigenous Analysis of Social and Environmental Relations in New Guinea* (Stanford: Stanford University Press, 2006), 79.

75 Fernando Santos-Granero, ed. "Introduction: Amerindian Constructional Views of the World," in *The Occult Life of Things. Native Amazonian Theories of Materiality and Personhood* (Tucson: The University of Arizona Press, 2013), 6.

76 Beth A. Conklin, "For Love or Money? Indigenous Materialism and Humanitarian Agendas," in *Editing Eden. A Reconsideration of Identity, Politics and Place in Amazonia*, eds. Frank Hutchins and Patrick C. Wilson (Lincoln: University of Nebraska Press, 2010), 139.

77 Hilda Soledad Pachon-Farias, *José Eustasio Rivera. Intelectual. Textos y documentos 1912–1918* (Neiva: Universidad Surcolombiana, 1991), 44.

78 Ibid, 45.

79 Camilo Domínguez, *Amazonia colombiana economía y poblamiento* (Bogotá: Universidad Externado de Colombia, 2005), 173

80 "Informe sobre una correría misional por los ríos Guaviare, Inírida, Atabapo, Guainía, Isana y Querari," June 16, 1961, Archivo General de la Nación (AGN), Ministerio de Gobierno, División de Asuntos Indígenas, Caja 190, Carpeta 1609, fol. 77.

81 Ibid.

82 Ibid.

83 Simón Uribe, *Frontier Road. Power, History, and the Everyday State in the Colombian Amazon* (Oxford: Wiley Blackwell, 2017), 33.

84 Ibid.

85 "Acta de recomendaciones para el gobierno comisarial," Puerto Inírida, ago. 20, 1965. AGG, Inírida, s/f.

86 "Decreto por el cual se ordena levantar el plan de Puerto Inírida, se establecen normas sobre desarrollo urbano y se dictan otras disposiciones," Puerto Inírida, March 11, 1966.

87 Tiberio de Jesús Acevedo, *Historia de Inírida* (Alcaldía Mayor de Inírida, Guainía, 2002), 96.

88 Ibid.

89 Ibid.

90 "Carta diriga al Señor Doctor Gregorio Hernández de Alba" Brujas (Guainía), 5 de mayo de 1965, AGN, Ministerio de Gobierno, División de Asuntos Indígenas, Caja 203, Carpeta 1819, f.1.

91 Ibid.

92 Rebecca Earle, "Algunos pensamientos sobre "El indio borracho" en el imaginario criollo," *Revista de Estudios Sociales* 29 (2008): 18–27.

84   Conversion Under Dispute

93 "Carta diriga al Señor Doctor Gregorio Hernández de Alba" Brujas (Guainía), 5 de mayo de 1965, AGN, Ministerio de Gobierno, División de Asuntos Indígenas, Caja 203, Carpeta 1819, f.1.

94 Ibid.

95 Paul Freston, *Evangelicals and Politics in Asia, Africa and Latin America* (New York: Cambridge University Press, 2001), 229.

96 David Stoll, "Higher Power: Wycliffe's Colombian Advance," in *Is God an American? An Anthropological Perspective on the Missionary Work of the Summer Institute of Linguistics*, eds. Søren Hvalkof and Peter Aaby (Copenhaguen: IWGIA and Survival International, 1981), 65.

97 "Informe dirigido al jefe de la División de Asuntos Indígenas del Ministerio de Gobierno," June 22, 1970, AGN, Sección República, Caja 216, Carpeta 2012, fol. 25–26.

98 Ibid.

99 Decreto Número 2263 de 1966. Por el cual se organiza y estimula la Integración Popular, con la participación del pueblo, el Gobierno y las entidades privadas. Archivo de la Gobernación del Guainía.

100 Ibid.

101 Ibid.

102 Informe sobre inventario de servicios y necesidades en la Comisaría Especial del Guainía, con destino al gobierno central. Puerto Inírida, 26 de Septiembre de 1968. Archivo de la Gobernación del Guainía.

103 Ibid.

104 Ibid.

105 Carta dirigida al Señor Reynaldo Cabrera, Comisario Encargado del Guainía. Puerto Inírida, Febrero 21 de 1966. Archivo de la Gobernación del Guainía.

106 Muller, *His Voice Shakes*, 178.

107 "Corregiduría Civil y Militar del Guaviare, Barranco Minas, Informativo 003," October 30, 1973, Archivo de la Gobernación del Guainía (AGG), nf.

108 The contempt of communism that Muller openly expressed brought her serious problems with guerrilla groups affiliated to FARC (Revolutionary Armed Forces of Colombia). In the last chapter of *His Voice Shakes the Wilderness*, Muller remembers that once a leader of FARC "entered a village at the end of a church conference. He was accompanied by a dozen heavily armed men and was asking for me. The Indians knew what he would do if he found me – either kidnap or kill." In the same chapter Muller recounts that one month later after this episode FARC did "kidnap Connie and Mari Cain´s son and wife along with the New Tribes Mission plane and two pilots." See Sophie Muller, *His Voice Shakes the Wilderness* (Sanford: New Tribes Mission, 1988), 189–190. The conflicts between New Tribes Mission's missionaries and FARC in Colombia acquired tragic dimensions in 1994 when Steve Welshy and Timoty Van Dike were kidnapped in the outskirts of Villavicencio and murdered a year and half later by members of FARC.

109 Ibid.

110 Ibid.

111 Ibid.

112 Ibid.

113 Matallana, "Ministerio de Defensa," 17.

114 Ibid, 82.

115 Ibid, 51.

116 Ibid.

117 Ibid.

118 Ibid, 74.

119 Muller, *His Voice Shakes*, 178.

Conversion Under Dispute 85

References

Beltrán, William Mauricio. *Del monopolio católico a la explosión pentecostal: pluralización religiosa, secularización y cambio social en Colombia*. Bogotá: Lecturas CES, 2013.

Calle, Bernardo J. *Caminos de* Esperanza. Mitú: Vicariato Apostólico de Mitú, 2014.

Carpenter, Joel. *Revive Us Again. The Reawakening of American Fundamentalism*. Oxford: Oxford University Press, 1997.

Comaroff, Jean, and John Comaroff. *Of Revelation and Revolution. Christianity, Colonialism and Consciousness in South Africa*. Chicago: The University of Chicago Press, 1991.

Conklin, Beth A. "For Love or Money? Indigenous Materialism and Humanitarian Agendas." In *Editing Eden. A Reconsideration of Identity, Politics and Place in Amazonia*, edited by Frank Hutchins and Patrick C. Wilson, 127–150. Lincoln: University of Nebraska Press, 2010.

De Jesús Acevedo, Tiberio. *Historia de Inírida*. Inírida: Alcaldía Mayor de Inírida, 2002.

De Vries, Hent. "Introduction. Before Around, and Beyond the Theologico-Political." In *Political Theologies. Public Religions in a Post-Secular World*, edited by Hent de Vries and Lawrence E. Sullivan, 1–88. New York: Fordham University Press, 2006.

Domínguez, Camilo. *Amazonía colombiana economía y poblamiento*. Bogotá: Universidad Externado de Colombia, 2005.

Earle, Rebecca. "Algunos pensamientos sobre "El indio borracho" en el imaginario criollo." *Revista de Estudios Sociales* 29 (2008): 18–27. https://doi.org/10.7440/res29.2008.01

Freston, Paul. *Evangelicals and Politics in Asia, Africa and Latin America*. New York: Cambridge University Press, 2001.

Gill, Anthony. *Rendering unto Cesar: The Catholic Church and the State in Latin America*. Chicago: University of Chicago Press, 1998.

Gow, Peter. "Forgetting Conversion. The Summer Institute of Linguistics Mission in the Piro Lived World." In *The Anthropology of Christianity*, edited by Fenella Canell, 211–239. Durham: Duke University Press, 2006.

Green, R. L. *Tropical Idolatry. A Theological History of Catholic Colonialism in the Pacific World, 1568–1700*. Lanham: Lexington Books, 2018.

Handman, Courtney. *Critical Christianity. Translation and Denominational Conflict in Papua New Guinea*. Oakland: University of California Press, 2015.

Hugh-Jones, Stephen. "Shamans, Prophets, Priests, and Pastors." In *Shamanism, History and the State*, edited by Nicholas Thomas and Caroline Humprey, 32–75. Ann Arbor: The University of Michigan Press, 1996.

Hvalkof, Søren, and Peter Aaby. "Introducing God in the Devil's Paradise." In *Is God an American? An Anthropological Perspective on the Missionary Work of the Summer Institute of Linguistics*, edited by Søren Hvalkof and Peter Aaby, 9–16. Copenhaguen: IWGIA and Survival International, 1981.

Johnston, Kenneth. *The Story of New Tribes Mission*. Sanford: New Tribes Mission, 1985.

Kirsch, Stuart. *Reverse Anthropology. Indigenous Analysis of Social and Environmental Relations in New Guinea*. Stanford: Stanford University Press, 2006.

Koselleck, Reinhart. *Futures Past, On the Semantics of Historical Time*. New York: Columbia University Press, 1985.

86 Conversion Under Dispute

Meyer, Birgit. *Translating the Devil: Religion and Modernity among the Ewe in Ghana*. Edinburgh: Edinburgh University Press, 1999.

Muller, Sophie. *Beyond Civilization*. Woodworth: New Tribes Mission, 1952.

Muller, Sophie. *His Voice Shakes the Wilderness*. Sanford: New Tribes Mission, 1988.

Muller, Sophie. *Jungle Methods*. Woodworth: Brown Gold Publications, 1960.

Pachon-Farias, Hilda Soledad. *José Eustasio Rivera. Intelectual. Textos y documentos 1912–1918*. Neiva: Universidad Surcolombiana, 1991.

Santos-Granero, Fernando. "Introduction: Amerindian Constructional Views of the World." In *The Occcult Life of Things. Native Amazonian Theories of Materiality and Personhood*, edited by Fernando Santos-Granero, 1–29. Tucson: The University of Arizona Press, 2013.

Stoll, David. "Higher Power: Wycliffe's Colombian Advance." In *Is God an American? An Anthropological Perspective on the Missionary Work of the Summer Institute of Linguistics*, edited by Søren Hvalkof and Peter Aaby, 63–76. Copenhaguen: IWGIA and Survival International, 1981.

Taussig, Michael. *Shamanism, Colonialism and the Wild Man*. Chicago: Chicago University Press, 1986.

Uribe, Simón. *Frontier Road. Power, History, and the Everyday State in the Colombian Amazon*. Oxford: Wiley Blackwell, 2017.

Van der Veer, Peter, "Introduction." In *Conversion to Modernities: The Globalization of Christianity*, edited by Peter van der Veer, 2–21. New York: Routledge, 1996.

Vilaça, Aparecida. "Indivíduos celestes. Cristianismo e parentesco em um grupo nativo da Amazônia." *Religao e Sociedade* 27, no. 1 (2007): 11–23. https://doi.org/10.1590/S0100-85872007000100002

3 Between Rupture and Continuity
The Politics of Conversion[1]

While Indigenous evangelical conversion became a political issue for the state, the local meanings of this process also varied between evangelical missionaries and Indigenous evangelicals. This chapter explores the *politics of conversion* in Guainía, comparing missionary narratives of conversion with Indigenous accounts of conversion. It describes how, since the 1940s, conversion to Christianity articulated new meanings and practices of indigeneity in this region. While lay and academic explanations tend to view evangelical conversion (not just among Indigenous groups) as rupture, this chapter shows that neither the missionaries nor the Indigenous populations in the Guainía view conversion only as rupture. Although they recognize the transformational process involved in conversion, they both emphasize cultural continuity, albeit for different reasons. Indigenous pastors and missionaries also combine narratives of rupture and narratives of continuity while articulating a new kind of indigeneity (Christian indigeneity), and a specific *politics of conversion* that postulates strong complementarities between Christianity and Indigenous values.

As we mentioned before, most accounts of the massive conversion of Indigenous communities to evangelical Christianity have explained it as a messianic phenomenon, suggesting that Sophie Muller, the first evangelical missionary to arrive to the region, was believed to be a messiah by Indigenous communities, echoing earlier messianic movements in the region during the mid-19th century.[2] Little attention has been paid to Indigenous narratives of conversion and how they relate to missionaries accounts of conversion and contemporary discourses of indigeneity. Predominant approaches to evangelical conversion in the Guainía focus on how Muller's message was couched "in almost the exact same terms as the early messiahs," provoking "a movement with strongly messianic and millennial overtones,"[3] while other interpretations of Indigenous conversions to Christianity in Amazonia emphasize how it consisted of "becoming white, half-civilized."[4] This chapter questions explanations about Indigenous conversion as a simple process of assimilation ("becoming white"), revealing how ideas and practices of conversion articulate new forms of being and becoming "Indian" in Guainía.

DOI: 10.4324/9781003370215-4

88 *Between Rupture and Continuity*

This chapter analyzes narratives of conversion produced by different generations of evangelical missionaries and Indigenous evangelicals. I suggest that Indigenous narratives of conversion should be understood in relation to missionary narratives of conversion, showing their dialogic nature.[5] Early missionary narratives conceive conversion as a simple replacement of "pagan" customs with Christian practices. The analysis of missionary and Indigenous narratives of conversion reveals a clear difference between contemporary missionary narratives of evangelizations that tend to view conversion as an individual transformation (not a collective one) and treat religion and culture as separate domains, and Indigenous narratives of conversion that consider conversion to be a cultural and collective transformation.

Contemporary missionary accounts of evangelization emphasize that conversion is the product of a personal decision that does not bring about major social or cultural change. In the case of Amazonia, Aparecida Vilaça shows how evangelical missionaries introduced specific "techniques of the self" to the Wari, the aim of which was the "constitution of an inner self as the locus for an 'intimate' relationship with God."[6] Missionaries claim that Indigenous culture does not undergo massive transformation, given that conversion is thought to be a change in personal beliefs, an inner transformation, but not a social or cultural one. Evangelical missionaries usually consider religion to be an inner and personal belief, while culture is seen as a simple collection of traits or things, which might include activities such as fishing and hunting. According to evangelical missionaries, natives are able to maintain their culture and identity, despite the changes that take place in terms of religious affiliation and beliefs. As Webb Keane points out, Christian missionaries usually attempt to define "what is cultural and what is religious," to distinguish one from the other, and leave each undisturbed.[7]

In fact, some missionaries even argue that Christianity has strengthened Indigenous culture through the translation of the Bible, leading people to read and use more their own language. The missionaries' assertion that they leave Indigenous culture unchanged is based on a separation of religion and culture, or a purification of them. By purification, following Bruno Latour, I refer to specifically modern practices that create distinct ontological zones which are supposed to work autonomously and have no relationship to each other.[8] Nonetheless, these missionary narratives that conceive conversion only as a personal transformation, not a cultural one, are contradicted by reports sent to the national government where missionaries have explicitly recognized that they are changing Indigenous patterns of life as a way of civilizing these societies.[9]

On the other hand, Indigenous evangelicals tend to associate evangelization with the arrival of civilization and the reformation of traditional custom. Becoming Christian is conceived as a learning process, a civilizing change that takes place in different spheres of life. Conversion, according to Indigenous evangelicals, brings changes in housing patterns, morality, social and political organization, ideas of personhood and community. Some

Indigenous evangelicals consider conversion to be a total social fact that involves changes in all realms of personal and social life. In fact, "discontinuity and rupture" tend to be the "aspects highlighted by native peoples, who insist on the originality of Christianity."[10] Peter Gow explores in the Peruvian Amazon how for Indigenous people of the Bajo Urubamba being "civilized" is not "opposed to an idyllic 'traditional' culture which has been lost, but to the ignorance and helplessness of the forest dwelling ancestors."[11] In the case of Guainía, contemporary Indigenous leaders do not see Christianity and indigeneity as opposed to each other. The embracing of Christianity is seen as part of their adaptation to the modern world and as a form of leverage with settlers, who treated them before as savages.

I respond in this chapter to Joel Robbins' argument that conversion entails a radical rupture from the past.[12] In contrast, based on my fieldwork in Guainía, I find that neither the missionaries nor the Indigenous population view conversion only as rupture. Although they recognize the transformational process involved in conversion, they both emphasize cultural continuity, albeit for different reasons. I draw here on the work of Birgit Meyer who argues that notions of rupture and continuity are defined in relation to each other. The break with "the past," as it were, presupposes its prior construction through remembrance and through Christian discourses of the past as pagan.[13] Pentecostalism, according to Meyer, "seeks a rupture from a 'tradition' or 'past' which it has previously helped to construct."[14] Finally, I show how the dichotomy between rupture and continuity falls short of explaining the kinds of transformations involved in the emergence of what I call here Christian indigeneity. I analyze how Indigenous leaders and missionaries use and combine narratives of cultural change and narratives of cultural continuity in strategic ways. These uses shape a specific *politics of* conversion, which, in turn, articulates complex relationships between Christianity and indigeneity.[15] *Politics of conversion* is understood here as the practices and narratives through which Indigenous communities in Guainía develop their "own" sense of what becoming Christian means, and the ways in which conversion to Christianity produces new meanings of indigeneity in this region. In this sense, embracing Christianity is seen by Indigenous leaders as a way of addressing the changes brought by colonization and modernity.

Early Missionary Narratives of Conversion

As I mentioned in Chapter 2, since the 1940s, the project of "reaching the unreached" became the *leitmotiv* of New Tribes missionaries across the globe. Most of the New Tribes Missionaries who visited Guainía in the Colombian Amazon after Sophie Muller's first visit in the 1940s shared the idea of contacting uncontacted tribes or reaching unreached tribes. Like other institutions such as the Summer Institute of Linguistics, New Tribes Mission (NTM) was a product of American evangelicalism and "its project of bearing the Good News to the last unreached people in the uttermost parts of

90   *Between Rupture and Continuity*

the earth."[16] Reaching these tribes entailed learning their languages, preaching the Gospel and founding "tribal churches." In her first book *Beyond Civilization* published in 1952, Muller presents her work as part of a "spiritual battle," a continual battle between the "powers of light and darkness," though "God is mightier that the Devil."[17] Muller combined in her narrative the possession of souls with possession of land, alluding to ways in which spirituality and materiality were intertwined in her project of evangelization. Muller used the trope of "possession" to frame and symbolize her vision of evangelization. She emphasized she was there to "re-possess" Indigenous territories and souls for Christ. Spreading the Word of God has usually been associated for New Tribes Missionaries with establishing "tribal" churches.

Despite the fact that Muller despised Indians' "witchcraft and evil practices," there are several references in her books to the idea of "going native" and becoming, to some extent, one of them. Muller recommends other missionaries not to take food supplies into the tribe, except for powdered milk since "it would make the covetous and take their eyes off the Word."[18] Muller believes that it's best to "eat native" and live off them, taking their food rather than providing them with food as was the case with other missionaries.[19] In *Jungle Methods*, Muller recalls how she used paddle in canoes by herself, but then realizing that because she had not the time and strength to do it, it was easier to delegate this job to the natives with all the advantages it brought: "In drifting along peacefully with the natives from place to place, you are not only received as 'one of them', but you save your strength for the real job."[20]

In *Jungle Methods*, Muller emphasizes that evangelization should start by awakening "their interest in the Word."[21] This process entailed learning the language of the "tribe" and teaching the members of the group to read and write their own language using syllable charts, following the Laubach method.[22] Finding audiences willing to hear the Word might require the help of former pupils that "will help you teach the new ones at the next village, and most important of all, you'll find eager ears and open hearts for the entrance of the Word of Life is you go with a tribal escort."[23] Muller not only trained Indigenous pastors and leaders, but also relied on the authority of well-known shamans. In the translation of the entire New Testament from Curripaco to Puinave, a former shaman named Julio helped Muller: "he was one of the witch doctors who had held sway over the village only half a year earlier. This man, who had made a clean break from his witchcraft, would turn out to be my most efficient and persevering helper."[24]

Muller used extensively oral and visual resources in her evangelical work. Oral indoctrination was used under the principle that "faith cometh by hearing," and under the conviction that "prayer changes things."[25] Given that the first words will make the greatest impression and become rooted in the minds of the natives, evangelization began with a set of "simple sentences about God, Satan and Salvation."[26] The emphasis placed by Muller on language on the Word resonates with how rhetoric is regarded by evangelicals to be the prime vehicle of conversion. As Susan Harding points out, "among orthodox Protestants, and especially among fundamentalists, it is the Word, the gospel of Jesus Christ, written, spoken, heard, and read, that converts the unbeliever."[27]

Indeed, one of the questions Muller asks herself in *Jungle Methods* is: "What brought about this mass change of heart from serving the devil to serving the Lord?" She replies saying it was done by "translating the Word into their language, by teaching them to read it, by inserting a question after every verse, thus making them think of what they read."[28] If the missionary was not able to communicate the main meaning of a verse, there was the risk of a twist "to incorporate some old heathen idea."[29] Something similar happened with rituals, Muller recounts how "these services, especially those such as baptism and the Lord's Supper, would turn into regular witchcraft ceremonies if they did not have the mode of service all down in black and white, with all the Scripture verses and songs written out in connection with each service."[30] Muller's enterprise was strongly focused on literacy and books: "you send out a thousand fundamental missionaries every time you send a thousand books through the tribe."[31] As mentioned in Chapter 2, protestant missions established a close relationship between literacy, conversion and civilization.

Muller also suggested that the realization of semiannual Bible conferences should be done at different times of the year in order to give the missionary the opportunity "to counsel, exhort and lead them on in the knowledge and the love of God."[32] Leadership of the missionaries was done through specific disciplinary technologies that involved appointing policemen in the evangelical meetings known in the region as *conferencias*. Bible study groups and conferences should make Indigenous churches self-governed and self-propagated throughout the tribes. However, despite all the efforts of Muller to convert and discipline different Indigenous groups, she recognized that her attempts could also fail. In *Jungle Methods* and his *Voice Shakes the Wilderness*, Muller mentions that drinking, smoking, dancing and "witchcraft went on as usual when I wasn't around. It seemed that reading had become an end in itself and was merely a ritual to most of them."[33] In fact, in *Jungle Methods* Muller recounts that she had to "get the Indians to think about what they were reading," because she noticed that "with their mouths they said, 'we all believe', but there was no real evidence of new life except for a faint flicker in some."[34] The idea of the "inconstancy of the savage soul" (in Portuguese *a inconstância da alma selvagem*) has been conspicuous in missionaries' constructed representations of Indigenous populations that were to be converted to Christianity. Eduardo Viveiros de Castro shows how the idea of the "inconstancy of the savage soul" originates in the missionary proselytization of the Tupinamba in Brazil during the 16th century.[35] Carlos Fausto, drawing on Viveiros de Castro's ideas, argues that this modality of "believing without faith" should be understood as part of an obscure desire of being the Other, but on the native's own terms.[36]

In conclusion, for these early evangelical missionaries, evangelization was about the replacement of "pagan" and "idolatrous" customs with Christian practices. This was the case with presenting and naming newborn babies.

92 *Between Rupture and Continuity*

Muller created a dedication service that was aimed at replacing the "witch-craft" ceremony that included "chanting and pounding on a basket all night."[37] Muller was clear in believing that "the dedication service has now replaced the witchcraft ceremony and teaches the parents how they should bring up their children."[38] In this sense, the first evangelical missionaries conceived of conversion as a change in belief and a replacement of practices, a "mass change of heart from serving the devil to serving the Lord," but above all a replacement of "witchcraft" with Christianity. Missionaries were very clear on the fact that changing "beliefs" entailed at the same time changing the practices that shaped and were part of those beliefs.[39] Such practices included traditional rituals and practices, such as naming newborn babies.

Contemporary Missionary Narratives of Conversion

Recent missionary versions of evangelization tend to be informed by contemporary anthropological concepts and visions of Indigenous peoples. Richard Johnson is a New Tribes missionary who came to the region in 1971 and lived there until 1995, when he was expelled by the FARC (Revolutionary Armed Forces of Colombia). When I did my fieldwork in Guainía in 2009, Richard frequently visited the capital of the province to work, with the help of Puinave Christians, on the improvement of the existing translation of the New Testament to Puinave. Richard has also done linguistic research on the Puinave language and is helping the Puinave to standardize their alphabet. The later initiative was carried out within broader projects of cultural revival that included recuperating traditional myths and practices.

Richard spent four years in Remanso on the Inírida River when he first visited the region in the 1970s. Christian converts received him warmly after being recommended by Sophie Muller. Richard told me that when he started his missionary work he had four initial assignments: (i) learning the language; (ii) learning what Puinaves believed[40]; (iii) understanding their culture; (iv) and finding out how much and how well Christian Puinaves understood the Bible. Richard and his wife started their work by trying to get extremely close to the Puinaves and get to know them on a personal basis. This was not an easy process. At the beginning, Richard told me, "things were not working very well," as they were considered outsiders and were treated with deference. Richard and his wife decided to ask the *capitán* of the community if they could be adopted in order to be treated as relatives.[41] A Puinave woman was willing to adopt Richard and treat him almost like a son, but more like a nephew, and Laura, his wife, was living with the same family. Laura had trouble getting to know Puinave women on a personal level. After a period of frustration, both Richard and Laura asked their consultant how to proceed. The consultant suggested that Laura should find her own family. Richard demonstrated extensive knowledge of how the Puinave kinship system worked, as he tried to explain to me that they had to find a family for Laura that had the appropriate relationship to Richard's family.[42] Puinaves use the Iroquois kingship

Between Rupture and Continuity   93

terminology, which differentiates between parallel and cross cousins. The same terms are used for brothers and parallel cousins, while different terms are used for cross cousins. Marriage rules established preferential marriage between cross cousins and prohibited marriage between parallel cousins, be them matrilateral or patrilateral.[43] This meant that Richard and his wife had to be situated in the kinship system as cross cousins, making their marriage possible. At the beginning Richard and his wife were simply observing, striving to be objective and to understand what was important for Puinaves. Richard wanted to learn the Puinave language, to know Puinaves on a personal level and to understand what they believed. Richard wanted to understand Puinave culture, their cultural concepts and meanings, in order to engage in meaningful conversations with them.[44] Getting to know the Puinaves on a personal level entailed participating in everyday activities. For instance, Richard recounted how he used to go with other Puinave men to cut fiber and used to bind the fiber into bundles for exchange. The fiber was later sold or traded for commodities with the *patrones*, white bosses who had control over the labor of Indigenous peoples in the region. Richard used those activities to learn catch phrases and common words as well as to get closer to the Puinaves.

Once Richard and Laura gained fluency in Puinave they started talking to people about their own experiences as Christians, "people wanted to hear about my own relationship with God," said Richard to me. Richard emphasized that his purpose was not to push anyone to become Christian. He did not consider evangelization to be an outward imposition: "We are not interested in people doing religious things, we are not interested in people doing religious rituals, we are not imposing religious ideas or beliefs."[45] To the contrary, he explained that evangelization is about provoking inner transformations, about convincing people in their "own hearts" about the "existence and work of God, as it is revealed in the Bible."[46]

Richard's vision of Indigenous conversion was completely informed by the idea of a free and autonomous subject who makes rational decisions based on the truth of facts or revelation. He understood conversion as an individual choice: "they as individuals have to choose,"[47] and claims that missionaries don't want to "change Puinave culture and see them become different as societies,"[48] since conversion is thought to be a change in the interiority of the self, a change that takes place in your "heart."

Nonetheless, conversion is also expressed in outward transformations that are the outcome of a process of self-reflection and self-evaluation. Accepting God entails a process of self-evaluation and making choices. Once you become Christian you have to evaluate your previous practices and beliefs and choose to drop those that are wrong or contradict your new beliefs. In this sense, Richard argues "we don't lose our culture when we become Christians,"[49] instead we just reject things from our culture that contradict our new beliefs. Put into Indigenous terms and practices, this means that Indigenous evangelicals should leave behind practices and beliefs associated with witchcraft. The possibility of leaving completely behind practices such

94 *Between Rupture and Continuity*

as sorcery remains questionable, as Richard himself recognizes that some Puinaves still "know myths but don't believe in them anymore."[50]

Consequently, Richard does not consider conversion to entail a radical rupture, as he believes that likeness between Christian and non-Christian Puinaves is maintained despite evangelization: "Christian Puinaves preserve more of their language and identity," they are "proud to be Puinaves."[51] It seems clear that he is operating under a notion of culture as a set of traits that can be divided between evil and good, where "evil traits" might be replaced by "Christian traits" without major consequences.[52] Richard is also drawing on ideas of culture as language. This is clear in his concern for and effort to learn Puinave's main cultural concepts and meanings, using their own language.

Richard assumes that culture and religion reside in separate domains, where culture is associated with traits such as language, and religion is considered to be pure inner belief. Christian missionaries try to purify and separate culture from belief as if one were not affected by the other. Nonetheless, it is possible "to tell" when someone is or is not an authentic Christian. Richard said explicitly that it is "very easy to imitate a real Christian, but you can differentiate spurious from authentic Christians."[53] Although the missionaries are supposed not to judge the relationship between the person and God, Richard claims that it is possible to tell when someone has a similar relationship with God to the one he himself has. In fact, when Christian Puinaves have stayed at Richard's house in Bogotá, he claims he can tell the difference between when Christian Puinaves are trying "to impress" him, and when they truly share similar responses and evaluations toward things. The authenticity of conversion and belief depends on a specific "relationship" or "engagement" with things that becomes explicit through social practice.[54]

Richards's vision of Indigenous conversion and culture is also shared by a Colombian missionary known as Luis Ordoñez, who lived for 25 years in the region, from the early 1960s. Ordoñez settled in the community of Tonina, on the Guainía River, where he established a school in which he taught native peoples mathematics, history and geography. This was before the state established boarding public schools in the region. Ordoñez holds the view that conversion to Christianity does not erase or eradicate what he understands as Indigenous culture, closely associated also with language and traits such as beliefs and legends. "You saw them, they are still Curripacos, they still speak their language, have their beliefs and legends," Ordoñez told me at his office in Bogotá.[55] He went further arguing that it is historically proven that when the Bible is translated to a specific language, this language endures more over time as it is increasingly used to read and talk about the Bible. This missionary was emphatic when he argued that traditional myths became part of Indigenous *folklore*, "they know myths but don't believe in them anymore, though some of them do," according to Ordoñez.[56]

Referring to *camajai*, a widely used poison associated with sorcery, Ordoñez said that it was impossible to eradicate the belief that *camajai* produces sickness. Those beliefs, in his own words, "stick to the minds of the people." Conversion in this sense is never absolute, as it is always already partial and incomplete. In fact, Ordoñez acknowledges that sorcery is real and has concrete effects: "sorcery, witch doctors can kill a person, we think it is not true, but it is true." What does it mean to say that Curripacos know myths but don't believe in them anymore, though some of them do? How can missionaries claim that they are not trying to change Indigenous culture, while simultaneously downgrading myths to folklore or just stories? Ordoñez leaves unexplained the fact that some Curripacos still believe in myths as well as in the real and concrete effects those "myths" have upon the everyday life and practices of Indigenous evangelicals in Guainía.

Evangelical missionaries saw their work as a complement to the policies that the national government designed for Indigenous groups from the 1960s onwards. On 22 June 1970, the secretary and legal representative of NTM sent a report to the chief of Indigenous affairs in the national government. In the section devoted to "morality," the report expressed that New Tribes missionaries have "helped in the transformation of Indigenous customs, in the responsibilities they have they have before other men, but especially before God and the Colombian Nation."[57] In a similar vein, the section of the report devoted to "culture" starts by saying that missionaries "fix nomadic and semi-nomadic people in favorable sites or in farms in order to raise their quality of life. They are taught to respect the laws and other civic duties of society, the nation and the family."[58] Despite the fact that Colombia has been historically a Catholic nation and the government has given tremendous power to the Catholic Church, NTM obtained its legal personality in Colombia on 23 May 1967. Six years earlier, the Summer Institute of Linguistics had reached an agreement with anthropologist Gregorio Hernandez de Alba (who was organizing Colombia's first Department of Indigenous Affairs) in order to "start an indigenist-oriented, government-controlled integration program and train national linguists."[59] While NTM had the support of the national government, missionaries affiliated to NTM caused friction with settlers on the ground. It is common to hear old settlers complain about the fact that Muller would turn Indigenous communities against them, demonizing settlers because they smoked and drank. In fact, as I will show in the next section, Indigenous evangelicals associate conversion with a civilizing process that reconfigured relationships with settlers or *colonos*.

Indigenous Accounts of Conversion

For most elders, pastors and former Indigenous missionaries, becoming Christian was associated with learning to read and write their own language.[60] Learning how to read the New Testament in Puinave or Curripaco was one of the main entrances to Christianity. The idea of a written language was unknown to most natives when Muller arrived in 1944. Both elder and young Indigenous evangelicals tend to think of conversion as the outcome of a clear-cut break from a "pagan" past to a Christian present.

96 *Between Rupture and Continuity*

Among elder Indigenous evangelicals, conversion is associated with becoming civilized, placing them on an equal level with white settlers, who usually depict the natives as savages or animals. For most Christian elders, the past was worldly, full of ignorance, violence and chaos. "My father that is deceased now used to be a worldly person," Feliciano Cayupare, a brother of one of the first Puinave missionaries, told me.[61] Evangelization is thought to produce a clear-cut break with the past, a learning process that changes local beliefs, customs and practices. Gerardo, an elder pastor of a Curripaco community in the upper Guainía River, told me that "before *señorita* Sophie came here, people used to live with their own culture."[62] I asked him how their culture was back then, and Gerardo replied that they had their own rituals and dances in which they would drink *chicha*. Culture here seems to be understood as customs (*costumbres*) and beliefs. Gerardo and his son, a teacher in a local boarding school, who was translating parts of our conversation, told me how "they" (meaning their predecessors) had their own gods who were considered sacred and respectable. The missionaries "used to call them the devil," according to Gerardo.[63] In this sense, the arrival of Muller is associated with leaving "that" culture behind and learning to live in a civilized way: "after she [Muller] taught them, they have civilization with this book [the Bible]. People know what civilization is about and know how to live here in this world."[64] When I asked Gerardo about the meaning of civilization, he said it was related to "learning how to live, having a house like this one, cleaning your patio."[65] In a broad sense, becoming civilized and Christian entailed material and bodily transformations: building single family houses with separate rooms for girls and boys, having correct manners and being polite, hosting in the correct way any visitor (even a white man), living in communities with several family houses gathered around a church and a communal meeting building, among others. All of these external signs work as indexes of inner and moral transformations.

Religious conversion among Indigenous communities nowadays is related to becoming a better person and this transformation can be seen through explicit material signs that include dress, bodily carriage, politeness and hospitality. In this sense, conversion can hardly be conceived a purely spiritual transformation, or a simple change in "beliefs," as evangelical missionaries sometimes present it.

Indigenous evangelicals also associate evangelization with discipline and following authority. Gerardo remembers vividly what it was like to travel on missionary trips with Muller:

> When you were traveling with her you had to know how it was to work with her (...) I am a pastor, but don't handle people how she did, just like the Bible (...) She was a *señorita* and she wouldn't wear shorts. She used pants, following the Bible (...) If you were going to take a bath you should do it far from her. Far from the women, like the Bible says.[66]

Between Rupture and Continuity 97

Discipline extended to other domains such as the naming of pastors and forbidding "sorcery." Policemen were also appointed to watch on people for each evangelical conference. For example, Gerardo told me how he became pastor not because he wanted to, but because Muller told him to. According to Gerardo, two years after she arrived in the Rio Guainía, Muller started "naming" both an elder and a pastor in each Indigenous community. These pastors and elders would help her organize the *conferencias*. Gerardo was one of the new pastors that Muller named and placed "in office." It seemed clear to Gerardo that he was obliged to become a pastor, and he was only 17 years old when Muller named him pastor in the community of Cejal: "Obliged, because she [Sophie] was smart, she noticed that I knew something about the Bible."[67] Gerardo summed up the story of his becoming pastor, saying that it was God who had chosen him. However, it wasn't until 1977, when Gerardo was approximately 40 years old (23 years after his "first conversion").[68] It is worth mentioning that Gerardo considers himself a botanist. He is familiar with a great variety of plants, and the remedies that can be produced from them, including those used to ward off sorcery.

On the other hand, most of the elders I had conversations with emphasized how Muller banned traditional rituals and practices associated with *payes*, such as drinking *chicha*, smoking tobacco and using hallucinogens such as *yopo*. People refer to these practices as customs (*costumbres*) they had before evangelization. Carlos Ramírez and his father Rodrigo described how Muller was able to convince people to give up the practice of traditional rituals. It was a slow process that took between three and five years. At the beginning Muller didn't forbid anything, she would watch them perform their rituals. When she realized people would listen to her, Muller started to reschedule traditional parties just for Sundays and only during the day. Once the leader of the community and the elders were convinced about the Word of God, Muller told them that the parties they had were a problem because people were killed in the midst of these "drinking parties." The elders began to recognize Muller was "right," and little by little she was able to convince them.[69] Finally, Muller named her own leaders who would also preach for her throughout the rest of the Curripaco communities. It was then, according to Carlos Ramírez and Rodrigo, that Muller started to organize services on Sunday in Cejal aiming to replace traditional rituals with Christian ceremonies. At the beginning, elders used to smoke in church or before entering the church, and Muller would scold them but they kept on doing it.

To some extent, becoming civilized and Christian is associated among native leaders' elders with "domesticating" or "pacifying" the white man. Scholarship about Indigenous memories in Amazonia has revealed the different "cosmologies of contact" created by Indigenous peoples using both mythical and historical accounts.[70] Pacifying or domesticating the white man refers not only to how Indigenous peoples appropriated commodities and practices associated with outsiders, it also refers to how Indigenous

98 *Between Rupture and Continuity*

populations were able to deter and neutralize, "pacify" to some extent, the violence and dangers associated with colonization.[71] Domesticating the white man refers to how Indigenous populations were able to empty the white men of "their aggressiveness, malignity, lethality, in few words, domesticate them."[72] Through this process Indigenous communities establish new relationships with the white men, reproducing themselves as societies "this time not against them, but through them, recruiting them for their own continuity and transformation."[73] The Indigenous appropriation of Christianity in the Colombian Amazon was crucial in this process of "domestication of the white man" as it established new relationships between settlers and Indigenous communities. The ways in which Christianity was used and transformed for "domesticating" the white man are also part of Indigenous *politics of conversion.*

Evangelization in Guainía is usually linked with the end of physical violence exercised by white traders (of rubber first and later fiber) on Indigenous men and women. In this regard, Gerardo told me how "since the arrival of Sophie, people live an organized life, they know what life is about, they don't run away anymore when the white man comes."[74] Gerardo recalled how white men used to call the "savages," they "didn't respect the people because they said that Indians were like animals (...) they did whatever they wanted."[75] In this sense, as native peoples became Christians and "civilized," they were able to gain the respect of the white men. This was part of the evangelical project of Muller. A Puinave elder repeated to me what Muller told him once: "Life is going to change, be ready. Lots of people will come here to live with you, organize yourselves, receive the people that arrive here, but demand respect. People will come and will want to abuse and exploit you, it is not necessary to fight with them, but demand respect. Don't kill them." Nonetheless, settlers do not share the claim that settlers or *colonos* stopped perceiving natives as savages after they became Christian. Some *colonos* still believe that Muller duped the natives and Christianity made them lazier. Furthermore, *colonos*' narrative of Indigenous conversion tends to reinscribe racial stereotypes of natives as inferior, easily duped and less civilized. However, Gerardo's account regarding the effects of Christianity upon power relationships between *colonos* and natives raises questions about the influence of Christianity upon racial hierarchies and discrimination in Guainía.

Christian Indigeneity

David López is a Puinave missionary who worked with Muller and studied in Argentina. He traveled to the United States and other countries in South America as part of his involvement in a pan Indian network of evangelical Indigenous churches and leaders called CONPLEI (Conselho Nacional de Pastore e Líderes Evangélicos Indígena) created in Brazil in 1991.[76] Indigenous missionaries developed a sensibility that makes them aware of the particularities that "Indigenous culture" brings to any evangelizing project.

Between Rupture and Continuity 99

In fact, David criticized white missionaries because they came to Indigenous communities and started telling people: "*Ah! That is sinful! That is wrong!*, without realizing that natives don't know what sin is, don't know what the word sin means."[77] According to David, white missionaries don't understand that natives have their own behavior, cosmology, forms, values, beliefs and history. In consequence, he believes that any missionary effort in order to be effective should first understand the native vision of things and what a native feels. Otherwise, conversion will remain insincere, and at a superficial level, as people might display external change, while their interior remains the same. Talking about his experience as a native on different trips, David said to me:

> I say and teach that we should preserve our identity, so that whoever you are, wherever you go, how many other languages you learn, and cultures you meet, you are still yourself. I think this is why I'm here. I have had opportunities to work in another city or in another country, but I will not rest until the Indian is aware of this. Until he can hold on to the sense of who he is. Until the Puinave remains Puinave, and the Curripaco remains Curripaco and holds onto his way of life, his way of eating, and fishing. But yes, he should have education, he should learn how the world is, he should learn to use the internet.[78]

David also praised contemporary white evangelical missionaries because they don't say they come to "change culture, they simply teach pure religion, and that's it."[79] The idea of evangelization as preserving and maintaining Indigenous culture echoes Johnson's arguments in the same direction, but contradicts Indigenous accounts of evangelization and conversion as cultural change. How is David able to combine a language of cultural change and transformation with a language that emphasizes cultural continuity and conservation? How can one reconcile the active defense of Indigenous culture and tradition with engagement in a process of radical change that is entailed in the idea of becoming Christian? Missionaries believe that it is possible to separate, or purify for this matter, the good from evil in any specific culture. Indigenous evangelicals renounce the "evil" practices of their own culture that include, according to David, "cultural and physical abuses," without losing their ethnic identity. A document called *plan de vida* was written by Curripaco and Yeral leaders and published in 2002. *Planes de vida* have been widely used in Colombia as a tool of development for programs in ethnic communities promoted by both governmental and non-governmental agencies. The *plan de vida* said that natives "wanted and should renounce" the ways in which their ancestors usually solved disputes with death, sometimes with "poison during the parties, in the midst of drunkenness."[80] The Indigenous leaders that wrote the *plan de vida* perceived their massive conversion to Christianity as part of the transformations that have been necessary to "preserve, adapt, and improve

100 *Between Rupture and Continuity*

themselves," preventing the "extinction or disappearance of our people."[81] Christianity appears here as mediating – the relationships between Indigenous communities and Western culture: "we have chosen the path of religiosity to come closer to Western culture, because it provides us with elements to counteract the most harmful of it and defend ourselves from external pressures."[82] This confirms how through the appropriation of Christianity, Indigenous communities in Guainía reconfigured the relationship with white settlers, "recruiting" Christianity for their own continuity.[83] In this sense, Christian practice has helped to "contain social deterioration as it is imposed by colonization."[84] This particular appropriation of Christianity is part of an Indigenous *politics of conversion* that puts into question any structural opposition between Christianity and indigeneity.

The *plan de vida* describes the strategy of permanence of Indigenous communities in their territory as a "process of hybridization" that combines the transmission of "ancestral knowledge" from parents to children, with the intelligence to adapt to cultural, economic, social and political changes from a "philosophy of salvation and solidarity."[85] Hybridity articulates an emergent articulation of indigeneity that might be called Christian indigeneity. This new type of indigeneity upholds Indigenous identity, despite the changes that have been brought by the appropriation of Christianity: "one of our strengths as Curripacos and Yeral, despite wanting to change behaviors of our ancestral history, such as drinking alcoholic beverages, is our Indigenous sensibility and feeling, nobody can take it away. We have this sensibility when we walk through the forest."[86] In this way, Indigenous evangelicals in Guainía do not find any contradiction between claiming an Indigenous identity and following Christian practices. Furthermore, Christianity becomes the medium through which "traditional customs and beliefs" are revived and maintained: "pastors and missionaries in the communities show the spiritual development that combined the gospel of Christ with our beliefs and custom. This revives our tradition in the services, in the sacred suppers and conferences, in the morning and afternoon prayers, in the dawn of the elders."[87] In this sense, practicing Christianity becomes a particular way of refashioning tradition and becoming Indian in Guainía. The *plan de vida* traces a continuity between Christianity and indigeneity, but it also recognizes political, economic and social changes (most of them associated with colonization) to which Indigenous communities have "adapted," in part, through the appropriation of Christianity.

Conclusion

This chapter compared missionary narratives of conversion that see conversion as an individual transformation and not a cultural one, with Indigenous narratives of conversion that consider conversion to be a collective transformation. As I have shown, these narratives should be understood in relation to each other and are not mutually incompatible. Each one reveals different elements of Indigenous conversion to Christianity. Indigenous pastors and missionaries have appropriated the narratives of conversion of non-Indigenous missionaries in order to develop their own sense and *politics of conversion* regarding what it means to be an Indigenous evangelical in Guainía.

Conversion to Christianity represented for Indigenous societies a break with the past, but it did not constitute a radical rupture, as some Indigenous evangelicals like to put it. Indigenous evangelicals uphold their "ethnic identity," most of them speak their native languages and some Indigenous communities maintain "traditional" practices of subsistence (such as horticulture, fishing and hunting). Furthermore, it is important to explore what Indigenous evangelicals mean when they claim to have made a "complete break with the past." Is it a way of resignifying external representations of themselves as "savages," and therefore of reclaiming their status as civilized subjects *vis-á-vis* white settlers? In this regard, Gallois and Grupioni point out that the appropriation of Christianity by Indigenous societies should be understood more as a political maneuver and not simply a religious phenomenon. This political maneuver enabled Indigenous societies to position themselves as equals in relation to the dominant society, appealing to the idea of equality among all God's children.[88] The embracement of Christianity changed the ways in which Curripacos and Puinaves relate to their own past and culture. Indigenous narratives of conversion reconstruct the pre-Christian past and "traditional culture" as "pagan" and violent, but simultaneously the political discourse of Indigenous leaders traces continuities between indigeneity and Christianity.

In this sense, missionaries and Indigenous evangelicals recognize the transformations involved in conversion to Christianity, but both emphasize cultural continuity for different reasons. Missionaries draw on the separation between religion and culture in order to argue that conversion is just a personal transformation, while Indigenous evangelicals see conversion as a way of carrying forward their own values and practices into the future.

Notes

1 An earlier version of this chapter was published as the journal article, Esteban Rozo, "Between Rupture and Continuity. The Politics of Conversion in the Colombian Amazon," *Social Sciences and Missions* 31 nos. 3–4 (2018): 284–309. https://doi.org/10.1163/18748945-03003007.

2 Earlier approaches to the massive conversion of Indigenous peoples in the Colombian Amazon to evangelical Christianity as a messianic phenomenon include Jonathan Hill and Robin Wright, "History, Ritual and Myth: Nineteenth Century Millenarian Movements in the Northwest Amazon," *Ethnohistory* 33, no. 1 (1986): 31–54; Stephen Hugh-Jones, "Shamans, Prophets, Priests, and Pastors," in *Shamanism, History and the State*, eds. N. Thomas and C. Humprey (Ann Arbor: The University of Michigan Press, 1996), 32–75l; and Robin Wright, "Prophetic Traditions among the Baniwa and Other Arawakan Peoples of the Northwest Amazon," in *Comparative Arawakan Histories: Rethinking Language Family and Culture Area in Amazonia*, eds. Jonathan Hill and Fernando Santos-Granero (Urbana: University of Illinois Press, 2002), 269–293.

102 *Between Rupture and Continuity*

3 Stephen Hugh-Jones, "Shamans, Prophets, Priests, and Pastors," in *Shamanism, History and the State*, eds. Nicholas Thomas and Caroline Humprey (Ann Arbor: The University of Michigan Press, 1996), 58.

4 Robin Wright, *Cosmos, Self and History in Baniwa Religion: For Those Unborn* (Austin: University of Texas Press, 1998), 97.

5 Mikhail Bakhtin, *The Dialogic Imagination* (Austin: University of Texas Press, 1981).

6 Aparecida Vilaça, "Culture and Self: The Different "Gifts" Amerindians Receive from Catholics and Evangelicals," *Current Anthropology* 55, no. 10 (2014): 322–332.

7 Webb Keane, *Christian Moderns: Freedom and Fetish in the Mission Encounter* (Berkley: University of California Press, 2007), 104

8 Bruno Latour, *We Have Never Been Modern* (Cambridge: Harvard University Press, 1993).

9 Archivo General de la Nación (Bogotá), Sección República, Caja 216, Carpeta 2012, Folios 25–26, Informe dirigido al jefe de la División de Asuntos Indígenas del Ministerio de Gobierno, Bogotá, 22 de junio de 1970.

10 Aparecida Vilaça, Conversão, predação e perspectiva. *Mana* 14, no. 1 (2008): 176.

11 Peter Gow, *Of Mixed Blood. Kinship and History in Peruvian Amazonia* (New York: Oxford University Press, 1991), 1–2.

12 Joel Robbins, "Continuity Thinking and the Problem of Christian Culture: Belief, Time, and the Anthropology of Christianity," *Current Anthropology* 48, no. 1 (2007): 5.

13 Birgit Meyer, "'Make a complete break with the past.' Memory and Post-colonial Modernity in Ghanaian Pentecostal Discourse," *Journal of Religion in Africa* 28, no. 3 (1998): 318.

14 Ibid.

15 Historian Keith P. Luria uses the notion of "politics of conversion" to account for how protestants in 17th-century France were reintegrated to the broader national and Catholic society through the conversion to Catholicism. Capuchin missionaries at the time used to legitimate the authority of the king based on religious reasons arguing that obedience to the king was based on the obedience to God. See Keith P. Luria, "The Politics of Protestant Conversion to Catholicism in Seventeenth-Century France," in *Conversion to Modernities: The Globalization of Christianity*, ed. P. van der Veer (New York: Routledge, 1996), 23–46.

16 Peter Gow, "Forgetting Conversion. The Summer Institute of Linguistics Mission in the Piro Lived World," in *The Anthropology of Christianity*, ed. Fenella Canell (Durham: Duke University Press. 2006), 216.

17 Muller, *Beyond Civilization*, 94.

18 Muller, *Jungle Methods*, 14.

19 Ibid.

20 Ibid.

21 Muller, *Beyond Civilization*, 22.

22 The Laubach method was created in the 1930s by Frank C. Laubach while working in the Philippines. The method originated as a way of teaching adults to read and write in their own language. The Laubach method emphasizes learning through association rather than through memory. Letters and sounds are introduced associating pictures with keywords.

23 Muller, *Jungle Methods*, 30.

24 Muller, *His Voice Shakes the Wilderness*, 102

25 Muller, *Beyond Civilization*, 97. Muller believed that the principle of "faith cometh by hearing" was also observed by communists: "Even the communists

are working in the "cold war" with their tireless repetition of denunciations and Godless ideology," see Sophie Muller, *Jungle Methods*, 23.

26 Muller, *Jungle Methods*, 60.

27 Susan Harding, "Convicted by the Holy Spirit: The Rhetoric of Fundamental Baptist Conversion," *American Ethnologist* 14, no. 1 (1987): 168.

28 Muller, *Jungle Methods*, 4.

29 Ibid, 4.

30 Ibid, 9.

31 Ibid, 9.

32 Muller, *Jungle Methods*, 23.

33 Muller, *His Voice Shakes the Wilderness*, 60.

34 Muller, *Jungle Methods*, 5.

35 Eduardo Viveiros de Castro, *A inconstância da alma selvagem e outros ensaios de Antropologia* (São Paulo: Cosac & Naify, 2002), 190.

36 Carlos Fausto (2005). "Se Deus fosse jaguar: canibalismo e cristianismo entre os Guarani (Séculos xvi–xx)," *Mana* 11, no. 2 (2005): 403.

37 Muller, *Jungle Methods*, 11.

38 Ibid.

39 Jean and John Comaroff emphasize how spiritual and material transformations went hand in hand in Protestant projects of evangelization: "the study of religious transformation (…) stems ultimately from oppositions (between matter and mind, the concrete and the concept, and so on) at the ontological roots of our social thought oppositions which persist despite growing agreement that the primary processes involved in the production of the everyday world are inseparably material and meaningful. The impact of Protestant evangelists as harbingers of industrial capitalism lay in the fact that their civilizing mission was simultaneously symbolic and practical, theological and temporal." See Jean Comaroff and John Comaroff, *Of Revelation and Revolution. Christianity, Colonialism and Consciousness in South Africa* (Chicago: The University of Chicago Press, 1991), 8.

40 Talal Asad points out that the modern understanding of belief originates in Europe in the 17th -century when religion (and later Natural Religion) was defined as a "set of propositions to which believers gave assent, and which could therefore be judged and compared between different religions and against natural science." According to Asad, our modern notion of belief is a privatized one that conceives belief as a "state of mind rather than as a constituting activity in the world." In this sense, it is impossible to separate belief from the worldly conditions and the material practices that produce it. See Talal Asad, *Genealogies of Religion. Discipline and Reasons of Power in Christianity and Islam* (Baltimore: John Hopkins University Press, 1993), 41–47.

41 Capitan is the chieftain in each Indigenous community. Few decades ago, chieftains were chosen by local politicians. Since the 1990s, chieftains have been democratically elected by each community for a period of one year.

42 Personal communication, February 27, 2009.

43 Gloria Triana, *Los puinaves del Inírida. Formas de subsistencia y mecanismos de adaptación* (Bogotá: Universidad Nacional de Colombia, 1985), 35.

44 Personal communication, February 27, 2009.

45 Personal communication, February 27, 2009.

46 Personal communication, February 27, 2009.

47 Personal communication, February 27, 2009.

48 Personal communication, February 27, 2009.

49 Personal communication, February 27, 2009.

50 Personal communication, February 27, 2009.

104 *Between Rupture and Continuity*

51 Personal communication, February 27, 2009.
52 According to Adam Kuper, the idea of culture as a random set of traits goes back to 1871, when Tylor defined culture or civilization as a "complex whole which includes knowledge, belief, art, morals, law, custom, and any other capabilities and habits acquired by man as a member of society." Kuper shows how the idea of culture as a set of traits was derived from the fact that Tylor "stated that a culture formed a whole, but his idea of a whole was a list of traits." It was until the 1930s when Boas and his students began to use the term culture in the plural, when "Boas did write about 'a culture' rather than 'culture', he wavered between describing it as an accidental accretion of traits and as 'integrated spiritual totality', animated by the 'genius' of 'a people'." This definition of culture as an "accidental" set of traits is an explicit rejection of the notion that a culture constitutes an integrated whole. See Adam Kuper, *Culture: The Anthropologists' Account* (Cambridge: Harvard University Press, 1999), 56–61.
53 Personal communication, February 27, 2009.
54 Michel de Certeau points out that belief should be understood "not as the object of believing (a dogma, a program, etc.) but as the subject's investment in a proposition, the act of saying it and considering it as true – in other words, a 'modality' of the assertion and not its content." See Michel de Certeau, *The Practice of Everyday Life* (Berkeley: University of California Press, 1988), 178.
55 Personal communication, March 3, 2009.
56 Personal communication, March 3, 2009.
57 Archivo General de la Nación (Bogotá), Sección República, Caja 216, Carpeta 2012, Folios 25–26, Informe dirigido al jefe de la División de Asuntos Indígenas del Ministerio de Gobierno, Bogotá, 22 de junio de 1970.
58 Ibid.
59 David Stoll, "Higher Power: Wycliffe's Colombian Advance," in *Is God an American? An Anthropological Perspective on the Missionary Work of the Summer Institute of Linguistics*, eds. Søren Hvalkof and Peter Aaby (Denmark: International Work Group for Indigenous Affairs and Survival International, 1981), 63–76.
60 It is necessary to point out that most of today's elders were very young when Sophie Muller arrived in the region in the 1940s. Most of them were between 7 and 15 years old. Ironically, this means that a lot of the elders, as some of them told me, did not understand what was going on when Sophie Muller arrived for the first time in the 1940s.
61 Personal communication, April 20, 2009.
62 Personal communication, July 14, 2009.
63 Personal communication, July 14, 2009.
64 Ibid.
65 Personal communication, July 14, 2009.
66 Personal communication, July 14, 2009.
67 Personal communication, July 14, 2009.
68 Personal communication, July 14, 2009.
69 Personal communication, August 28, 2009.
70 Regarding the discussion about the relationship between myth and history among Amazonian societies, as well as Indigenous form of making history and representing the past, see *Rethinking History and Myth. Indigenous South American Perspectives on the Past*, ed. Jonathan Hill (Urbana: University of Illinois Press, 1988); Terence Turner, "Ethno-Ethnohistory: Myth and History in Native South American Representations of Contact with Western Society," in *Rethinking History and Myth. Indigenous South American Perspectives on the Past*, ed. Jonathan Hill (Urbana: University of Illinois Press, 1988), 235–281; Carlos Fausto and Michael Heckenberger, "Introduction. Indigenous History and the History of the "Indians,"" in *Time and Memory in Indigenous Amazonia*,

Between Rupture and Continuity 105

eds. Carlos Fausto and Michael Heckenberge (Gainesville: University Press of Florida, 2007), 1–43.

71 Bruce Albert, "Introdução," in *Pacificando O Branco. Cosmologias do contacto no Norte-Amazonico*, eds. Bruce Albert and Alcida Ramos (São Paulo: Editora Unesp, 2000), 9–21.

72 Manuela Carneiro da Cunha, "Apresentação," in *Pacificando O Branco. Cosmologias do contacto no Norte-Amazonico*, eds. Bruce Albert and Alcida Ramos (São Paulo: Editora Unesp, 2000), 7–8.

73 Ibid.

74 Personal communication, July 14, 2009.

75 Personal communication, July 14, 2009.

76 CONPLEI has its headquarters in Brazil. Some of the main objectives of CONPLEI as they are announced in the website of the organization are: promoting union and confraternity among pastors and other Indigenous evangelical leaders, represent Indigenous evangelical churches and support them in issues related to civil society and constituted public powers, defend, safeguard and fight for Indigenous rights (www.conplei.org.br).

77 Personal communication, March 3, 2009.

78 Personal communication, March 3, 2009.

79 Personal communication, March 3, 2009.

80 ONIC, *Plan de Vida Curripaco y Yeral* (Bogotá: Ediciones Turdakke, 2002), 34.

81 Ibid, 36.

82 Ibid, 37.

83 Manuela Carneiro da Cunha, "Apresentação," 7.

84 ONIC, *Plan de Vida Curripaco y Yeral*, 36.

85 Ibid, 37.

86 Ibid.

87 Ibid, 29.

88 Dominique Tilkin Gallois and Luís Donisete Benzi Grupioni, "*O índio na Missão Novas Tribos*," in *Transformando os deuses: os múltiplos sentidos da conversão entre os povos indígenas no Brasil*, ed. Robin Wright (Campinas: Unicamp, 1999), 77–129.

References

Albert, Bruce. "Introdução." In *Pacificando O Branco. Cosmologias do contacto no Norte-Amazonico*, edited by Bruce Albert and Alcida Ramos, 9–21. São Paulo: Editora Unesp, 2000.

Asad, Talal. *Genealogies of Religion. Discipline and Reasons of Power in Christianity and Islam*, 41–47. Baltimore: John Hopkins University Press, 1993.

Carneiro da Cunha, Manuela. "Apresentação." In *Pacificando O Branco. Cosmologias do contacto no Norte-Amazonico*, edited by Bruce Albert and Alcida Ramos, 7–8. São Paulo: Editora Unesp, 2000.

Comaroff, Jean, and John Comaroff. *Of Revelation and Revolution. Christianity, Colonialism and Consciousness in South Africa*. Chicago: The University of Chicago Press, 1991.

De Certeau, Michel. *The Practice of Everyday Life*. Berkeley: University of California Press, 1988.

Fausto, Carlos. "Se Deus fosse jaguar: canibalismo e cristianismo entre os Guarani (Séculos xvi–xx)." *Mana* 11, no. 2 (2005): 403. https://doi.org/10.1590/S0104-93132005000200003

Fausto, Carlos, and Michael Heckenberger. "Introduction. Indigenous History and the History of the "Indians."" In *Time and Memory in Indigenous Amazonia*,

106   *Between Rupture and Continuity*

edited by Carlos Fausto and Michael Heckenberger, 1–43. Gainesville: University Press of Florida, 2007.

Gallois, Dominique Tilkin, and Luís Donisete Benzi Grupioni. "*O índio na Missão Novas Tribos.*" In *Transformando os deuses: os múltiplos sentidos da conversão entre os povos indígenas no Brasil*, edited by Robin Wright, 77–129. Campinas: Unicamp, 1999.

Gow, Peter. "Forgetting Conversion. The Summer Institute of Linguistics Mission in the Piro Lived World." In *The Anthropology of Christianity*, edited by Fenella Canell, 211–239. Durham: Duke University Press, 2006.

Gow, Peter. *Of Mixed Blood. Kinship and History in Peruvian Amazonia.* New York: Oxford University Press, 1991.

Harding, Susan. "Convicted by the Holy Spirit: The Rhetoric of Fundamental Baptist Conversion." *American Ethnologist* 14, no. 1 (1987): 167–181.

Hill, Jonathan, ed. *Rethinking History and Myth. Indigenous South American Perspectives on the Past.* Urbana: University of Illinois Press, 1988.

Hill, Jonathan, and Robin Wright. "History, Ritual and Myth: Nineteenth Century Millenarian Movements in the Northwest Amazon." *Ethnohistory* 33, no. 1 (1986): 31–54.

Keane, Webb. *Christian Moderns: Freedom and Fetish in the Mission Encounter.* Berkley: University of California Press, 2007.

Kuper, Adam. *Culture: The Anthropologists' Account.* Cambridge: Harvard University Press, 1999.

Latour, Bruno. *We Have Never Been Modern.* Cambridge: Harvard University Press, 1993.

Luria, Keith P. "The Politics of Protestant Conversion to Catholicism in Seventeenth-Century France." In *Conversion to Modernities: The Globalization of Christianity*, edited by Peter van der Veer, 23–46. New York: Routledge, 1996.

Meyer, Birgit. "'Make a Complete Break with the Past.' Memory and Post-Colonial Modernity in Ghanaian Pentecostal Discourse." *Journal of Religion in Africa* 28, no. 3 (1998): 316–349.

Muller, Sophie. *Beyond Civilization.* Woodworth: New Tribes Mission, 1952.

Muller, Sophie. *His Voice Shakes the Wilderness.* Sanford: New Tribes Mission, 1988.

Muller, Sophie. *Jungle Methods.* Woodworth: Brown Gold Publications, 1960.

ONIC. *Plan de Vida Curripaco y Yeral.* Bogotá: Ediciones Turdakke, 2002.

Robbins, Joel. "Continuity Thinking and the Problem of Christian Culture: Belief, Time, and the Anthropology of Christianity." *Current Anthropology* 48, no. 1 (2007): 5–38.

Stephen, Hugh-Jones. "Shamans, Prophets, Priests, and Pastors." In *Shamanism, History and the State*, edited by Nicholas Thomas and Caroline Humprey, 32–75. Ann Arbor: The University of Michigan Press, 1996.

Stoll, David. "Higher Power: Wycliffe's Colombian Advance." In *Is God an American? An Anthropological Perspective on the Missionary Work of the Summer Institute of Linguistics*, edited by Søren Hvalkof and Peter Aaby, 63–76. Copenhaguen: IWGIA and Survival International, 1981.

Triana, Gloria. *Los puinaves del Inírida. Formas de subsistencia y mecanismos de adaptación.* Bogotá: Universidad Nacional de Colombia, 1985.

Turner, Terence. "Ethno-Ethnohistory: Myth and History in Native South American Representations of Contact with Western Society." In *Rethinking History and*

Myth. Indigenous South American Perspectives on the Past, edited by Jonathan Hill, 235–281. Urbana: University of Illinois Press, 1988.

Vilaça, Aparecida. "Conversão, predação e perspectiva." *Mana* 14, no.1 (2008): 173–203. https://doi.org/10.1590/S0104-93132008000100007

Viveiros de Castro, Eduardo. *A inconstância da alma selvagem e outros ensaios de Antropologia.* São Paulo: Cosac & Naify, 2002.

Wright, Robin. "Prophetic Traditions among the Baniwa and Other Arawakan Peoples of the Northwest Amazon." In *Comparative Arawakan Histories: Rethinking Language Family and Culture Area in Amazonia,* edited by Jonathan Hill and Fernando Santos-Granero, 269–293. Urbana: University of Illinois Press, 2002.

4 Christianity, Materiality and the Critique of Modernity[1]

This chapter analyzes how different views of materiality reveal different understandings and relationships to modernity, closely associated with ideas about civilization (for Catholic missionaries) and/or "worldliness" (for Indigenous evangelicals). Specifically, I describe how Indigenous evangelicals in the Colombian Amazon developed specific ideas about materiality and how these shaped their perception and use of specific objects and commodities. It was common for evangelical missionaries to associate the use of certain objects or instruments among Indigenous communities with demon worship, while the possession of commodities was related to "worldliness." The evangelical critique of materiality was developed on two fronts: the destruction of objects that were used in shamanic practices or traditional rituals and the restriction of material possessions or the accumulation of commodities.

While Catholic missionaries in Vaupés relied heavily on commodities and material objects within their work, evangelical missionaries affiliated to New Tribes Mission tried to destroy material objects with sacred value for Indigenous communities. This practice of destroying such material objects has been common in several projects of political and religious reform, as well as in broader missionary enterprises.[2] Muller draws on colonial and Catholic interpretation of "Indigenous religion" as "demon worship" arguing that the natives she met could not pray, because they were "possessed by the Devil." Muller thought that "Devil worship" could be hampered or attacked by "suppressing or transforming material manifestations of the spirit world."[3]

The second part of the chapter looks at how evangelical missionaries affiliated to New Tribes Mission, in the region since 1940, tried to restrict practices of object and commodity accumulation among Indigenous evangelicals, arguing that things or possessions would "tether them" and limit their agency. Indigenous evangelical churches had grown out of the New Tribes Mission evangelizing work in the 1940s and many of them were still active during my fieldwork. By Indigenous evangelicals in this chapter I refer to the members of *Iglesias Bíblicas Unidas* (United Biblical Churches), a regional "association" of Indigenous churches that was created in the 1980s. Indigenous evangelicals and churches among the Curripacos and Puinaves groups in Guainía developed an ongoing critique of materiality through the idea of "worldliness" (*lo mundano*),

DOI: 10.4324/9781003370215-5

Christianity, Materiality and Critique of Modernity   109

producing a selective appropriation of modernity. "Worldliness" is related to both material things (money, radios, etc.) and specific deeds, thoughts or desires. This chapter shows how Indigenous evangelicals were not so much concerned with the possessions of material things as such, but more so with the values and attitudes that certain objects or technologies might help disseminate.

This chapter develops further discussions within the anthropology of Christianity regarding how Christianity happens materially and how materiality mediates different moral apprehensions of modernity.[4] In the context of Amazonia, Indigenous theories of materiality and objects challenge simplistic or modern understandings about the relationships and frontiers between subjects and objects.[5] In addition, modernity in Amazonia was not necessarily associated with "the rise of reason," but more with different projects of colonization, including extractive economies, gold mining, state building, the armed conflict and the work of missionaries, among others.

The last section of this chapter shows how some of the objects and commodities initially introduced by Catholic missionaries and *colonos* alike (such as mirrors, *machetes*, rudders, and boats) were later depicted in images that evangelical missionaries used to teach the Bible. "Worldliness" in these images is related with both material things (money, radios, etc.) and specific deeds, thoughts or desires. Indigenous evangelicals were not so much concerned with the possessions of material things as such, but more with the values and attitudes that certain objects or commodities might help disseminate. While some anthropologists point out that "consumerism" appears to be a characteristic feature of lowland South American Indians,[6] the status and role that different objects or commodities might play among Amazonian Indigenous societies remains ambiguous.[7] The high demand for "Western trade goods" among native Amazonian peoples should be situated "withing a broader economy of desire with roots in historical experiences of colonization."[8]

Witchcraft, the Devil and Destroying Sacred Objects

As it was described in Chapter 2, the Devil had an important place in Sophie Muller's narrative about Indigenous rituals and religious practices. Echoing earlier Catholic missionaries, Muller frequently described local rituals and religious practices in terms of "demon worship" or witchcraft. Still today, Indigenous evangelicals considered Satan or the Devil to be "the chief of the sorcerers." For instance, in *Beyond Civilization*, Muller describes a traditional Curripaco ritual known as *pudáli* in the following way:

> It seemed like a calling together of all the demons in creation. Moving along in a slow, funeral-like procession, they blew on long, tube-like poles, swaying them slowly from side to side, in time with the hollow notes that issued forth and re-echoed through the jungle. One could easily associate these weird strains with witchcraft or demon worship, especially on a moonlight night in the heart of the jungle.[9]

110 *Christianity, Materiality and Critique of Modernity*

According to Jonathan Hill, *pudáli* were ritual ceremonies closely linked with "subsistence activities of the yearly agricultural and fishing cycles."[10] *Pudáli* involved wife and food exchanges, as well as ritual dances where flutes and trumpets were played. Muller perceived traditional Indigenous rituals as a clear sign of demon worship, a sort of "funeral-like procession" where tube-like poles (or flutes) were blown. Muller associates the "hollow notes" of the flutes with witchcraft or demon worship. In her books, Muller refers to shamans as "witch doctors" and to their practices as "professions of faith." Muller translated the Curripaco word *malirri* (shaman) as "witch doctor." She considered the "witch doctors" to be her "chief rivals" and described how "they blew on their patients, and chased evil spirits away with a carved gourd rattle."[11] "Witch doctors," according to Muller, would "suck on the patients arm," and then, using "a piece of wood hidden in their mouth," would extract it and say "this came out of your arm and now you will get well."[12] Furthermore, Muller went as far to compose a song named "Simon the sorcerer" after following closely the practices of her "chief rivals."

Muller recognized the authority and power of well-known shamans over their constituents. In fact, once they became Christian, she relied on their traditional authority and used it to her advantage. For instance, in the translation of the entire New Testament from Curripaco to Puinave, a former *malirri* named Julio helped Muller: "he was one of the witch doctors who had held sway over the village only half a year earlier. This man, who had made a clean break from his witchcraft, would turn out to be my most efficient and persevering helper."[13] In her first book, Muller depicts the witch doctor of Canyo Iwiali and a stone that "appears to have been handed down for generations," giving him authority to practice witchcraft.[14] It was the Devil who had led them for generations into witchcraft and sorcery. It was the Devil who had taught them everything they knew.

In the case of Muller's narrative, the main difference traced between missionaries and natives was framed in terms of Christianity vs. witchcraft. Furthermore, Muller not only used the Devil to explain Indigenous religious practices but also referred to the presence of the Devil in her writings, and to demons and evil spirits while traveling throughout the region. The Devil seemed to have a real presence in Muller's daily work as a missionary and he tried to distract her attention before the meetings she organized "with all the filth and sickness and flies and dogs," as well as with the bites of "fire ants." In *Beyond Civilization*, Muller recounts how "missionaries here believe in demon possession more than those in the States." Specifically, Muller describes how:

> (...) one is more sensitive [here] to the invisible forces. One's friends and family form a protective smoke screen that desensitizes one, I guess. Anyway, last night, we seemed to be surrounded by demons. Even the Indians from Tunuí couldn't pray. They seemed to be held tongue-tied. I prayed aloud that the Lord would release them from the Devil's grip so they could pray, and then some of them came through to the Lord, it seemed.[15]

Christianity, Materiality and Critique of Modernity   111

The idea that some of the "Indians" could not pray because they were "possessed by the Devil" has been widely used by missionaries in the representation and interpretation of "Indigenous religions" and rituals in different colonial contexts. For instance, *The Jesuit Relations* from New France in the 17th century described the Iroquois as "possessed by the demon." Since then, it was common that missionaries described so-called "animism" or "spirit worship" in terms of "demoniacal possession."[16] Up until the 1940s anthropologists thought that "demoniacal possession" constituted a "specialized from of spirit intrusion" that happened "without invocation."[17] Paul C. Johnson points out how "possessed action came to be viewed as the opposite of *individual* action- accountable, contract-worthy, transparent, and properly civil – in early modern social theories that became the template for almost all political states."[18] In this sense, the "figure of the 'possessed' helped define the proper sort of individual in relation to which the state was imagined."[19]

As mentioned in Chapter 3, Muller used the trope of "possession" to symbolize her vision of evangelization: "These people seem like 'empty houses, swept and garnished', waiting to be occupied. I pray that the Lord will be allowed to take possession of each one, so that the Devil doesn't return in power (...)."[20] In *Jungle Methods* published in 1960, Muller describes the main task of a missionary when he or she comes into a village: "he must realize that he is there to 'possess it [the village]' for the Lord. He must say to himself, 'Yes, I shall possess it for Christ'."[21] Therefore, Muller's ambivalent use of "possession" shows how "spirit possession" indexed "overlapping issues of the ownership of territory and bodies" or the problem of "controlling interior lives of peoples encountered in newly occupied lands."[22]

One of the main strategies that Muller and other evangelical missionaries used to remove what they considered to be witchcraft or demon worship was pushing their "followers" to destroy sacred instruments (such as flutes) associated with different traditional rituals or practices. As I mentioned at the beginning of this chapter, the destruction of material objects with sacred value has been common in several projects of political and religious reform. In fact, Muller's song about Simon (the sorcerer) is about how he will dispose of the objects he uses in "sorcery" and return them to the Devil.

However, the persecution of "idolatry" in the hands of missionaries or religious authorities is not new in Latin America. Since the 17th century, using the existing bureaucracy associated with the Spanish Inquisition, Church and Crown tried to extirpate among Indigenous communities under their rule what they considered to be idolatrous practices. In fact, during the colonial period, the bureaucracy of the Inquisition included the figure of the "visitors of idolatry," who were usually missionaries or members of religious orders such as the Jesuits. These "visitors of idolatry" seemed to be convinced that "everything that could be done for the conversion of the natives would be in vain if the evil were not extirpated by the roots" and this entailed the "severe punishment of adult idolaters."[23]

112 *Christianity, Materiality and Critique of Modernity*

Ricardo López, a Curripaco whose father is a pastor and who grew up in the Upper Guainía River, told me how Muller had instructed all the pastors to destroy and throw to the river the sacred instruments and objects used in traditional rituals. The idea behind this kind of actions was that destroying the material support of "sorcery" or "witchcraft" was a way of transforming the "beliefs" that supported those practices or the spirits that might inhabit those objects.[24] Some of the instruments thrown to the river were, for instance, flutes associated with different kinds of rituals. For example, *Yurupary* is a widely known initiation rite in Northwest Amazonia involving the use of flutes and trumpets made from section of the trunk of paxiuba palm. *Yurupary* is a secret men's cult that centers on the "use of sacred instruments that women and children are forbidden to see."[25] *Yurupary* is a culture hero that is also present in the myths of different Indigenous groups in Vaupés. According to Stephen Hugh Jones, "a theme common to most of these stories is that of a hero being burned alive on a fire, often as a punishment for an act of cannibalism. From the ashes of this fire springs a paxiuba palm which is subsequently cut up into sections to make the Yurupary instruments."[26] The instruments used in these rituals "represent the living dead, the first ancestors of humanity."[27] In this sense, sacred or ritual objects in Amazonia put into question modern conceptions of things as inanimate beings as well as ideas of the human as distinctive and superior to the material world.

Recent and classic ethnographies show how it is common in Amazonian ontologies, that "things – or at least some things – are considered to be subjectivities possessed of a social life."[28] Indigenous distinctions between humans and nonhumans in Amazonia are irreducible to Western distinctions between nature and culture. Evangelical missionaries thought that destroying or throwing sacred instruments into the river would eradicate the practices and beliefs that went along with those objects. Birgit Meyer shows how the "Protestant rejection of sacred objects as 'idols' or 'fetishes' went along with a heavy emotional investment" in these same objects."[29] Protestant missionaries had to deal in one way or another with objects and different notions of materiality in order to bring about the "true faith."[30]

David López, the Puinave missionary that criticized white missionaries in Chapter 3 for ignoring Indigenous culture and feelings, told me a story about the sacred flutes used in Yurupary. Some years ago in *Chorro Bocón*, a Puinave community on the Inírida River, some men who were fishing found a flute that was used in traditional rituals on a small branch next to the river. Flutes were hidden before, under the water in places considered sacred.[31] Nobody wanted to touch the flutes because they had the belief, according to David, that if someone saw or touched the flutes, women especially, they could die. "But there was a trap," David told me. It wasn't the flute, that "piece of wood," that killed people, he explained. It was the people who spied on each other and killed with poison those who touched or played the flute. People in *Chorro Bocón* feared the flute. When David arrived there, they had the flute hidden in a kitchen. David wanted to see the flute, but they wouldn't

Christianity, Materiality and Critique of Modernity   113

let him. He told them: "let me go inside, I don't care if I die." He then took the flute outside, showed it to everyone and told them: "look, look at this, nobody is going to die here." As Webb Keane points out, "one of the chief aims of the work of purification, as undertaken by Protestant missionaries, is to establish the proper locus of agency in the world by sorting out correct from mistaken imputations of agency."[32] Indigenous evangelical missionaries like David despise the belief that certain kinds of objects (like flutes) might possess agency in themselves. This, for them, is idolatry. David was trying to explain to the people in Chorro Bocón that the flute had no agency in itself, and that seeing it otherwise, was a mistaken imputation of agency. Instead, David attributed agency to the men that were in charge of watching the flutes. However, it is difficult to know if David and other evangelical missionaries succeeded in their effort to purify agency and establish an ontological divide between humans and nonhumans, culture and nature.

Evangelical Christianity and Worldliness

Regardless of Indigenous evangelicals criticizing the possession of material things, evangelical missionaries also relied on objects such as Bibles, catechisms and songbooks (translated to Indigenous languages), flannelgraphs, images and radios for their work.[33] Since the 1940s, Indigenous evangelicals in the Colombian Amazon developed a specific understanding of modernity through ideas about "worldliness" (*lo mundano*).[34] The idea of *lo mundano* entailed a critique of material possessions or commodities as possible sources of moral derailment. Nonetheless, the high demand for "Western trade goods" among native Amazonian peoples is part of "a broader economy of desire with roots in historical experiences of colonization."[35] Moreover, economic exchange and "trade goods" in Amazonia are intertwined with the "boom-bust cycles that mark the collecting of natural commodities" in this region.[36] In Amazonia, as Harry Walker points out, consumption and commoditization are "often closely linked to the nature of modernity as lived experience."[37]

Despite Indigenous evangelicals and missionaries rejecting some practices or values associated with modernity as "worldly," evangelical Christianity should not be understood as inherently anti-modern given that they relied heavily on modern technologies and objects as part of their daily practices. In fact, some of these objects (such as *machetes* or outboard motors) appeared in images that were used by missionaries and members of Indigenous churches to articulate specific understandings of the Bible and Christianity. As I will show in this section, through the idea of "worldliness," Indigenous evangelicals developed a moral understanding of modernity and condemned specific practices such as the possession of material things or "vices" such as smoking, drinking, or dancing.

In 2009, as mentioned in Chapter 3, I met Feliciano Cayupare, brother of one of the first Puinave missionaries in Caño Ucata (Venezuela). Most of the Indigenous evangelicals I encountered during fieldwork were members

114 *Christianity, Materiality and Critique of Modernity*

of churches affiliated to *Iglesias Bíblicas Unidas* (United Bible Churches), a regional "network" of Indigenous churches that was created in the 1980s. Feliciano explained to me that his deceased father was a worldly person because he was Catholic, drank alcohol and participated in traditional parties or rituals where flutes were played and *chicha* was consumed. For most Christian elders, the past was worldly, full of ignorance, violence and chaos. The idea of "worldliness" [*lo mundano*] constitutes one of the main categories through which Indigenous evangelicals articulate their personal and social experience. Among younger Indigenous evangelicals it was common to think of worldliness as something related to the possession of material things. A Curripaco evangelical missionary said to me once that,

> In Maroa [a town in Venezuela] I have seen brothers, I have always said: why brothers are you tied up to material things? Why? Some sisters and brothers have told me: I can't go, I can't go to the Holy Supper or the Conference because we are going to be there 2 or 3 days and nobody watches my house, because I have refrigerator, television, washing machine. Things tied them down, the things of this world tied them down, do you understand? This is what happens today.

The idea of being "tied down" to "material things" such as a "refrigerator, television or a washing machine" refers to how property can also possess people and jeopardize the idea of the autonomous subject or individual. Nonetheless, modern individuals can also be defined by property or by their possessions to the extent that "individual freedom" can also become a "function of possession."[38] The project of liberating oneself from "things" that might limit one's agency is also part of what Webb Keane calls the moral narrative of modernity. In this narrative "progress is not only a matter of improvements in technology, economic well-being, or health" but is, above all, "about human emancipation and self-mastery."[39] Specifically, the moral narrative of modernity links "moral progress to practices of detachment from and revaluation of materiality."[40] In addition, Protestant ontology, according to Keane, defines the value of the human in terms of its superiority to the material world.[41]

Indigenous evangelicals perceived material possessions as a hindrance to Christian practice and belief. Furthermore, Indigenous representations of "worldliness" were not reduced to material things or objects. Rodrigo, a deacon from one of the Indigenous churches close to the capital of the province of Guainía, told me once how before he became Christian he used to get drunk with his cousin: "*We used to drink with him in the discos, smoked, everything. Our talk was about this world: women, money, getting drunk, all that. We did not congregate, nor did we join in worship One day I entered the service and the pastor preached to me.*" In this sense, worldliness, according to Indigenous evangelicals, refers not just to material things or possessions, but it also includes places, vices, ways of talking, specific deeds and thoughts. Indigenous understandings of "worldliness" refer not only to material things

Christianity, Materiality and Critique of Modernity   115

but also to "immaterial things" such as thoughts, desires and vices. Therefore, as Opas and Haapalainen point out, "the relation between the material and immaterial does not submit to fixing."[42] Mathew Engelke shows that "the repudiation of the material is a selective process" and "what sustains projects of immateriality in religious practice is always the definition of what counts as materially dangerous."[43] In this sense, following Engelke, the notion of *worldliness* developed by Indigenous evangelicals is also a "project of immateriality," as it defines a set of objects, things or commodities that might be considered potentially dangerous in moral terms.

For most Indigenous evangelicals living a life "separated" from worldliness "meant going about one's life according to a different outlook" and a "distinctive morality."[44] For instance, a *mestizo* pastor who worked with Christian Puinaves for several years explained to me how it is possible to tell if someone is Christian or not by the way they carry their body. Good manners and proper behavior are usually associated with being a good Christian. As I described in Chapter 3, becoming civilized and Christian entailed, for Indigenous evangelicals, material and bodily transformation related to how they build houses, how they attend visitors and community-oriented ways of life.

The relationship that Indigenous evangelicals establish with "worldliness" can take different forms. Worldliness cannot be totally left behind once you become Christian, because it can still haunt you and will be part of the world you live in. Weber's description of Protestantism as "this-worldly asceticism" has been criticized because it privileges "a particular view of Protestantism as a rational, disenchanting religion that transcends the body, the senses, and outward religious forms."[45] This "dematerialized" understanding of Protestantism leaves aside the "value attributed to bodies, things, texts and gestures, so as to make the divine tangible in the immanent."[46] Therefore, the struggle that Indigenous evangelicals establish against worldliness has to be carried out in "this world" and has to become tangible. The alleged renunciation of worldly values, ideas or practices had to take place out here in this world and in everyday life. Daniel Miller shows how even the most radical critiques of materiality, as well as the goal of transcending our attachment to material life, have to be expressed in material form.[47]

According to a booklet called *The Christian Life* used by Indigenous evangelical pastors and missionaries that are part of *Iglesias Bíblicas Unidas* (United Bible Churches), conversion entails not only becoming a "new" person, but also a different kind of person. A young pastor from the Puinave community of Chorro Bocón showed me the booklet in October 2009. It was made by evangelical missionaries in 1972 based on the first Protestant translation of the Bible done in 1569 by Spanish theologian and reformer Casiodoro de Reina.[48] The booklet explains that, in order for conversion to happen, the "spiritual man," guided by the will of God, is supposed to leave behind the "natural man" that lives for the "things of this world." In other words, "being born again" is part of the transit from the "carnal" or "natural man" to the "spiritual man."[49] The carnal man has heard or knows about

116 *Christianity, Materiality and Critique of Modernity*

the Holy Spirit, but he doesn't obey it or God's will, the flesh controls him.[50] The natural man has not received the Holy Spirit and, therefore, he cannot know or understand anything about God's will. Unlike the "natural" man, the "spiritual" man is controlled by the Holy Spirit, obeys him and follows God's will. When the Holy Spirit starts to control the "believer" from then on he is "spiritual."[51] During my time in Guainía in 2009, these were common ideas that circulated in booklets and printed materials used by Indigenous evangelical pastors and missionaries.

However, this ideal vision of conversion and believer did not correspond necessarily with real experiences of converts. It was common, for example, to hear stories about Indigenous evangelicals that had gone astray and returned to a "worldly life." Indigenous evangelicals refer to this kind of backsliding as *descarriarse*, which can be translated as "to go astray" or to "fall off the wagon," showing how there are also failed conversions. Converts can easily go back and forth between a Christian and a worldly life.

During my fieldwork in the Upper Rio Negro, I met Alonso, a Curripaco from Venezuela who had been the pastor of the Venezuelan border town of San Carlos since the year 2000. Alfonso was baptized at the beginning of the 1980s in San Carlos, but he left his community and traveled around. In July 2009 he told me that when he went astray he traveled a lot and visited different cities in Amazonia and the eastern plains (*llanos orientales*). Alonso said that when he was a "worldly" person, "I traveled over there, in order to know life, in order to preach better." To some extent, this pastor was suggesting that it is not possible to preach effectively unless you know the "things of the world" or unless you had led a worldly life before. The more you know about the "things of the world," the better you can preach knowing worldliness and what it entails is essential for staying the course and leading a virtuoso Christian life. It is common for Indigenous evangelicals to go back and forth between a worldly life and Christian practice. The positive connotation that a "worldly" past has for living a virtuous Christian life in the present produces an odd complementarity between "worldliness" and evangelical Christianity in this context. As Minna Opas points out, Christian denominational adherences in Amazonia are "best understood as unstable forms of belonging that require constant reproduction."[52] In Amazonia social discrepancies or tensions within Indigenous communities and families are expressed through religious disputes regarding, for example, denominational affiliations. The next section of the chapter addresses how "worldliness" and modernity were framed in images that circulated among Indigenous pastors and missionaries.

Images, Objects and the Critique of Modernity

Despite the emphasis on literacy and translations of the Bible into Indigenous languages, New Tribes Missionaries also relied heavily on images (which also included texts in Spanish and quotes from the Bible). David Morgan shows how since the late 18th century in England and the United States the

Christianity, Materiality and Critique of Modernity   117

"printed images of a highly abstract and allegorical character had long appealed to even the staunchest Puritans."[53] Mass-produced and hand-painted images, according to Morgan, became a "new moral technology" that "supplemented the Protestant apparatus of conversion."[54] Furthermore, Morgan describes how 19th- and early-20th-century Protestants increasingly found that act of looking at mass-produced images as "an act imbued with the power of belief or to make one believe."[55]

Some Indigenous Christian elders keep images made and circulated by evangelical missionaries as part of their work in their houses. Some of these images are also hung on the walls of the churches where Indigenous evangelicals hold their services. In 2009, I saw the original versions of some of these images at the Biblical Institute in Caño Ucata across the border in Venezuela. The images were displayed in the offices of the Biblical Institute, where I had the chance to meet Indigenous missionaries who were trained and worked there. The images distributed by evangelical missionaries established symbolic associations between the Bible and different kinds of objects that were familiar to natives. The Bible was compared with mirrors, swords (*machetes*), food, milk, seeds, brakes and rudders, among other objects. This kind of comparisons disseminated ideas throughout Indigenous communities of what it meant to become Christian. For instance, comparisons between the Bible and a mirror articulated specific understandings of conversion (see Figure 4.1).

This image is divided into two parts, the upper part has the title *the Bible is milk and food* and shows a healthy female baby drinking milk from a feeding bottle on the left side and the right side shows an undernourished male baby. The lower part of the plate (see below) has the title *is a mirror*. Pablo, one of the Indigenous pastors I met during my fieldwork, explained to me, in his own words, what the idea of the Bible as a mirror consisted of:

> if one doesn't look at one's face in a mirror, one doesn't know what is going on with one's face. The same thing happens with the Bible. The Bible shows that one is a sinner before God. Then, one takes the mirror and looks, look what I have on my face, I am ashamed. Did I go over there at noon like this? It is the shame that is shown by the mirror. In the same way, the Bible shows our sins before God.

The Bible, according to Pablo, shows us "who we really are" before God and shames us of our "dirtiness" and sins. It is here that estrangement comes into play as we are not really who we thought we were. Pablo thought he was doing well and being a good man before becoming Christian, but later he realized that there was nothing good about his previous life. Without objects such as a mirror or a Bible it would be impossible for us to know who we "really" are and recognize ourselves as sinners before God. More than simply reflecting our own selves as they are, the Bible gives us back a negative image of ourselves, it *shows all the evil we have*, Pablo told me. The Bible as a mirror becomes an object that can mediate the sincerity of

118 *Christianity, Materiality and Critique of Modernity*

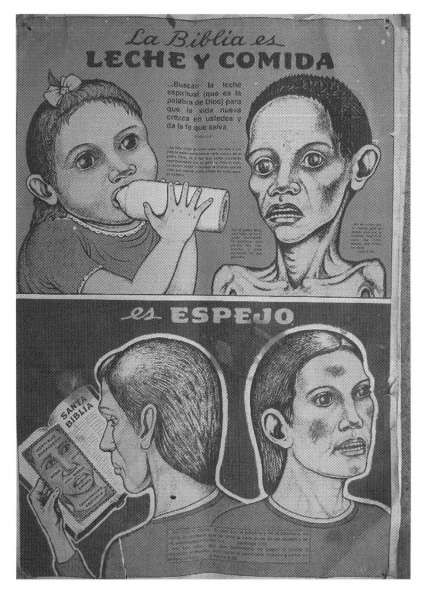

Figure 4.1 The Bible as milk and food, the Bible as mirror.
Source: Picture taken by the author.

conversion, but also reveals how sincerity can be considered "something tangible."[56] The importance of what can be "observed" in others' actions and behavior is crucial here. In a similar way to other Indigenous Christian churches, "it is actions seen, not speech heard that reliably informs people about their fellows."[57]

Christianity, Materiality and Critique of Modernity 119

Going back to the image, you can see a person looking at his face in the Bible. There are dirty spots around his face, signs of specific sins associated with "worldliness": lies and drunkenness in his forehead, theft and hate on each cheek, wasteful spending between his nose and mouth, deception in his chin, rudeness and fornication in his throat. The Bible then works as a mirror, but a particular kind of mirror that enables specific forms of self-estrangement, pushing people to see things that were not there before. On the upper left corner of this image there is an inscription that reads: "Through the Bible, the young man sees his sins and says: 'I'm dirty, I want to be cleansed by Christ.'" In this sense, only through the Bible can the "young man" see his sins and recognize himself as a sinner before God. Nonetheless, the image also refers to those who don't "obey" the Bible, to those who don't follow the modes of recognition or misrecognition suggested in the metaphor of the Bible as mirror: "So the Bible says: 'The one who listens to the word and doesn't obey is like a man that looks at his dirty face in a mirror and goes away, forgetting how he was.'"[58] In this sense, there is explicit reference in the image to those who "give testimony of following Christ and return to the world."

Other objects such as boats, engines, brakes, rudders and swords (*machetes*) appear frequently in the images that circulate among Indigenous evangelicals. In another image at the Biblical Institute that I also saw on the wall of a church, the Bible is compared with a brake and a rudder (see Figure 4.2). The plate draws on the book of James and is entitled *the Bible is brake and rudder*.[59] On the upper left it reads: "with the brakes we can manage (*manejar*) the whole body,"[60] and in brackets it reads: "So, too, through the Bible we can put the brake on evil desires and walk with our God." On the upper right it reads: *With a rudder it guides them through (...) the path of life*. Underneath this it reads: *Without a rudder the driver cannot avoid the rocks in the river... In the same way, without the Bible we are not aware of the temptations that can destroy our life*. The image uses local metaphors to convey a message that makes sense for those who read it or see it. In the Amazon, boats are the most common medium of transportation, rudders are used to stir the boats and rivers are part of daily life.

In the image below (see Figure 4.2) there is an explicit comparison between the boat and life, the rudder and the Bible. In a similar way, each of the rocks on the river has a particular inscription: drugs, alcohol, impurity, jokes and evil friends. All these inscriptions are associated with worldly things. Underneath the rider and the horse there is a short paragraph that reads: *the reins are tied to each side of a steel bar in the mouth of the horse, with this break the owner can guide it through the path it should travel. So too the Holy Spirit is guiding us through the Bible in the dangerous path of this world until we reach our home in heaven*.

The comparison of the Bible with a brake and a rudder emphasizes self-discipline and control of ones' own desires. Obeisance to God starts with self-discipline, which is only possible through the action of the Word, according to Pablo, the Puinave pastor: *discipline is what comes out of the Word, you*

120 *Christianity, Materiality and Critique of Modernity*

Figure 4.2 The Bible as brake and rudder. The Bible as sword of the spirit.
Source: Picture taken by the author.

see me here, like disciplined. I am here disciplined, but it is not because you disciplined me, it is not because the pastor disciplined me; it is just because I am disciplined by the Lord, with the help of what he told me, all that he gives us. Despite Pablo's belief that it is the Word and the Lord that discipline him, there are also practices by which members of Indigenous churches are disciplined. I had the chance to participate in meetings of Indigenous churches called *conferencias* where Indigenous policemen were appointed in order to watch their fellowmen and kin during the conference, following the instructions in the catechism.[61] *Conferencias* were hosted every two or three

Christianity, Materiality and Critique of Modernity 121

months, through a rotation system, by different Indigenous evangelical communities and could last between four or five days which included services, sharing of food and non-alcoholic drinks, as well as listening to "Christian music" of different genres. In fact, during one of these meetings in 2009, a fellow Indigenous evangelical actually caught me smoking a cigarette and I was accused in public the next day during the service by the pastor who had taken me there. In these *conferencias* each of the appointed policemen was given a long spear made of wood at the beginning, so people could identify them. These Indigenous Christian police had to watch over all the attendees of the conference, making sure everybody, including non-Christians (as me), followed the rules during these events.

The recently appointed policemen told the people at the conference that although they were in charge of keeping an eye on them, attendees should also police the policemen, because they could also make mistakes. The idea of Indigenous evangelicals as "soldiers of God" appears in the same poster where the Bible is compared with a break and rudder. In this image the Bible is "sword of the spirit," and you can see a person wearing an armor with a "helmet of salvation," a "breastplate of justice," a "belt of truth" and holding a sword which is the Bible ("the word of God is sharper than any sword"). During my fieldwork, I would often hear comparisons between the Bible and *machetes*, some of the pastors would say the Bible is like a *machete* because if you don't know how to use it, you can cut your hand at some point.

These images also condense local understandings of worldliness and modernity. Ideas about "worldliness" were addressed in these images distributed by evangelical missionaries. This image (see Figure 4.3) pictures a sitting native who is smiling because he has a large amount of coins and two bundles of bills in front of him. On his t-shirt it says "tied-up by business and pleasures," below this there is another sign that reads "love for money" and on top of the two bundles of bills it says "more and more." In the background of the images there are plants with thorns and a cross inscribed with: "take your cross and follow me," yet to the left of the cross is another sign that says "no time to serve."

The image comes with a long explanation underneath that goes like this:

Christ talked about the ones tied to thorns: "(...) the ones that listen to the word, but the thirst [*afán*] for this world, the deception of wealth and pleasures that drown the word and don't bear fruit." This comparison talks about things that block [*tapan*] the voice of God and take away the desire to live for him. What today stops us from thinking of God is the music of the devil, the one that invites demons to enter the households through television, radio, and cassettes expelling [*echando fuera*] the Holy Spirit. The world also calls us everywhere to enjoy in things that don't have value [*no valen*] and waste time, instead of reading and teaching the bible to the ones who don't know that they are lost and that there is forgiveness and salvation in Christ.

122 *Christianity, Materiality and Critique of Modernity*

Figure 4.3 "Tied-up by business and pleasures."
Source: Picture taken by the author.

According to this explanation of the image, money is one of the "things that block [*tapan*] the voice of God and take away the desire to live for him." Televisions and radios are also among the things that scare away the Holy Spirit from households.[62] Nonetheless, from the explanation in the image it seems clear that it is not technology in itself, which puts Christian values, virtues or practice, in jeopardy, but the desires and values that technology helps to disseminate or provoke (the "music of the devil" that expels the Holy Spirit). The references to the "things of the world" or the "thirst [*afán*] for this world, the deception of wealth and pleasures that drown the word," should not be ignored given that "worldliness" [*lo mundano*] constitutes one of the main categories through which Indigenous evangelicals articulate their personal and social experience.

The idea that the "things of this world" tie up Christians returns us to the question of how certain objects or possessions might limit the agency of individuals. Therefore, Indigenous evangelicals could try to refuse specific "types of material forms," but they could simultaneously "make use of these forms for other means."[63] This explains why the problem that missionaries

Christianity, Materiality and Critique of Modernity   123

find with radios, cassettes and televisions is not in their ownership, but in how they might be used or in what they might provoke in those who use them. Moreover, the problem is how these objects might become vehicles of inappropriate desires, thoughts and values; what missionaries call the "music of the devil."

In this chapter I showed how Indigenous evangelicals develop a complex and ambiguous relationship with modernity. Local ideas and practices associated with modernity might include the practices of missionaries, informal mining and illegal activities, colonization and different state-making projects, among others. However, contemporary Indigenous evangelicals are "modern" in terms of the selective use of modern technologies, devices and commodities. Indigenous evangelicals develop a contentious relationship with certain values and attitudes of modernity that might be disseminated or accelerated through specific objects or technologies. This contentious relationship leads to a sort of evangelical "moral modernity," which frames and mediates local experiences and transactions with the modern. This selective and particular relationship that Indigenous evangelicals develop with modernity is condensed in the idea of *lo mundano* [worldliness].

Conclusions

In this chapter I analyzed how different notions of materiality among evangelical missionaries and Indigenous evangelicals framed specific experiences of Christianity and modernity in the Colombian Amazon. Specifically, this chapter focuses on how Christianity "happens materially," considering the contingent and relational nature of the objects or commodities that might be perceived as morally dangerous or not. The first part of the chapter showed how destroying the material support of Indigenous religious practices was a way of transforming the "beliefs" that sustained those practices. Furthermore, Indigenous notions of materiality put into question the clear cut divisions between subjects and objects. In this context, Christian materialities have to interact with Indigenous ontologies in which boundaries between persons and things, subjects and objects, are not totally clear, and objects are "endowed with subjectivity."[64] Moreover, the different relationships that evangelical missionaries and Indigenous evangelicals establish with materiality reveal different understandings of Indigenous culture, modernity and civilization.

At the same time, evangelical missionaries tried to "reform" Indigenous culture through the destruction of sacred object and tried to limit and control (at least rhetorically) the accumulation, possession and use of different kinds of commodities, arguing these would interfere with Christian practice. This chapter described how Indigenous evangelicals frame their experience of modernity through the notion of "worldliness" (*lo mundano*), which included not only material possessions, but also visiting certain places, acquiring specific vices, ways of talking, as well as specific desires or thoughts.

124 *Christianity, Materiality and Critique of Modernity*

Through the idea of "worldliness" (*lo mundano*), Indigenous evangelicals and churches developed an ongoing critique of materiality, producing a selective appropriation of modernity.

Notes

1 A previous version of this chapter was published in: Rozo, Esteban. "Christianity, Materiality, and the Critique of Modernity in the Colombian Amazon," in *Indigenous Churches. Anthropology of Christianity in Lowland South America*, eds. Elise Capredon, César Ceriani and Minna Opas (Cham: Palgrave Macmillan, 2023), 85–107.
2 See Webb Keane, *Christian Moderns: Freedom and Fetish in the Mission Encounter* (Berkeley: University of California Press, 2007); and Sabine MacCormack, *Religion in the Andes* (Princeton: Princeton University Press, 1997).
3 Webb Keane, *Christian Moderns*, 135.
4 Minna Opas and Anna Haapelainen, "Introduction: Christianity and the Limits of Materiality," in *Christianity and the Limits of Materiality*, eds. Minna Opas and Anna Haapelainen (New York: Bloomsbury Academic, 2017), 1–33; Birgit Meyer and Dick Houtman, "Introduction. Material Religion. How Things Matter," in *Things. Religion and the Question of Materiality*, eds. Dick Houtman and Birgit Meyer (Fordham: Fordham University Press, 2012), 1–23; Webb Keane, *Christian Moderns: Freedom and Fetish in the Mission Encounter* (Berkeley: University of California Press, 2007); Harry Walker, "Demonic Trade: Debt, Materiality, and Agency in Amazonia," *The Journal of the Royal Anthropological Institute* 18, no. 1 (2012): 140–159.
5 Fernando Santos-Granero, "Introduction: Amerindian Constructional Views of the World," in *The Occcult Life of Things. Native Amazonian Theories of Materiality and Personhood*, ed. Fernando Santos-Granero (Tucson: The University of Arizona Press, 2013), 1–32.
6 Stephen Hugh-Jones, "Yesterday's Luxuries, Tomorrow's Necessities: Business and Barter in Northwest Amazonia," in *Barter, Exchange and Value. An Anthropological Approach*, eds. Caroline Humphrey and Stephen Hugh-Jones (Cambridge: Cambridge University Press, 1992), 42–74.
7 Harry Walker, "Demonic Trade: Debt, Materiality, and Agency in Amazonia," *The Journal of the Royal Anthropological Institute* 18, no. 1 (2012): 140–159; Fernando Santos-Granero, "Introduction: Amerindian Constructional Views of the World," in *The Occcult Life of Things. Native Amazonian Theories of Materiality and Personhood*, ed. Fernando Santos-Granero (Tucson: The University of Arizona Press, 2013), 1–32.
8 Harry Walker, "Wild Things: Manufacturing Desire in the Urarina Moral Economy," *The Journal of Latin American and Caribbean Anthropology* 18, no. 1 (2013): 51–66.
9 Sophie Muller, *Beyond Civilization*, 30.
10. *Pudáli* ceremonies were "held in two-part cycles between local sib groups of different phratries who were either actually or potentially related to one another as kinsmen to affines;" see J. Hill, *Wakuénai Society: A Processual-Structural Analysis of Indigenous Cultural Life in the Upper Rio Negro Region of Venezuela*. Unpublished Ph.D. dissertation, Indiana University, 1983, 319–320.
11 Sophie Muller, *Jungle Methods*, 20.
12 Ibid.
13 Sophie Muller, *His Voice Shakes the Wilderness*, 102.
14 Sophie Muller, *Beyond Civilization*, 123.
15 Sophie Muller, *Beyond Civilization*, 51.

Christianity, Materiality and Critique of Modernity   125

16 John L. Nevius, *Demon Possession and Allied Themes* (Chicago: Fleming H. Revell Company, 1895).

17 Kenneth M. Stewart, "Spirit Possession in Native America," *Southwestern Journal of Anthropology* 2, no. 3 (1946): 324.

18 Paul C. Johnson, "Spirits and Things in the Making of the Afro-Atlantic World," in *Spirited Things: The Work of "Possession" in the Afro-Atlantic World*, ed. Paul C. Johnson (Chicago: University of Chicago Press, 2014), 1.

19 Ibid.

20 Sophie Muller, *Beyond Civilization*, 53.

21 Sophie Muller, *Jungle Methods*, 16.

22 Paul C. Johnson, An Atlantic Genealogy of "Spirit Possession," *Comparative Studies in Society and History* 53, no. 2 (2011): 396.

23 Pablo Joseph de Arriaga, *The Extirpation of Idolatry in Perú* (Lexington: University Press of Kentucky, 1968), xviii.

24 Missionaries also promoted the destruction of magic plants or poisons, in particular, they tried to restrict the use of a poison called *camajai*, which is made out of the bark of a tree. During my fieldwork in 2009, I heard stories of people who were severally ill, some of them died, after being poisoned with *camajai*. Ricardo López told me how Muller tried to ban *camajai*. Muller ordered the pastors to throw the "poison" into the river. The pastors replied to Muller saying "[w]e can throw away the *camajai* but we can get more there in the hills." Ricardo used this story to point out that *camajai* was always going to be available because the hills (where you can find the plant from which it is made) would always be there.

25 Stephen Hugh-Jones, *The Palm and the Pleiades: Initiation and Cosmology in Northwest Amazonia* (Cambridge: Cambridge University Press, 1988), 4.

26 Ibid, 6.

27 Ibid.

28 Fernando Santos-Granero, "Introduction: Amerindian Constructional Views of the World," in *The Occcult Life of Things. Native Amazonian Theories of Materiality and Personhood*, ed. Fernando Santos-Granero (Tucson: The University of Arizona Press, 2013), 1–32.

29 Birgit Meyer and Dick Houtman, "Introduction. Material Religion. How Things Matter," in *Things. Religion and the Question of Materiality*, eds. Dick Houtman and Birgit Meyer (Fordham: Fordham University Press, 2012), 7.

30 Ibid.

31 According to Stephen Hugh-Jones, the sacred flutes are associated with the Yurupary cult that is widespread among Indigenous communities in Northwest Amazonia. The cult embraces all adult men and "new members being incorporated through rites of initiation at which they are shown the Yurupary instruments for the first time." Like other secret men's cults, Yurupary is centered "on the use of sacred musical instruments that women and children are forbidden to see. These cults serve to express and to reinforce a fundamental division between the sexes that permeates almost every aspect of society." See Stephen Hugh-Jones, *The Palm and the Pleiades: Initiation and Cosmology in Northwest Amazonia* (Cambridge: Cambridge University Press, 1988), 4.

32 Webb Keane, *Christian Moderns: Freedom and Fetish in the Mission Encounter* (Berkeley: University of California Press, 2007), 54.

33 Sophie Muller said that "you send out a thousand fundamental missionaries every time you send a thousand books through the tribe." See Muller, *Jungle Methods*, 7.

34 Authors such as Bruce M. Knauft argue that "modernity is often characterized in terms of consciousness of the discontinuity of time: a break with tradition," and an increased sense of the passage of time "marked by progress and improvement

126 *Christianity, Materiality and Critique of Modernity*

vis-a vis the past," see ed. Bruce Knauft, *Critically Modern. Alternatives, Alterities, Anthropologies* (Bloomington: Indiana University Press, 2002), 7. This definition of modernity also raises the question of which cultural features fit in one or another mode of being modern and which are left behind as backward-looking or traditional? In a similar vein, Webb Keane suggests that "modernity is, or ought to be, a story of human liberation from a host of false beliefs and fetishisms that undermine freedom," recognizing also the limitations of reducing history to a single narrative, excluding "alternative ideas about modernity," see Webb Keane, *Christian Moderns*, 5.

35 Harry Walker, "Wild Things: Manufacturing Desire in the Urarina Moral Economy," *The Journal of Latin American and Caribbean Anthropology* 18, no. 1 (2013): 52.

36 William H. Fisher, *Industry and Community on an Amazonian Frontier* (Washington, Smithsonian Institution Press, 2000).

37 Harry Walker, Wild Things, 52.

38 C. B. Macpherson, *The Political Theory of Possessive Individualism: Hobbes to Locke* (Oxford: Oxford University Press, 1962), 3.

39 Webb Keane, *Christian Moderns*, 6.

40 Ibid.

41 Ibid, 71.

42 Minna Opas and Anna Haapelainen, "Introduction: Christianity and the Limits of Materiality," in *Christianity and the Limits of Materiality*, eds. Minna Opas and Anna Haapelainen (New York: Bloomsbury Academic, 2017), 2.

43 Mathew Engelke, "Dangerous Things: One African Genealogy," in *Things. Religion and the Question of Materiality*, eds. Dick Houtman and Birgit Meyer (Fordham: Fordham University Press, 2012), 40.

44 Joel Carpenter, *Revive Us Again. The Reawakening of American Fundamentalism* (Oxford: Oxford University Press, 1997), 63.

45 Birgit Meyer, "Aesthetics of Persuasion: Global Christianity and Pentecostalisms's Sensational Forms," *South Atlantic Quarterly*, 109, no. 4 (2010): 743.

46 Ibid.

47 Daniel Miller, "Materiality: An Introduction," in *Materiality*, ed. Daniel Miller (Durhman: Duke University Press, 2012), 1.

48 Casiodoro de Reina was a Spanish monk and reformer born in 1520, who was persecuted by the Inquisition, in part, because of his covert translation into Spanish of the New Testament known as "Biblia del Oso."

49 La vida cristiana, p. 18.

50 Ibid, 20.

51 Ibid, 26.

52 Minna Opas, "Keeping Boundaries in Motion: Christian Denominationalism and Sociality in Amazonia," *Anthropological Quarterly* 92, no. 4 (2019): 1074.

53 David Morgan, *Protestants and Pictures: Religion, Visual Culture, and the Age of American Mass Production* (Oxford: Oxford University Press, 1999), 5.

54 Ibid.

55 Ibid, 6.

56 Minna Opas, "Organic Faith in Amazonia: De-indexification, Doubt, and Christian Corporeality," in *Christianity and the Limits of Materiality*, eds. Minna Opas and Anna Haapelainen (New York: Bloomsbury Academic, 2017), 71.

57 Joel Robbins, *Becoming Sinners. Christianity and Moral Torment in a Papua New Guinea Society* (Berkley: University of California Press, 2004), 142.

58 The complete quote of James 1:22–25 is: "Be doers of the word, not hearers only, deceiving yourselves. For if anyone is a hearer of the word and not a doer, he is like a man that looks at his natural face in a looking-glass; for after looking at

Christianity, Materiality and Critique of Modernity   127

himself, he goes away and at once forgets what he was like. But anyone that looks at the perfect law that makes men free, and stands by it, being not a hearer that forgets, but a doer that acts, that shall be happy in his work."

59 The complete quote in James 3:1–5 is: "Not many of you must become teachers, my brethren; remember that we teachers shall be judged more severely than others. In many ways we all fall into sin. If any man falls into no sin of speech, he is a perfect man, able to control his whole body. If we put the bridle into a horse's mouth to make it obedient, we can turn its whole body. Ships, also, big as they are and drive by violent winds, are turned about, as you see, with a very small steering-oar, wherever the will of the steers-man chooses. So the tongue is a small organ, but it boasts of great things. See how large a forest a small flame sets on fire!."

60 In Spanish *manejar* refers to both "manage" and "drive" in the sense of providing direction.

61 In *Jungle Methods* (1960), Muller refers to the job of policemen in conferences saying that they "will look into each house before each meeting to see that no one hides away from God's Word. They will also watch entrances of Conference building to see that whoever leaves meeting, quickly returns. If someone refuses to attend meetings, the leaders must tell them to leave the Conference, also any who wants to commit sin. The policemen will watch to see that no one walks around after the evening meeting. They will watch the children that they do not play bad (immorally). They must not let unbelievers bring drink or cigarette to the Conference. You must all respect these men and come when they call you, since they will be helping our Lord to keep Satan out of this Conference," see Sophie Muller, *Jungle Methods* (Woodsworth: Brown Gold Publications,1960), 49.

62 When missionaries settled in Guainía in the 1940s there were no TVs, tape recorders or players, just a few radios if any at all. I was told that some missionaries gave Indigenous evangelicals radios which could only tune one Christian radio station known as *Radio Trans Mundial*. This means that the plates missionaries used were probably made after the end of the 1950s, when the television was brought for the first time to Colombia under the military rule of Gustavo Rojas Pinilla (1953–1957) or even later.

63 Ingie Hovland, Beyond Mediation: An Anthropological Understanding of the Relationship Between Humans, Materiality, and Transcendence in Protestant Christianity, *Journal of the American Academy of Religion* 86, no. 2 (2018): 14.

64 Fernando Santos-Granero, "Introduction: Amerindian Constructional Views of the World," 11.

References

Carpenter, Joel. *Revive Us Again. The Reawakening of American Fundamentalism.* Oxford: Oxford University Press, 1997.

De Arriaga, Pablo Joseph. *The Extirpation of Idolatry in Perú.* Lexington: University Press of Kentucky, 1968.

Engelke, Mathew. "Dangerous Things: One African Genealogy." In *Things. Religion and the Question of Materiality*, edited by Dick Houtman and Birgit Meyer, 40–61. Fordham: Fordham University Press, 2012.

Fisher, William H. *Industry and Community on an Amazonian Frontier.* Washington: Smithsonian Institution Press, 2000.

Hill, Jonathan. *Wakuénai Society: A Processual-Structural Analysis of Indigenous Cultural Life in the Upper Rio Negro Region of Venezuela.* Unpublished Ph.D. dissertation. Indiana University, 1983.

128 *Christianity, Materiality and Critique of Modernity*

Hovland, Ingie. "Beyond Mediation: An Anthropological Understanding of the Relationship Between Humans, Materiality, and Transcendence in Protestant Christianity." *Journal of the American Academy of Religion* 86, no. 2 (2018): 1–29. https://doi.org/10.1093/jaarel/lfx054

Johnson, Paul C. "An Atlantic Genealogy of "Spirit Possession."" *Comparative Studies in Society and History* 53, no. 2 (2011): 393–425.

Johnson, Paul C. "Spirits and Things in the Making of the Afro-Atlantic World." In *Spirited Things: The Work of "Possession" in the Afro-Atlantic World*, edited by Paul C. Johnson, 1–22. Chicago: University of Chicago Press, 2014.

Keane, Webb. *Christian Moderns: Freedom and Fetish in the Mission Encounter.* Berkeley: University of California Press, 2007.

Knauft, Bruce ed. *Critically Modern. Alternatives, Alterities, Anthropologies.* Bloomington: Indiana University Press, 2002.

MacCormack, Sabine. *Religion in the Andes.* Princeton: Princeton University Press, 1997.

Macpherson, C. B. *The Political Theory of Possessive Individualism: Hobbes to Locke.* Oxford: Oxford University Press, 1962.

Meyer, Birgit. "Aesthetics of Persuasion: Global Christianity and Pentecostalisms's Sensational Forms." *South Atlantic Quarterly* 109, no. 4 (2010): 741–763. https://doi.org/10.1215/00382876-2010-015

Meyer, Birgit, and Dick Houtman. "Introduction. Material Religion. How Things Matter." In *Things. Religion and the Question of Materiality*, edited by Dick Houtman and Birgit Meyer, 1–23. Fordham: Fordham University Press, 2012.

Miller, Daniel. "Materiality: An Introduction." In *Materiality*, edited by Daniel Miller, 1–50. Durhman: Duke University Press, 2012.

Morgan, David. *Protestants and Pictures: Religion, Visual Culture, and the Age of American Mass Production.* Oxford: Oxford University Press, 1999.

Muller, Sophie. *Beyond Civilization.* Woodworth: New Tribes Mission, 1952.

Muller, Sophie. *Jungle Methods.* Woodworth: Brown Gold Publications, 1960.

Muller, Sophie. *His Voice Shakes the Wilderness.* Sanford: New Tribes Mission, 1988.

Nevius, John L. *Demon Possession and Allied Themes.* Chicago: Fleming H. Revell Company, 1895.

Opas, Minna. "Keeping Boundaries in Motion: Christian Denominationalism and Sociality in Amazonia." *Anthropological Quarterly* 92, no. 4 (2019): 1069–1097. https://doi.org/10.1353/anq.2019.0061

Opas, Minna, and Anna Haapelainen. "Introduction: Christianity and the Limits of Materiality." In *Christianity and the Limits of Materiality*, edited by Minna Opas and Anna Haapelainen, 1–33. New York: Bloomsbury Academic, 2017.

Robbins, Joel. *Becoming Sinners. Christianity and Moral Torment in a Papua New Guinea Society.* Berkley: University of California Press, 2004.

Santos-Granero, Fernando. "Introduction: Amerindian Constructional Views of the World." In *The Occcult Life of Things. Native Amazonian Theories of Materiality and Personhood*, edited by Fernando Santos-Granero, 1–32. Tucson: The University of Arizona Press, 2013.

Stephen, Hugh-Jones. *The Palm and the Pleiades: Initiation and Cosmology in Northwest Amazonia.* Cambridge: Cambridge University Press, 1988.

Stephen, Hugh-Jones. "Yesterday's Luxuries, Tomorrow's Necessities: Business and Barter in Northwest Amazonia." In *Barter, Exchange and Value. An Anthropological*

Christianity, Materiality and Critique of Modernity   129

Approach, edited by Humphrey Caroline and Hugh-Jones Stephen, 42–74. Cambridge: Cambridge University Press, 1992.

Stewart, Kenneth M. "Spirit Possession in Native America." *Southwestern Journal of Anthropology* 2, no. 3 (1946): 323–339.

Viveiros de Castro, Eduardo. *A Inconstância da alma selvagem e outros ensaios de Antropologia*. São Paulo: Cosac & Naify, 2002.

Walker, Harry. "Demonic Trade: Debt, Materiality, and Agency in Amazonia." *The Journal of the Royal Anthropological Institute* 18, no. 1 (2012): 140–159.

Walker, Harry. "Wild Things: Manufacturing Desire in the Urarina Moral Economy." *The Journal of Latin American and Caribbean Anthropology* 18, no. 1 (2013): 51–66.

5 Indigeneity, Development and Extractivism

This chapter describes how, beginning in the 1960s, the national government started to implement development programs aimed at integrating Indigenous groups in the Amazon region into the body politic of the nation. The first part of the chapter analyzes how the implementation of development programs entailed the establishment of an indigenist bureaucracy that was concerned with adapting those programs to the specific "cultural" realities of Indigenous groups in that region. The ways in which the state governed Indigenous groups changed over time as did the actors and institutions that were in charge of governing Indigenous populations. During the 1960s Catholic missionaries, who since the 19th century had controlled the tutelage and education of Indigenous groups and claimed to "civilize" them, were replaced by an indigenist bureaucracy. This bureaucracy attempted to "develop" and "integrate" Indigenous groups into the nation. However, development did not imply "cultural assimilation" in this case. State bureaucrats including anthropologist Gregorio Hernández de Alba[1] tried to adjust or "customize" development policies to Indigenous cultural practices and realities.[2] This process of adjusting development programs to Indigenous realities is what I call here "developmental indigenism."

While developmental indigenism focused more on educational programs and the training of Indigenous leaders who would later serve as brokers between Indigenous communities and the state, starting in the 1980s the national government began to develop and promote gold prospecting and extraction in the region. While official initiatives for the extraction of gold failed, there had been, since the 1970s, informal gold mining practiced in the Colombian Department of Guainía with the participation of Indigenous miners. The second part of this chapter explores how local governance of gold mining was shaped in Guainía through *de facto* agreements between Indigenous communities and miners. Specifically, this second part of the chapter analyzes how the arrangements and agreements between miners and *indígenas* that made informal mining in Guainía possible were not necessarily opposed to state rule or state policies that regulated this activity. Indigenous and non-Indigenous miners wanted to be recognized as "traditional miners" in the eyes of the state and to legalize their activities. Efforts to legalize

DOI: 10.4324/9781003370215-6

Indigeneity, Development and Extractivism 131

informal mining included the request in 1992, by some Puinave communities, to create an Indigenous Mining Zone (IMZ) on the Inírida River. This request was approved in December 1992 by the Ministry of Mining and Energy. Nonetheless, after 2012 informal mining was criminalized by the state which produced different kinds of conflicts between miners and state authorities. At the same time, state prosecution led to the formation of political alliances between Indigenous miners and settlers. State policies and the socio-environmental conflicts derived from mining also reshaped the relationships and subjectivities of both miners and *indígenas* working in gold extraction.

Developmental Indigenism[3]

On June 26, 1959, Gregorio Hernández de Alba, the director of the recently established National Indigenist Institute of Colombia, sent a letter to the *indios* of Vaupés Department greeting them and putting himself at their service. Fifteen days later the missionaries of the Apostolic Prefecture of Vaupés sent with enthusiasm to Hernández de Alba a translation of the letter in Tukano, the predominant Indigenous language of the region.[4] Although, according to the available sources, it is impossible to know who prepared the translation of the letter, it is obvious that there was in interest in adapting the content of the letter to the Indigenous public to whom it was directed. In the letter, Hernández de Alba emphasized that *indígenas* had rights and duties, because just as "the other Colombians who live in the cities, we are sons of the same Colombian fatherland."[5] Hernández de Alba asserted that "the *indígena* has the right that his language, good customs, and social bonds be respected, [as well as] his right to land, education and to prosper in his economy."[6] This recognition of specific rights associated with cultural difference (language, customs, land and education) constitutes a significant change regarding the project of "cultural assimilation" and civilization of Indigenous groups. Developmental indigenism preceded the multicultural reform that took place in Colombia at the beginning of the 1990s.

In Colombia, until the mid-20th century the relationship between Indigenous communities and the state was mediated by the "civilizing" work and practices of evangelization deployed by Catholic missionaries. After the 1950s this relationship changed when the state created indigenist policies, introducing a new political sensibility based upon the idea of creating productive and educated Indigenous citizens. Indigenous groups were incorporated into the nation as citizens with their own rights and duties. State officials such as Hernández de Alba became part of the articulation of new sensibilities regarding the state administration of Indigenous affairs in Colombia. In this same period, the government designed laws aimed at redefining the terms of the relationship between the state and Indigenous groups, and undertaking alternatives to assimilation through the concept of social integration. In the Conclusions of the 5th Interamerican Indigenist Congress (1964), the concept of social integration was defined as "the national unity of all the inhabitants

132 *Indigeneity, Development and Extractivism*

of a country, but not of their identity and not even of their fundamental similarity."[7] Social integration required the "progressive development of mutual adjustments, but not the absolute homogenization of all the population."[8] If the idea of civilization or assimilation entailed a radical cultural transformation, the concept of social integration supposes the transformation only of those "cultural traits" considered dysfunctional for national development.

One of the juridical assets used to "integrate" Indigenous groups to national development was Law 81 of 1958, which "inaugurates a new stage of indigenist action." For the first time, the relationships between the state and Indigenous groups were framed in terms of development and not in terms of forced assimilation or *reducción*, as had happened previously with Catholic missionaries (see Chapter 1). In a similar vein, the first National Indigenist Plan of Colombia in 1966 established the importance of generating a "new type of land tenure [among Indigenous groups] that would simultaneously protect and expand production and stimulate income and consumption."[9] The concept of "social integration" underlying developmental indigenism proposed to protect certain aspects of Indigenous cultures while developing others at the same time. This tension raises a fundamental question: How can you simultaneously protect and "develop" Indigenous culture? In the letter that Hernández de Alba sent to the Indigenous groups of Vaupés he suggested that the state should protect "good Indigenous customs" in order that their bodies can be "healthier (…), receive better education and can produce more, improving their conditions of poverty."[10]

This project of simultaneously protecting and developing Indigenous groups was based upon the idea of dividing Indigenous culture between good and bad traits. This project consisted in comprehending culture as an aggregate of unrelated elements that is possible to separate between good/bad or useful/useless, so that it is desirable to transform only those cultural traits that are conceived of as dysfunctional in terms of development ideals. The idea of culture as a set of traits can be traced back to 19th-century evolutionism and the work of anthropologists such as Edward B. Tylor.[11] Although it is presented in apparently neutral or technical language, the project of moralizing "cultural traits" (good/useful customs *versus* bad/useless customs) of Indigenous groups resonates with strategies previously used by Catholic and evangelical missionaries, as is shown in Chapter 3. In another letter sent on June 26, 1959, to the apostolic prefect of Mitú, Hernández de Alba displays this "new" indigenist sensibility that reconsiders the role of the missionary as the main state agent in the frontier regions of the country:

> The missionary, not only as pastor of souls, disseminator of Christian doctrines of charity, justice and human equality that arise from the words of Christ, but also constituting the vanguard of civilization and the sense of the fatherland, deserves the respect, the appreciation of citizens and the support of the State which should, in turn, expect, determined support of missionaries in all the campaigns aimed at the global

Indigeneity, Development and Extractivism   133

improvement and effective and useful incorporation of its Indigenous population, for several centuries marginalized, rejected or unknown.[12]

In this new context, the civilizing role of missionaries was reimagined so it would not be restricted to saving souls, but should also expand to disseminating values of citizenship and democratic rights (justice, equality, etc.) among the Indigenous population located on the margins of the nation. Furthermore, missionaries would stop being the only representatives of the nation in frontier territories so as to start working hand in hand with the emergent indigenist bureaucracy that was entailed in the creation of new political-administrative units (such as *comisarias*) in frontier regions such as Amazonia. Instead of opposing the work of missionaries, these new bureaucrats would learn from the long-accumulated experience of missionaries among Indigenous groups. This process of state officials approaching missionaries can be seen in the correspondence between Hernández de Alba and Catholic missionaries based in Mitú, Vaupés.

In this sense, developmental indigenism emerged toward the end of the 1950s following on the work that Catholic and evangelical missionaries had undertaken among Indigenous groups. Developmental indigenism entailed a new relationship between the state and Indigenous communities mediated by a language of rights and duties, under a new legal framework that promoted, at least rhetorically, equality among its citizens. Developmental indigenism went hand in hand with the creation of a specialized bureaucracy in Indigenous groups as well as the design of governmental policies that were suited to the particularities and specificities of these groups in frontier regions. Instead of civilizing Indigenous communities, which implied their cultural transformation, developmental indigenism articulated practices and discourses aimed at developing and integrating these communities into the body politic of the nation while at the same time protecting their culture.

Customizing Development in a Frontier Region

As mentioned in the first two chapters of the book, the establishment of provinces (or *comisarias*) in the Colombian Amazon, which were new political and administrative units, was part of an attempt to expand the sovereignty of the state in frontier regions. The *comisaría* of Guainía was established in 1965 and the *comisaría* of Guaviare in 1977. In these new territories specific ways of governing Indigenous groups emerged, first through Catholic missionaries who were in charge of the tutelage and education of these groups, and later through an indigenist bureaucracy that was represented through such state officials as Gregorio Hernández de Alba and was sensitive to "cultural difference." Indigenist bureaucrats were concerned with adapting public policies of the time (most of them associated with development programs) to the specific realities of Indigenous groups in the Amazon region. Indigenist development takes place in provinces such as Guainía through programs, decrees as well as

134 Indigeneity, Development and Extractivism

state officials who were part of an emergent indigenist bureaucracy. The main tenets of developmental indigenism were deployed in policies and programs aimed at Indigenous groups. For instance, in August 1973, the Secretary of State issued a decree (1741) with norms directed to "corporations and foundations constituted to develop activities related with Indigenous communities."[13] The decree was part of new state indigenist policy aimed at "teaching the [Indigenous] communities the advanced techniques of economic exploitation and facilitating their incorporation into national development under equal conditions, with respect for cultural autonomy."[14] This decree synthesizes the new indigenist sensibility directed at developing Indigenous groups while simultaneously respecting their "cultural autonomy."

The protection of Indigenous autonomy, within a context of development, entailed "customizing" development to Indigenous culture and worldviews, as well as a double adaptation between the state and Indigenous groups: some traits of Indigenous culture and social life had to be adjusted to development ideals and discourse, while state programs and policies were adapted to cultural specificities of Indigenous communities. However, some of these programs also ignored Indigenous practices and worldviews. One of the programs promoted by the decree of 1973 consisted of teaching the *indígenas* the "correct protection and use of natural resources." Ideas about teaching Indigenous communities how to exploit the land and protect natural resources are at odds with contemporary visions of Amazonian Indigenous peoples as "ecological natives."[15] Since the 1980s, as an outcome of transnational alliances and transcultural encounters Amazonian native leaders became prominent in the international public sphere of environmental activism. According to Conklin and Graham a "middle ground of Amazonian eco-politics" emerged on the "assertion that native peoples' views of nature and ways of using natural resources are consistent with Western conservationist principles."[16] Nonetheless, what the Colombian government understood by 1973 as the correct use of natural resources did not necessarily follow environmentally sustainable practices. In fact, as will be demonstrated in the second part of this chapter, the Colombian government commenced developing gold prospecting in some places of Guainía beginning in the 1980s.

Furthermore, the decree promoted teaching Indigenous communities the "advanced techniques of economic exploitation," as well as training indigenous promoters in "social development," including areas as diverse as health, agricultural extension, literacy, cooperativism and community action [*acción comunal*]. Decree 1741 also established three criteria to be followed by public institutions associated with developing educational programs for Indigenous groups. First, Indigenous education should be bilingual, "imparted in Spanish and in the community members' own language." Second, the design of academic programs had to be consistent with "the characteristics of the *indígena*, wholly respecting their cultural values;" and, third, the academic calendars should be adapted to the "system of life" of the Indigenous population, which entailed devoting specific times of the year for fishing or hunting, among other activities.

Indigeneity, Development and Extractivism   135

A clear example of how developmental indigenism worked on the ground can be seen through the program of "home improvers" which Hernández de Alba promoted as director of the National Indigenist Institute. On July 4, 1966, Amalia Torres presented to the Secretary of Government with her report as "home improver" for the month of June of that same year. After a short description of the family structure and the health conditions of two Indigenous homes, Torres concluded her report saying:

> I wanted to reach the heart of these natives, above all, through persuasion with the purpose of instilling upon them the need of paying attention to their health, providing them with instructions about personal hygiene, in their dress, in their housing, [in the] preparation of food, [in] not drinking water without boiling it first, because in it you can find the seedbed of disease germs, etc. ... As the secretary is already familiar with the idiosyncrasy of the natives, you can easily conclude that they are reluctant and they give you the impression of having little interest in the instructions, but I am convinced that with insistence and patience I will achieve my objective and that of the regional government, which is, to uplift the moral and material level of the Indigenous population.[17]

The main idea underlying this letter in terms of promoting material and corporal transformations in order to reach "inner transformations" resonates strongly with the rhetoric of missionaries. At the same time, the attempt of Torres to "reach the heart" of the natives shows how material and moral improvement went hand in hand and could also work from the inside out: changing their hearts in order to achieve their "material improvement." Hygiene, for example, required a new frame of mind and new ways of relating to one's own body. However, the "idiosyncrasy" of the "natives" that Torres was supervising appears as the main obstacle that local officials could face regarding the material and moral improvement of local dwellers. Torres thought that local officials could overcome this obstacle with their own effort and persistence. This combination of the "will to improve" and the idea of "reaching the natives," no matter how far distant they live, is also present in a report sent to the head of Indigenous affairs by a local official that worked in the same office: "The Indigenous people of the upper Inírida (River) are truly deprived of any assistance due to the transportation difficulties in that zone (...) Our work team made a huge human effort with which they have been occupied all this time and it fills us with satisfaction that those people integrated within the commission can say: yes, you can reach the *indígena!*."[18] In this sense, self-sacrifice and effort became crucial virtues among the emergent indigenist bureaucracy in charge of "reaching out" to the natives.

The national plan of rural health designed for Guainía in 1977 included guidelines in order to adapt state health programs to the "rainforest conditions" and the cultural particularities of the Indigenous groups. The plan was presented as a specific "modality for the rainforest," and Guainía was

136 *Indigeneity, Development and Extractivism*

represented as a "huge territorial extension of a rainforest type crossed by rivers and streams of difficult navigation that constitute the only communication routes."[19] The plan also recognized the existence of "different ethnic groups with cultural and settlement patterns highly dispersed throughout rivers and streams, barely accessible and very little attended in their basic needs."[20] The state officials of the regional health office tried to design specific programs adapted to the geographical and demographic particularities of Guainía such as the dispersed pattern of Indigenous settlements and communities. In fact, the plan suggested a specialized model of health attention that could "give to each [ethnic group] a special treatment regarding the services being offered." Therefore, while the "home improvers" tried to change the hygiene practices of Indigenous families, the health plan of Guainía sought to adapt state policies and practices to "rainforest conditions." Despite the fact that the plan criticized the precariousness of health attention in Guainía, the plan did not change the health conditions in the region at large as can be clearly seen in a document written and signed by Curripaco Indigenous leaders in June 1980 and directed to the national secretary of health:

> We address your honor [Secretary of Health] in order to request your intervention in helping us with the drug supply of the Health Post, medical and dental services. Provision of the Health Post, outboard engine, beads, first aid equipment. There is a Health Post completely abandoned in a small village where more than three hundred people live, all of us "INDIGENAS," where we are safeguarding our Colombian sovereignty over the border from Venezuela, bearing poverty, misery and diseases of all kinds. Because of this your honor we turn to you because the services of Guainía have not been concerned at all for these far-flung regions that are marginalized by our Colombian government.[21]

In addition to the complaints of these Indigenous leaders regarding the abandonment and marginalization they attribute to the Colombian government, it is important to point out how these Indigenous leaders have appropriated the notion of sovereignty that is explored in the first chapter of this book. Furthermore, since the 1960s, it was common for local Indigenous leaders to send written requests or formal letters to state officials in Bogotá. In the letter sent to Hernández de Alba on May 5, 1965, analyzed in Chapter 2, complaining about the behavior of the first group of state officials sent to establish the new capital of Guainía, the Puinaves who signed the letter also requested "help in tools, seeds, schools for our children. Medications for sick people, because in San Fernando, Venezuela, we receive little attention; given that we are Colombians it is our government that should help us."[22] In this sense, lay notions of sovereignty and nationhood were appropriated by Indigenous subjects in Guainía as part of their interactions with the state. Specifically, when Indigenous signatories of letters to the government presented themselves as Colombians who were concerned with "safeguarding our Colombian sovereignty over the border with Venezuela," they were

Indigeneity, Development and Extractivism   137

positioning claims and demands before the state using the same language that they had appropriated from state officials.

State programs associated with developmental indigenism emphasized the training of local populations, including *indígenas* and settlers who "were in conditions of transmitting messages to their communities that were comprehensible [for them]."[23] This emphasis of developmental indigenism on training local leaders who could serve as cultural brokers between the state and local communities became clear in 1974 when the secretary of education of Guainía designed a plan to train Indigenous bilingual assistants in order to overcome the "difficulty of communication between white professors and the Indigenous community."[24] Indigenous bilingual assistants were chosen from among those who were at least in 5th grade and who showed qualities associated with leadership. The figure of Indigenous bilingual assistants was already being promoted by Gregorio Hernández de Alba as head of the Indigenist Institute. Indigenous bilingual assistants were also trained to serve as health promoters within their communities. Through the training of Indigenous bilingual assistants as translators for education purposes and health promoters the state tried to guarantee their "participation in the social and cultural development of the region," showing their "will to improve" (*deseo de superación*) and interest to serve "their offspring."[25] While Decree 1741 of 1973 and the education program of Guainía of 1974 emphasized the importance of bilingual teaching in both Spanish and different Indigenous languages, an Indigenous bilingual assistant reported in August 1976 that the Curripaco *capitán* of the community of Caranacoa (on the Upper Rio Negro) "suggested the appointment of white professors so they can teach the [Indigenous] kids to speak in Spanish, as something needed in order to communicate with the white sirs [*señores blancos*]."[26] In this sense, the attempts made by state officials such as Gregorio Hernández de Alba to "customize" development into Indigenous terms and language were confronted with Indigenous demands for learning Spanish and being part of the world of the "white sirs," becoming fluent in the language most *colonos* used for trading and different purposes. This shows how Indigenous people were not resisting development or civilization *per se*, but were also adapting to colonization and mobilizing practices which would enable them to compete with the "white man" in his own language and terms. As Nancy Appelbaum points out, colonization is not merely "a top-down process of imposed submission"; effective colonizing has "historically involved the participation of the colonized, who have simultaneously adapted to colonization."[27]

Indigenous Appropriations of Development

The Indigenous appropriations of the "languages of the state" and the discourse of development became clear in different letters that Indigenous communities sent to the regional authorities. For example, in April 1979, a group of *indígenas* from Laguna Colorada on the Guaviare River sent a letter the *comisario* of Guainía in which they referred to their "yearning for progress"

138 *Indigeneity, Development and Extractivism*

and their "desire to live with more dignity as the man of 1970 deserves it."[28] In the letter, the Indigenous people of Laguna Colorada requested from the *comisario* roof tiles of zinc so they could "establish a town with the same perspective as those built by the civilized."[29] One year later, in 1980, Curripacos from San José, on the Guainía River sent a petition to the *corregidor*, the Board of Communal Action of Puerto Colombia and the traders of Puerto Colombia and San Felipe, requesting their support for "developing a community work project in order to explore and find a favorable terrain for the opening of a road or trail that will enable us to communicate the Guainía River with the Inírida River."[30] This project of exploration was presented as an initiative from the *indígenas* of San José, which was also "voluntary" and "free." In the letter the *indígenas* from San José represented themselves as "natives and those familiar with the region."[31] The petition responded to the possibility of "finding a 'short cut' that will enable us to move to the capital when it is needed because the frontier closes or because of problems with the transit of the route Maroa-Yavita (which) are very frequent and well known by all of us."[32] *Indígenas* were requesting the supplies needed to explore the terrain and offered in exchange their "own and voluntary initiative" as well as the support of other fellow *indígenas*: "all of us know the conditions of terrain, and we will collaborate with fellow *indígenas* in order to expand and make adequate the trail, making it easier to use."[33]

The letters sent by *indígenas* expressing their desire to explore routes, build roads and establish towns in a way similar to "civilized people" puts into question the need to protect Indigenous culture, which underlies developmental indigenism. Furthermore, the Indigenous "desire for civilization" expressed in these letters contends against the idea that only settlers or *colonos* were interested in colonization or practices such as establishing new towns or building roads. In this sense, it is not possible to say that Indigenous groups in the Colombian Amazon region resisted the state or colonization *tout court*; the relationships these groups established with colonization and the state were more complex. Anthropologist David Gow argues that "resistance to the state" does not necessarily mean "opposition to it"; rather it is the "demand to be recognized as Indigenous and to be treated as citizens, to become a vital part of the nation."[34] The petitions expressed in the letters sent to state officials should be understood in terms of demanding more attention and recognition from the state, as well as more participation in practices entailed in development and colonization.

Indigenous appropriations of development can also be traced through the establishment of "leaders schools" designed for training Indigenous leaders that would teach different "skills" to their constituents. In 1975, in a place known as Laguna Colorada on the Guaviare River, a "leaders school" was established. The school was created in order to "train a group of young people that will later help their community as teachers, health promoters, manager of cooperatives, guides in agriculture and lots of other things."[35] In the minutes of this event, two types of leaders were defined in the report:

Indigeneity, Development and Extractivism   139

natural and "trained" [*capacitado*]. A natural leader is defined as the one who without being literate or *capitán*, is "capable of organizing the community; everybody obeys him, respects him and goes with him to work;" whereas a trained leader is defined as the one who "knows the problems of his community and becomes prepared to work better within his community."[36] The duties of a leader were defined along three lines that included moral, political and pedagogical obligations. According to the report, the first duty of a leader was to "provide his services within the community and help the others."[37] Specifically, according to the report, the Indigenous leader should "worry more about his Indigenous brothers than a white person [*un blanco*] and he can provide his services with more love and dedication, because he knows better their way of thinking [*su pensamiento*]."[38] In this sense, Indigenous leaders were understood to be connected to their constituents through affection and shared ways of thinking.[39]

The three main duties of an Indigenous leader included: presenting the problems of the community to those who might help resolve them, causing people to respect the land and the rights of the community, and teaching to the community what are the rights and duties of "herself" [*de ella misma*]. The notion of community emerges here as a homogenous and unified collective entity, as well as a political subject with rights and problems of its own. The notion of community promoted by the state was also indigenized, as white teachers and Indigenous leaders appropriated it, and it began to include other issues such as land and culture. Another of the topics taught in the leaders school was about the "*indígena* and his culture," where prospective Indigenous leaders learned that the "thought of the white man is different from the thought of the *indígena*."[40] Among the differences in thought pointed out in the report, we find the idea that "for the *indígena* the land is sacred, because his parents were born there and provides him with food; for the white man it is a thing to make money."[41] Therefore, Indigenous leaders taught their constituents about that which made them different from the "white man."

Within this ideological framework, the "disintegration of community" was presented as one of the main problems to be confronted. This was directly related to lack of land, work and means of subsistence. This alleged process of "community disintegration" consisted of "living separately from the family, each person with different thoughts, working alone, forgetting his or her own language and customs."[42] According to the directors of the leaders school, Indigenous leaders must "defend their customs and traditions" and for this purpose they created a newspaper called "*malicia indígena* [Indigenous malice] in order to defend their land and reinforce their culture."[43] The newspaper was intended to show "all the problems of the *indígenas*," as well as "to narrate [*contar*] their customs in order to not forget everything [passed] from their grandfathers."[44] In this way, the category of a "political community" with rights and needs of its own (represented by a leader who knows those needs and rights) was articulated with essentialized notions of culture, custom, tradition and land. While the state had promoted the idea of community as

140 *Indigeneity, Development and Extractivism*

part of developmental policies aimed at attaining the integration of marginal groups into the body politic, in the Colombian Amazon this same idea was "customized," appropriated and incorporated into Indigenous politics. White teachers implemented the idea of establishing a school for Indigenous leaders, while articulating at the same time an indigenist agenda that emphasized the defense of Indigenous communities, of their land and culture. The indigenist agenda of some of the white teachers hired by the regional government also informed Indigenous politics at a local and regional level in different ways.

In September 1977 in Laguna Colorada, located on the Guaviare River, the director, teachers and students of the leaders' school organized the *Tercer Congreso de Indígenas* [Third Congress of *Indígenas*]. Several *capitanes* and leaders from different communities and ethnic groups of the Guaviare and Vichada Rivers attended the meeting. The written minutes of the event start with a list of all the people who attended the Congress, with their respective ethnic affiliation. They defined a leader as the "one who knows the necessities of his community and helps to resolve them."[45] Evidently, this definition is almost the same as the one that was given to the bilingual assistants in their vacation course: a "thinking person that identifies the problems and needs of his tribe and looks for solutions that respond [to them]."[46] As part of the process of creating the first Indigenous political organization in the region, leaders and members of the leaders' school appropriated specific notions of leadership promoted by the regional government within the context of state-building practices. In this sense, emergent Indigenous leaders and political organizations became agents of change and were incorporated into state-directed projects of cultural and social change. The state mediated, to some extent, the direction and sense of cultural and social change, as it approved and promoted specific projects of transformation, while it rejected others (such as Christian evangelization).

The records of the event give a basic definition of what a congress is and what it is useful for: "a meeting of people seeking something."[47] The opening words of Carlos Gómez (a white teacher and director of the leaders school) refer specifically to the purpose of the congress:

> The *indígenas* in Colombia are running out [*acabando*] because they have too many enemies. Out of the 25 million inhabitants of Colombia, half a million correspond to Indigenous population. The struggle is unequal but with ORGANIZATION it is possible to overcome in order to defend the originality of the Colombian. This half a million is spread out throughout Colombia; in the Congress we look for unity of the areas of Guainía and Vichada to join them to other [areas] of the country.[48]

As can be inferred from here, indigenist discourses were actively produced and promoted by white teachers themselves. The emphasis of these discourses on union and pan-tribal forms of organization should not be dismissed, as it constituted a new way of conceiving and articulating indigeneity. Two

Indigeneity, Development and Extractivism   141

Indigenous leaders that spoke after Carlos Gómez emphasized that "all united: guahibos, piapocos, cubeos, curripacos, piaroas, tucanos and puinaves; is the only hope of "getting ahead" [*salir adelante*]. Both leaders argued: "the solution to our problems is in our hands, we don't have to wait until they come to tell us, we ourselves have to fight."[49] In another part of the document the question about "what do you look for with this Congress?" was raised. Some Guahibo leaders replied saying things such as: "help from the government," "ask for a *reserva* [reservation] if there is a law that offers them" and "have ideas to create cooperatives."[50] A Guahibo leader was clearer in saying that he was there to "get to know the desires of others, while knowing my desire. I didn't come to ask for a present, I came to learn and teach to all of my people."[51] In addition to this, the memories of the Congress also include the transcription of – five letters written by people who attended the event.

The letters refer to specific petitions and concerns that leaders brought to the Congress, assuming that making these concerns public might help to resolve them. For instance, the first letter addresses the conflicts which had arisen on the Uva River between some natives and a *colono* called Luis Batía who would neither allow them cross his backyard [*patio*], nor slash trees of *mure* (a native palm tree), something which natives had done for years, nor have their crops where Luis lived.[52] The author of the letter made the formal request in the name of "all the Indigenous communities" that this "man be expelled from here soon; we assume no liability for his life if he keeps bothering us."[53] The authors of two other letters expressed their interest in participating in the Congress and reaching agreements with all of the *capitanes*. Both letters included demands for land or *reserva* [reservation], as well as references to "claiming our rights." A fourth letter also made reference to "the limits of what belongs to us" regarding the presence of *colonos* in territory historically inhabited by natives, something the author of the letter framed in terms that "it is our limit and I am making clear my right because my grandparents lived in this part, then, we are natives of Vichada."[54] A fifth letter signed by the *capitán* of a community called *Murciélago* [Bat] presented the "most urgent needs of the community," hoping they could be resolved soon. So-called "urgent needs" were described as specific "working tools," among which were requested: 5 hand saws, hammers, brushes, 75 kilos of assorted nails, shovels, mattocks, axes, a dozen *machetes*, a dozen drills, 300 sheets of zinc with nails included, a 25 [horsepower] outboard engine for "common benefit," a power plant, and the list goes on to include barbed wire and a radio phone. The letter finished with a request to stop the exploitation by unscrupulous merchants that "don't hesitate to charge three times the value of first necessity goods."[55]

As it is clear from the diversity of demands deployed in these letters, there was no common theme or agenda held by all of the participants in the Congress. However, these letters and their rhetoric revealed new ways of communicating with the state and constituted what some authors call "languages of the state."[56] For instance, the language of rights articulated a vocabulary in terms

142 *Indigeneity, Development and Extractivism*

of which Indigenous communities could frame their claims and demands. It should not be taken for granted that most of these claims and demands were framed in a collective voice through the language of "community" and were collectively signed since some of these demands such as the letter with the long list of "working tools" were also based on material things.

Development and Mining[57]

Developmental indigenism was installed in Guainía in the 1970s, focusing mainly on educational programs and the training Indigenous of leaders who would later become brokers between their communities and the state. Starting in the 1980s the national government began to develop gold prospecting in the region, specifically in the *Serranía de Naquén* (see Map 5.1). By 1978, the government had already developed the Radargammetric Amazon Project which recognized the possibility that there existed rocky formations having potential for gold production. In 1987, the Ministry of Mining and Energy, together with Ecopetrol, promoted gold prospecting in Guainía.[58] In an article published in 1988, the president of the mining project of Guainía stated that with "this project that state would be able to reconcile the global economic effort at generating reserves (*divisas*) and fiscal resources

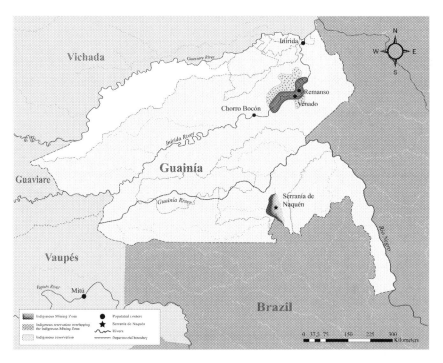

Map 5.1 Map of Guainía with the Indigenous Mining Zone and Indigenous Reservations.

Indigeneity, Development and Extractivism 143

in order to make possible the national integration of frontier zones through a model of social and economic development that would guarantee a sustainable supply of renewable natural resources."[59] The access of experts and technicians working for institutions such as the Colombian Geological Service (Ingeominas) to the *Serranía de Naquén* in the Upper Guainía River was made possible through the use of helicopters – more than 100 heliports were built in all the area. Two basecamps and several dispersed camps were also established in the area. All of these activities entailed substantive interventions into, and transformation of, the environment in order to make possible state-sponsored gold prospecting.

Years before the mining project of Guainía, as early as the1970s, Curripaco families were already extracting gold using rudimentary technologies in mining seasons of about three months per year.[60] Following the mid-1970s, attracted by the state campaign that promoted a better future with gold extraction, a number of settlers (*colonos*) began to arrive to Puerto Maimache in *Serranía de Naquén*.[61] Despite gold extraction being initially promoted by the state in Maimache, by the 1990s Revolutionary Armed Forces of Colombia (FARC) exercised *de facto* control in the region. FARC members controlled the entrance and exit to the mining zones and promoted "social cohesion" by imposing their own rules.[62]

During the 1980s, in Guainía state-sponsored mining had coexisted with the informal mining practiced by settlers and natives alike. Once the official mining project of Guainía ended in the 1990s, informal initiatives started to proliferate in the region. Some of these initiatives reached legal status and were formalized for a period of time through the figure of IMZs.[63] At the same time, at the beginning of the 1990s, Brazilian settlers and miners (also known in the region as *garimpeiros*) began to extract gold on the Inírida River. Unlike the state-sponsored mining that was conducted "underground," informal mining on the Inírida River was carried out by dredging the river from mining rafts with an engine for the dredges and a synthetic sieve to retain the sand being removed from the river bed (see Figure 5.1). Once the river bed has been removed with the dredges the sand is run through a set of synthetic carpets (made in Brazil) that retains parts of the sand containing gold nuggets. The sand in the sieves is later mixed with mercury, an amalgam is produced and then the gold nuggets are separated from the mercury using an instrument called in Spanish *retorta* (mining retort).

While Colombian and Brazilian settlers promoted informal gold extraction using mining rafts and small dredges, different Puinave Indigenous communities from the Inírida River made a request in 1990 to the Ministry of Mining and Energy for the creation and delineation of an IMZ in the middle basin of the Inírida River. This request for creating an IMZ was approved in December 1992 by the Ministry of Mining and Energy in a resolution that established an area of 47.769 hectares and 3.811 square meters in the middle basin of the Inírida River for this purpose (see Map 5.1). This area overlaps the jurisdiction of the Puinave reservation (*resguardo*) of Remanso-Chorro

Figure 5.1 Mining raft with dredges for extracting gold.
Source: Picture taken by the author.

Bocón. IMZs were not only implemented in Guainía. As Catalina Caro points out, up to 17 declarations of IMZs existed in Colombia; the province of Cauca, in the Andes, is the region having the most IMZs.[64] At the beginning, IMZs were thought of as a figure for organizing mining activities in Indigenous territories.

The resolution that officially established the IMZ in Guainía provided that "some *indígenas* wish to exploit the alluvial deposit using small dredges, given that use of the current practice of *barequeo* (artisanal gold mining) it is not economically profitable for them."[65] When the IMZ was established the national Indigenous Organization of Colombia (ONIC) filed a rights injunction (*tutela*) against the establishment of the IMZ. It was resolved in their favor and the mayor of the capital (Puerto Inírida) cancelled the licenses to operate in the area. In 1993 the Ministry of Mining and Energy suspended the "illegal exploitation of gold on the Inírida and Guainía Rivers and their affluents."[66] In this sense, the constitution of IMZs did not bring into effect better organized mining activities in this region. Instead it unearthed the conflicts that existed around the appropriation of gold revenues in Guainía.[67] IMZs have become a challenge for Indigenous local governments because this juridical figure may allow for the advancement of medium or large-scale gold mining.[68]

Indigeneity, Development and Extractivism   145

In regard to the state resolution that sought to interrupt mining in the region, the Association of Small Miners of Guainía indicated in June 1993 that they would not obey such resolutions because they considered them to breach their right to work.[69] In 1997 the miners that worked in the IMZ created the Cooperative of Miners of Colombia (Coolmicop), which had more than 300 affiliated members, including Indigenous and non-Indigenous miners. In one brochure, the cooperative defined itself as a: "(…) cooperative of solidary character, created by a group of traditional Indigenous miners that live from gold (…) its main objective is to obtain the mining titles and environmental licenses that will allow the practice of mining without interruptions for the mining community that has traditionally lived from that." The formalization of mining activities has formed part of the main political objectives of the Cooperative since its beginning. This demonstrates how miners have wanted their practices to be recognized and regulated by the state through mining titles and environmental licenses. Furthermore, local and regional authorities supported the regulation of mining activities on the Inírida River. In 2005, Indigenous and non-Indigenous miners commenced their own process for recognition of titles and paid for their own environmental impact survey, while local environmental authorities included in their plan of action for the years 2007–2011 the adoption of measures effecting the "implementation of clean technologies in mining activities."[70]

During the 1990s gold extraction was definitely established on the Inírida River and, more recently, on the Atabapo River which marks the border with Venezuela. Most of the Indigenous communities that live in the IMZ depend directly or indirectly upon the revenues from gold extraction for their own subsistence. In December 1993, Gustavo Rodríguez, the leader of the Puinave community of Cerro Nariz, told me that the five communities which form part of the Remanso-Chorro Bocón reservation, which includes more than 1,400 people, have been working in mining for more than 20 years. Rodríguez told me that most of them "live out of pure mining" and that mining is very useful for them. Nonetheless there are Indigenous leaders such as Ignacio Sánchez who argue that Indigenous communities and political organizations have a clear position regarding mining. Other Indigenous leaders who promoted the IMZ said that some communities would sometimes "defend mining and sometimes not." For Ignacio Sánchez the problem is not who conducts the mining, whether it be settlers or Indigenous communities. The problem is the technology used (dredges and mercury) and the environmental damage this may cause.

In this region Indigenous communities have been historically divided regarding gold mining within Indigenous reservations. Some Indigenous leaders and members of Indigenous communities support and benefit from gold mining, while other leaders oppose gold extraction in Indigenous territories head-on. Geographer Anthony Bebbington argues that in Latin America "some Indigenous populations are engaging with extraction not only for the very pragmatic reason of extracting benefits, but also in order to see how far

146 *Indigeneity, Development and Extractivism*

the extractive economy can be used as a means of consolidating territories."[71] It is problematic to assume that Indigenous communities are inherently opposed to extractivism or always resist capitalism.[72] Furthermore, some Indigenous leaders and communities have changed their positions about gold mining in their territories over time.

In this sense, informal mining has not always been prosecuted, criminalized and labeled illegal by the state in Guainía. Since the end of the 1980s official and informal initiatives promoting gold mining have coexisted and are shaped in relation to each other. These categories and practices (formal/informal, legal/illegal) are usually relational.[73] It is not possible to understand separately official and informal initiatives promoting gold mining. While engaged in my field work in 2013, informal miners would often quote the slogan the government of Juan Manuel Santos used in its official propaganda about mining ("mining for everyone") as a way of proving how their participation in gold extraction was legitimate.

Local Governance of Mining: Agreements and Relationships between Miners and Indigenous Communities

Even if small-scale gold mining has been described as a practice "out of control," associated in some cases with criminality, there have been in Guainía for a number of years customary norms and agreements that regulate informal gold mining within the region. In 2010 a new mining code that restricted mining in zones of forest reservations was issued. Despite the absence of mining titles and environmental licenses, Indigenous communities have developed agreements and *de facto* rules with miners in order to allow the operation of mining rafts within their territories and reservations. As Ardila and Galvis point out, informal gold extraction in regions such as Amazonia has been mediated by agreements and disputes around the "material and symbolic appropriation of mining resources," which entail "different forms of political authority and relationships with the state."[74] Therefore, informality should not be understood as a legal or social status, but instead as a *modus operandi* that is not necessarily opposed to state legislation or bureaucracy. In fact, as High point outs in the case of Mongolia, rather than considering illegality as merely that which is not endorsed by the law, it is possible to approach illegality as a "legal construction that separates and dissociates particular forms of sociality from their wider cultural validation."[75]

In December 2013, I made my first visit to a mining camp where a Brazilian married to an Indigenous woman lived, with a settler from the Caribbean coast. I was there with the president of Coolmicop and two researchers that worked for the GOMIAM project.[76] The president of Coolmicop told us the resolution that established the IMZ stipulated that Indigenous communities are allowed to make agreements with "third parties" for specific works. The permits that Indigenous authorities gave to miners in order to work in their territories were conditioned upon making payment to Indigenous communities

Indigeneity, Development and Extractivism   147

and hiring an Indigenous work force for gold extraction.[77] Through these *de facto* agreements between miners and Indigenous authorities, the payments received by the Indigenous miners and the communities in accordance with the amount of gold they extracted from the river were established. Each mining raft requires ten people in order to operate it, and they are distributed in two shifts of four people each who operate under the direction of a diver or an administrator. These payments and agreements allow the miners to present themselves as representing a source of progress for the region. One of them was proud of the amount of gold a "cook" (usually an Indigenous woman) could earn in a mining camp for one month, about 30 grams. This amount of gold was more in pesos than what a medical doctor could be paid.

The Brazilian miner who lived in the camp had a notebook where he kept a record of all the transactions he had made with Indigenous communities. Several pages of the notebook had signatures of the *capitanes* with the amount of gold they had received. According the president of Coolmicop, the documents and minutes (*actas*) also served as a proof of the existence of "traditional mining" in Guainía. In this sense, informal mining does not necessarily challenge state rationality or bureaucracy;[78] instead, it produces its own bureaucratic practices and documents that imitate official practices and documents.[79] It is important to point out that these forms of local governance had the support of regional environmental institutions such as the CDA (Corporation for the Development of Amazonia) who gave advice to miners regarding the use of clean technologies. CDA also distributed an instrument called *retorta* among the miners which allowed them to separate the gold from mercury and reutilize the mercury several times over. This kind of instrument was introduced throughout all the Amazon region.[80]

Even if most of the time the work of Indigenous miners was limited to the operation of mining rafts, some Indigenous miners were able to purchase their own mining rafts. That happened with the Indigenous communities of Chorro Bocón, Zamuro and Remanso. Unlike the rafts that were built and administered by "white" miners, Indigenous mining rafts did not give to the community a weekly percentage depending on the amount of gold they obtained; instead they extracted gold for specific events. These events could be related with Christian practices such as the Holy Supper or *Conferencias* (conferences). Christian values and practices also played an important role in the agreements and in the ways in which Indigenous communities used the revenues they obtained from mining. For instance, agreements with miners included the prohibition of selling liquor, cigarettes and practice of prostitution in the mining camps.

The ways in which relationships between *colonos* (settlers) and Indigenous communities were transformed through these agreements, and customary norms became clear through the public demonstrations that took place on the streets of Puerto Inírida on October 13, 2013. Few days previously, marines and the police of Guainía conducted a military operation against informal mining called Operation Oxygen. During this operation five rafts that

148   *Indigeneity, Development and Extractivism*

were extracting gold within the limits of the IMZ were confiscated. Eleven Indigenous people were detained but were later released because their arrest was declared illegal. In the demonstrations there were non-Indigenous and Indigenous miners walking together and holding up posters that said "The small traditional miners are from the region, whites and Indigenous here and here we stay." In these demonstrations both settlers and Indigenous miners would position themselves before the state as "traditional miners," emphasizing their shared experiences and interests. These inter-ethnic alliances intensified the "dispute about the redefinition of the legal/illegal subjects and practices in Guainía."[81] The invocation of traditional mining, which included settlers and Indigenous miners, was a crucial resource used by small miners in their efforts and struggles aimed at legalizing and formalizing their activities. In fact, Law 1382 of 2010 defines "traditional mining" as that "developed by groups of persons or communities that exploit state mines without titles inscribed in the national mining registry and can prove that mining has been developed in a continuous way for five years, through technical and commercial documentation."[82]

While for state authorities the absence of mining titles and environmental licenses was a way of classifying informal miners as illegal, the miners appropriated the state's definition of traditional mining as a way of substantiating the traditional character of their activities. Therefore, in order to be recognized as a traditional miner by the state one must produce "technical and commercial documentation." This explains why "white" miners had notebooks where they had a written record of all the transactions made with Indigenous authorities and communities. Informal miners made particular uses and interpretations of existing state laws in order to prove their "traditionality." As Veena Das points out, the law is brought into the framework of everyday life through "the performance of its rules in modes of rumor, gossip, mockery and mimetic representation."[83] The president of Coolmicop told me several times that it was easier to prove their traditionality in a region such as Guainía where a high percentage of its population is Indigenous.

Moreover, the emphasis that miners placed upon the notion of Indigenous autonomy, whose origin dated back to the Political Constitution of 1991, became a way of defending gold extraction in Indigenous territories. On social networks such as Facebook, Indigenous supporters of mining criticized the military operations against mining saying that "... Attorney Porras and the police department of Guainía are destroyer terrorists that don't know Indigenous laws ... they lie to the people and make illegal arrests of people who have nothing to do with the mining rafts ... accusing them of destroying the environment." The uses miners make of notions such as Indigenous autonomy or Indigenous law demonstrate how categories produced by the state are appropriated to legitimize the agreements that make informal mining possible in the region. At the same time, new discourses were displayed regarding the meaning of gold to Indigenous communities. For example, on December 1, 2015, during a sort of "legal clinic" that the National Mining

Indigeneity, Development and Extractivism   149

Agency organized in Inírida, a Puinave pronounced the following discourse before the state officials and the audience:

> I am from the Puinave ethnic group and we have been, since millennial times, miners by nature (...). We were born next to gold (...) it is the main source of our lives. We live out of that, there is no *indígena* that is not also a miner, I assure you one hundred percent that we are sons of gold and live with that (...) but when the helicopters fly above of our communities, they plunder that, right? They take away all the people, the stuff with which they have to work, what is the destroyed there? The soul, the heart of Indigenous people, which hurts us a lot.

This intervention, which was applauded by the attendees at the "legal clinic," shows how the notion of traditional mining also draws on the idea of "ancestrality" which is attributed to the Indigenous groups of Guainía. In consequence, gold extraction not only transformed local notions of indigeneity through the figure of the ancestral Indigenous miner, but also drew settlers closer to certain ideas of ancestrality through the notion of the traditional miner. The president of Coolmicop also asserted his status as *mestizo* given that his mother was Indigenous. These new discourses of indigeneity challenge, among others issues, hegemonic representations of Indigenous communities as "ecological natives," advocates of the environment or active anti-capitalists.[84]

Conflicts and Environmental Disputes between Traditional Miners and the State

Beginning in 2012, the national government, with Juan Manuel Santos as president, adhered to decision 774 of 2012 of the Andean Community of Nations. This decision pushed the members of the Andean Community to "confiscate, seize, immobilize, destroy, demolish, make unusable and neutralize the goods, machines and supplies used in illegal mining."[85] This agreement ordered the armed forces to protect and defend the environment, while it defined the "exploration and exploitation without mining title and environmental license" as a great threat to the environment and national security. This new function of the armed forces of the state contributed to the militarization of environmental protection.[86] Those miners who continued to extract gold by use of artisanal and mechanized instruments, without environmental licenses or mining titles, were classified by the state as "illegal miners."[87]

In addition to Operation Oxygen, on June 23, 2014 another military operation was conducted on the Atabapo River, which delineates the border with Venezuela. In this operation the national army and the police used dynamite to destroy 11 rafts, while 10 people were detained. Four of the detained were Puinave and six were settlers. The prosecutor presented charges against them that included exploitation of gold deposits without having a mining license

150 *Indigeneity, Development and Extractivism*

inscribed in the national register, and for environmentally damaging strategic ecosystems. The detained members of Indigenous communities requested that their case to be transferred to the Indigenous Special Jurisdiction and this request was fulfilled. The settlers remained under house arrest until the year 2015. Consequently, the case was divided between Indigenous and non-Indigenous detainees. The participation of the armed forces demonstrates how informal mining has been criminalized while also associating it with the sponsorship of armed groups.

Some of the miners who were detained told me how their rafts have been destroyed several times, but that they were rebuilt so as to recover what they lost in the military operations. The main paradox of these ways of confronting informal mining is that they are not able to end this practice. The military operations also polluted the rivers given that the rafts were blown up with gallons of diesel inside the rafts and in the engines used for the dredges. The deleterious effects of military operations resulted in the miners viewing the state as a source of social and environmental conflict. When I told the president of Coolmicop that my research was also about socio-environmental conflicts his immediate reply was: "it is the state which causes conflict here."

In response to the military operation of June 23, 2014, there were more public demonstrations where not only Indigenous and non-Indigenous miners participated, but also regional state officials, members of the local council, the Mayor of Puerto Inírida and the governor of the department. Military operations were seen by miners as suspicious actions by presenting a risk to their lives and personal integrity, but also for the disrespect of their "jurisdictional norms."[88] Public demonstrations became a way of defending the agreements and customary norms that regulated gold extraction in the region, thereby putting into collision different forms of governance. Nonetheless, *de facto* agreements between miners and Indigenous communities were incomprehensible for the state. One of the posters used in these public demonstrations said: "Yes to Indigenous traditional mining, not to multinational corporations."

The prosecution some institutions of the state exercise against informal mining in Guainía clashes with the formalization programs the National Mining Agency promotes in the region and with the attempts made by miners to join those programs. While for the Ministry of Mining, illegal mining is associated with the absence of mining titles and environmental licenses, for the Ministry of Defense "illegal mining is that which criminals develop in order to fund their criminal activities."[89] In this sense, within the same state there are contradictory definitions of what illegal mining is. The ongoing judicialization of miners represents a risk for the programs of formalization developed by the National Mining Agency. According to the president of Coolmicop, "when the mining boards [*juntas mineras*] take place there will be no one who can access the formalization programs,"[90] because detained miners will be in court or will have been convicted. In addition to the clashes between national ministries (specifically, those between the Ministry of Mining and the Ministry of Environment) the changing positions of regional

Indigeneity, Development and Extractivism   151

authorities such as the CDA regarding informal mining produce an effect of illegibility among miners which makes it difficult to understand why the state prosecutes them using violent practices.[91]

In reaction to the official accusations of environmental contamination, the miners began to articulate a discourse that emphasized the protection of the environment. A Brazilian miner told me that they were concerned about not polluting the river. He said to me he was careful to not pour diesel fuel into the river while also discarding the garbage from of the mining camps several meters away from the shore of the river. This miner emphasized that up to 95% of mercury was reused and the sand polluted with mercury was also buried several meters away from the shore. Another Indigenous miner told me, in July 2014, that there was no mercury contamination because "there were no deformed children born; all of them were normal."[92] In Puerto Inírida there were also rumors about the possible contamination of the river with mercury. A biologist who worked in town told me she preferred to eat scaled fish rather than catfish because the latter could retain more mercury than the former.

The disputes between miners and the state transformed into disputes regarding possible ecological and environmental damage by one or the other. These disputes also included the production of evidence that could prove those damages. According to the president of Coolmicop, in the military operation of 2013 no mercury was found aboard the rafts. The president said to me: "they can't prove anything because everything was blown away."[93] In order to convict the miners for ecological damage, the prosecutor would have to prove, using a scientific assessment, which could take several months to complete, that the rafts were actually polluting the river. As Roberston and Farelly point out, the contamination caused by mercury is not only a "technical issue," but has to do more with the entanglements that emerge between miners and specific materials to the extent that mercury can be considered co-constitutive of certain types of mining.[94] Furthermore, the multiple versions of the facts that circulate in Puerto Inírida regarding mercury contamination can produce what sociologist Javier Auyero calls "toxic uncertainty."[95] One doesn't know whether or not the fish you eat in Puerto Inírida is toxic. Toxic uncertainty is part of a "labor of confusion" that has the effect of sharing (mis)understandings regarding risk and environmental contamination. This labor of confusion works as a "blinder" that minimizes the potential damage that mercury can produce and becomes part of everyday life.[96] Therefore, miners in Guainía do not have the same ideas of risk as other social actors who are external to their situation of exposure may have.

When President Santos visited Puerto Inírida in July 2014 in order to sign decree 1275, which declared the "fluvial star" of Inírida a Ramsar site, the president of Coolmicop gave Santos a document in which he claimed that: "since the year 2004 we have participated in different formalization programs offered by the government, expressing our interest in formalizing our activities. At present we have requests that have not been attended to: requests for concession contracts, traditional mining and special reserve zones

152 *Indigeneity, Development and Extractivism*

for mining." In this way the defense of traditional mining became a way of drawing closer to the state and making the local forms of regulating the access and distribution of gold legitimate.

In a public demonstration in May 2015 in front of the administrative tribunal of Cundinamarca in Bogotá, the miners of Guainía were present in support of the miners association from Cauca. In this demonstration the miners of Guainía held posters that said: "the traditional miners are not enemies of the environment." The environmental discourse of traditional miners can also articulate environmental subjectivities.[97] Another of the posters that the miners held out said: "the mining people (*pueblos mineros*) demand respect for our tradition and culture." The use of the idea of "people" (*pueblo*) as a group with its own tradition and culture demonstrates how the political strategies of miners have taken on an "ethnic" undertone, which also produced new articulations of indigeneity. Traditional miners combine the defense of mining with the protection of the environment and the use of ethnic categories in their discourse. While "traditionality" for the state is associated with practicing mining outside of the existing legal frameworks, for small miners the idea of "traditionality" is informed by the concept of ancestrality attributed to the Indigenous groups of Guainía and this is what makes their informal practices legitimate before the state.

Conclusions

The first part of this chapter analyzed how, starting in the 1960s, state policies directed toward Indigenous communities in the Amazon became concerned with cultural differences and adapted to local realities, while Indigenous communities began to demand access to development plans, health services and lessons in the Spanish language. The notion of "developmental indigenism" entailed a new relationship between the state and Indigenous communities in which the former adapted its policies to "Indigenous customs" and the latter demanded access to development and material improvement. Indigenous appropriations of development included the incorporation of "languages of the state" through which demands for material improvement, or better health or education, were made incorporating specific notions of rights, culture and community. Indigenous communities were not passive objects of development policies, but they sought interactions with state functionaries at the local and national level through written correspondence in order to place their demands for development in their own terms.

The second part of the chapter describes how, after the 1980s, the state promoted gold prospecting and extraction in the region. However, after these official initiatives failed, Indigenous and non-Indigenous miners (most of whom were settlers from other parts of the country and Brazilian miners) developed their own rules and agreements in order to regulate the access and distribution of gold. While local state authorities initially supported informal mining with technical assistance, after the year 2012 the state began to

Indigeneity, Development and Extractivism 153

criminalize and undertake military operations against small-scale miners in Guainía as a way of confronting "illegal mining." In response to accusations of environmental contamination, miners articulated an environmentalist discourse and reframed their practices in terms of "traditionality." This chapter shows how the strategic appropriation of legal categories such as "traditional mining" also produced new notions of indigeneity, as well as new uses of ideas of ancestrality and "Indigenous autonomy." In this context, indigeneity was mobilized, not to defend "ancestral territories" or the environment but to make small-scale gold mining legitimate within Indigenous territories.

Notes

1 Gregorio Hernández de Alba was a Colombian ethnologist and archeologist considered to be one of the founders of anthropology as a profession in Colombia. Since 1935 de Alba held different positions in State institutions such as the Archeological National Service and the National Indigenist Institute.

2 Writing about Indigenous politics in Peru, Shane Greene argues that *customization* refers both to *"specific acts* and to a *structural process* of constrained creativity." Greene defines customization along three different lines. First, customization has to do with "the interdependent nature of social values and social actions, which are in turn dependent on the dialectic of structural repetition and practical transformation (...) it indexes the dynamic relation between those things we do without thinking and those things we do with purpose." Second, customization refers also to a "stage of *getting accustomed* to something that at first appears to be foreign but becomes a bit more familiar over time," involving a "process of domestication in which social actors are both forced into and desirous of establishing a proper relationship with a foreign object that has appeared or imposed itself on them." Third, any project of customization is "constrained by the politics of customization in which it is enmeshed." In this sense, the reach and creativity of specific acts of customization depend "heavily on the structures of power that inevitably constrain them," see Shane Greene, *Customizing Indigeneity. Paths to a Visionary Politics in Peru* (Stanford: Stanford University Press, 2009), 17–18.

3 Part of the ideas used in the first two sections of this chapter was developed in the article: "Rozo, Esteban y Carlos del Cairo. Indigenismo desarrollista: Estado y diferencia cultural en una frontera amazónica (1959–1980)," *Historia Crítica* 65 (2017): 163–182. https://doi.org/10.7440/histcrit65.2017.08.

4 "Carta dirigida al Señor Doctor Don Gregorio Hernández de Alba," Mitú, July 10, 1959, in AGN, República, *Ministerio de Gobierno, División de Asuntos Indígenas*, caja 6, carpeta 1, f.20.

5 Ibid.

6 Ibid.

7 Jimena Perry, *Caminos de la antropología en Colombia: Gregorio Hernández de Alba* (Bogotá: Ediciones Uniandes, 2006), 94.

8 Ibid.

9 Hugo Burgos and Gonzalo Pesantez, "Plan nacional indigenista de Colombia: 1966–1969," *América Indígena* XXVII, no. 4 (1967): 779.

10 "A los caciques, jefes e indígenas del Vaupés," Bogotá, June 26, 1959, in AGN, Sección República, Fondo *Ministerio de Gobierno, División de Asuntos Indígenas*, caja 6, carpeta 1, f.18.

11 As I mentioned in Chapter 3, Adam Kuper argues that the idea of culture as a random set of traits goes back to 1871, when Tylor defined culture or civilization

154 Indigeneity, Development and Extractivism

as a "complex whole which includes knowledge, belief, art, morals, law, custom, and any other capabilities and habits acquired by man as a member of society." See Adam Kuper, *Culture: The Anthropologists' Account* (Cambridge: Harvard University Press, 1999), 56–61.

12 Gregorio Hernández de Alba, "Carta dirigida al Reverendísimo Monseñor Heriberto Correa, Prefecto Apostólico de Mitú," Bogotá, June 26, 1959, in AGN, República, *Ministerio de Gobierno, División de Asuntos Indígenas*, caja 6, carpeta 1, f.17.

13 "Decreto 003 de 1965. Por el cual se declara oficialmente establecido dentro de su territorio el primer Gobierno de la Comisaría Especial del Guainía y se dispone conmemorar esta fecha," Puerto Inírida, February 5, 1965.

14 Ibid.

15 Astrid Ulloa, *The Ecological Native: Indigenous Peoples Movements and Ecogovernmentality in Colombia* (London: Routledge, 2005).

16 Beth A. Conklin and Laura Graham, "The Shifting Middle Ground: Amazonian Indians and Eco-Politics," *American Anthropologist* 97, no. 4 (1995): 695–710.

17 "Informe de labores de mejoradora de hogar dirigido al secretario de gobierno," Inírida, July 4, 1966, in Archivo de la Gobernación del Guainía (AGG).

18 "Informe sobre la comisión realizada a Morichal Garza Alto Inírida," Inírida, November 15, 1977, in AGN, Sección República, Fondo *Ministerio de Gobierno, División de Asuntos Indígenas*, caja 96, carpeta 4, f.86.

19 "El plan nacional de salud rural en el Guainía. Planteamiento de una modalidad para regiones selváticas," Bogotá, February 13, 1977, in AGN, Sección República, Fondo *Ministerio de Gobierno, División de Asuntos Indígenas*, caja 96, carpeta 4, f.93.

20 "El plan nacional de salud rural," f.93.

21 "Carta dirigida al Doctor Jaramillo Salazar, Ministro de Salud", Vereda San José, 8 de junio de 1980, AGG, sf.

22 "Carta diriga al Señor Doctor Gregorio Hernández de Alba," Brujas (Guainía), May 5, 1965, in AGN, Sección República, Fondo *Ministerio de Gobierno, División de Asuntos Indígenas*, caja 203, carpeta 1819, f.1.

23 "El plan nacional de salud rural en el Guainía. Planteamiento de una modalidad para regiones selváticas", Bogotá, 13 de febrero de 1977, AGN, Ministerio de Gobierno, División de Asuntos Indígenas, Caja 96, Carpeta 4, f .93.

24 "Curso vacacional para capacitación de auxiliares bilingües," Puerto Inírida, October 13, 1976, in AGG.

25 "Curso vacacional para capacitación."

26 José Jacinto Morales Mondragón, "Acta de visita No.1," Caranacoa (Guainía), August 24, 1976, in AGG.

27 Nancy P. Appelbaum, *Muddied Waters. Region, and Local History in Colombia, 1846–1948* (Durham: Duke University Press, 2003), 12.

28 "Carta dirigida al Señor Comisario Especial del Guainía," Laguna Colorada (Guainía), April 1, 1979, en AGG.

29 "Carta dirigida al Señor Comisario."

30 "Petición dirigida al Corregidor Comisarial, Junta de Acción Comunal y Comerciantes de Pto. Colombia y San Felipe," San José (Guainía), July 19, 1980, in AGG.

31 Ibid.

32 Ibid.

33 Ibid.

34 Peter Gow, *Indigenous Modernity and the Moral Imagination* (Durham: Duke University Press, 2008), 3.

35 "Tercer Congreso de Indígenas. Río Guaviare y Vichada," Laguna Colorada (Guainía), September 12 –17, 1977, in AGG.

36 Ibid.

Indigeneity, Development and Extractivism   155

37 Ibid.
38 Ibid.
39 Ethnographic research about the "aesthetics of conviviality" in Amazonia shows how some Indigenous societies tend to "disdain the sociological" and instead place an "affective emphasis" in their interpersonal relations and everyday life. In this context, the "sense of community" entails both moral and political meanings, as well as the production of "an aesthetics of action" which informs at the same time specific "styles of relating" that vary among and within Indigenous communities in Amazonia. See Joanna Overing and Alan Passes, "Introduction: Conviviality and the Opening Up of Amazonian Anthropology," in *The Anthropology of Love and Anger. The Aesthetics of Conviviality in Native Amazonia*, eds. Joana Overing and Alan Passes (New York: Routledge, 2000), xi.
40 Ibid.
41 Ibid.
42 Ibid.
43 In this context, "Indigenous malice" has an ambiguous meaning and it is an expression often used in ordinary language and conversations in Colombia. On one hand, the notion of "Indigenous malice" tends to reinscribe negative stereotypes of natives as treacherous, untrustworthy and evil. At the same time, "Indigenous malice" might also be associated with cunningness when one is doing, for example, business with someone else. However, in both cases the notion of "Indigenous malice" is associated with negative behavior (i.e. dupe or being duped by someone else) in opposition to contemporary ideas of native Amazonians as noble savages or ecological natives.
44 Ibid.
45 Tercer Congreso de Indígenas. Rio Guaviare y Vichada. Laguna Colorada Septiembre 12–17, 1977, in AGG.
46 "Curso vacacional para capacitación."
47 Ibid.
48 Ibid.
49 Ibid.
50 Ibid.
51 Ibid.
52 According to the letter, Luis had inherited the piece of land where he lived from his father-in-law, which probably means that Luis was married with an Indigenous woman.
53 Tercer Congreso de Indígenas. Rio Guaviare y Vichada. Laguna Colorada Septiembre 12–17, 1977, in AGG.
54 Ibid.
55 Ibid.
56 Thomas Blom Hansen and Finn Stepputat, *States of Imagination. Ethnographic Explorations of the Postcolonial* (Duke University Press, Durham, 2001).
57 Part of the ideas used in the last three sections of this chapter was developed in the article: Rozo, Esteban. "Mineros e indígenas: gobernanza local, extracción de oro y disputas ambientales en Guainía," *Revista Colombiana de Antropología* 58, no. 3 (2022): 34–58. https://doi.org/10.22380/2539472X.2323.
58 Ecopetrol is the state agency in charge of petroleum exploration and extraction in Colombia.
59 Jorge Bendeck Olivella. "El proyecto minero del Guainía y el desarrollo socioeconómico del área fronteriza," *Revista del Centro de Estudios Colombianos* 47 (1988): 53.
60 ONIC (Organización Nacional Indígena de Colombia), "Cronología de la minería en el Guainía," *Hojas de Selva* (October–November 1990): 13.
61 Mónica Valdés, "En el Guainía. Minas de oro y hambre," *Hojas de Selva* (October–November 1995): 12.

156   *Indigeneity, Development and Extractivism*

62 Ibid.

63 IMZs were defined in the article 122 of the Mining Code of 2001 as an "area defined by the mining authority within an Indigenous territory through a technical visit in which the mining potential of the area is established." An IMZ should be formally requested by the "traditional authority" of the Indigenous community to the Ministry of Mines and Energy, while the exploitation of the IMZ can be realized by Indigenous communities through a concession contract. Nevertheless, the concession contract is by itself not sufficient for the extraction of gold in an IMZ; an environmental license and paying the "superficiary canon" are also required, see Diana Alexandra Mendoza, *Estudio de caso: minería en territorios indígenas del Guainía en la Orinoquia y la Amazonia* (Bogotá: Programa de Naciones Unidas para el Desarrollo, 2012), 44.

64 Catalina Caro Galvis, "Minería en el norte del Cauca indígena. Prácticas territoriales y transformaciones socioespaciales en los resguardos indígenas nasa del municipio de Santander de Quilichao, Cauca, Colombia," in *Extractivismo minero en Colombia y América Latina*, eds. Barbara Göbel y Astrid Ulloa (Ibero-Amerikanisches Institut / Universidad Nacional de Colombia, 2014), 259.

65 Resolución número 326334 del 17 de diciembre de 1992 por la cual se señala y delimita la Zona Minera Indígena.

66 Diana Alexandra Mendoza, *Estudio de caso: minería en territorios indígenas del Guainía en la Orinoquia y la Amazonia* (Bogotá: Programa de Naciones Unidas para el Desarrollo, 2012), 83.

67 Carlos Ariel Salazar, Franz Gutiérrez y Martín Franco, *Guainía. En sus asentamientos Humanos* (Bogotá: Instituto Sinchi, 2012), 82.

68 Catalina Caro Galvis, "Minería en el norte del Cauca indígena. Prácticas territoriales y transformaciones socioespaciales en los resguardos indígenas nasa del municipio de Santander de Quilichao, Cauca, Colombia," in *Extractivismo minero en Colombia y América Latina*, eds. Barbara Göbel y Astrid Ulloa (Ibero-Amerikanisches Institut/Universidad Nacional de Colombi, 2014), 259.

69 ONIC (Organización Nacional Indígena de Colombia), "Cronología de la minería en el Guainía," *Hojas de Selva* (October–November 1990): 13.

70 Fernando J. López-Vega, "Desafíos de la movilización minera interétnica en el río Inírida, Guainía, al posconflicto en Colombia," in *Extractivismos y posconflicto en Colombia: retos para la paz territorial*, eds. Astrid Ulloa y Sergio Coronado (Bogotá: Universidad Nacional de Colombia, 2016), 275.

71 Anthony Bebbington, "Underground Political Ecologies: The Second Annual Lecture of the Cultural and Political Ecology Specialty Group of the Association of American Geographers," *Geoforum* 43, no. 6 (2012): 8.

72 For a further discussion on these topics, see Astrid Ulloa, *La construcción del nativo ecológico: complejidades, paradojas y dilemas de la relación entre los movimientos indígenas y el ambientalismo en Colombia* (Bogotá: ICANH, 2004); Stuart Kirsch, "Indigenous Movements and the Risks of Counterglobalization: Tracking the Campaign against Papua New Guinea's Ok Tedi mine," *American Ethnologist* 34, no. 2 (2007): 303–321.

73 For a further analysis on informality, see Sarah Muir, "Recursive In/formality. Time and Ideology in a Distributed Monetary System," *ANUAC* 6, no. 2 (2017): 77–83; Keith Hart, "The Informal Economy," *The Cambridge Journal of Anthropology* 10, no. 2 (1985): 54–58.

74 Ángela Castillo Ardila and Sebastián Rubiano Galvis, *Territorios, autonomías locales y conflictos en Amazonia y Pacífico (1975–2015)* (Bogotá: Ediciones Uniandes, 2019), xvi.

75 Mette M. High, "The Cultural Logics of Illegality: Living Outside the Law in the Mongolian Gold Mines," in *Change in Democratic Mongolia. Social*

Indigeneity, Development and Extractivism   157

Relations, Health, Mobile Pastoralism, and Mining, ed. Julian Dierkes (Leiden: Brill, 2012), 251.

76 GOMIAM is a knowledge network on small-scale gold mining and social conflicts in the Amazon, set up in the period 2010–2016. During the project, GOMIAM compared states, environments, local populations and miners by means of research, dissemination and policy advocacy activities in Bolivia, Brazil, Colombia, Peru, Suriname and French Guyana.

77 Luis Álvaro Pardo Becerra and Aída Sofía Rivera Sotelo, "¿Qué minería aurífera, por quiénes y con fines de qué desarrollo? Una mirada a la minería aurífera en la ZMI Remanso Chorrobocón," *Opera* 14 (2014): 112.

78 Keith Hart, "The "Informal Economy," *The Cambridge Journal of Anthropology* 10, no. 2 (1985): 54–58; Daniella Gandolfo, "Formless: A Day at Lima's Office of Formalization," *Cultural Anthropology* 28, no. 2 (2013): 278–298.

79 Veena Das, *Life and Words. Violence and the Descent into the Ordinary* (Berkeley: University of California Press, 2007).

80 Leontien Cremers and Marjo de Theije, "Small-scale Gold Mining in the Amazon," in *Small-scale Gold Mining in the Amazon. The Cases of Bolivia, Brazil, Colombia, Peru and Suriname,* eds. Leontien Cremers, Judith Kolen and Marjo de Theije (Amsterdam: Cedla, 2013), 10.

81 Fernando J. López-Vega, "Desafíos de la movilización minera interétnica en el río Inírida, Guainía, al posconflicto en Colombia," in *Extractivismos y posconflicto en Colombia: retos para la paz territorial,* eds. Astrid Ulloa y Sergio Coronado (Bogotá: Universidad Nacional de Colombia, 2016), 282.

82 "Ley 1382 de 2010. Por el cual se modifica la Ley 685 de 2001 Código de Minas."

83 Veena Das, *Life and words. Violence and the Descent into the Ordinary* (Berkeley: University of California Press, 2007), 162.

84 Astrid Ulloa, *La construcción del nativo ecológico: complejidades, paradojas y dilemas de la relación entre los movimientos indígenas y el ambientalismo en Colombia* (Bogotá: ICANH, 2004); Stuart Kirsch, "Indigenous Movements and the Risks of Counter Globalization: Tracking the Campaign against Papua New Guinea's Ok Tedi mine," *American Ethnologist* 34, no. 2 (2007): 303–321; Beth A. Conklin and Laura Graham, "The Shifting Middle Ground: Amazonian Indians and Eco-Politics," *American Anthropologist* 97, no. 4 (1995): 695–710.

85 "Decisión No. 774 del 30 de julio de 2012 de la Comunidad Andina de Naciones."

86 Nancy Peluso and Michael Watts, eds. *Violent Environments* (Ithaca: Cornell University Press, 2001).

87 Luis Álvaro Pardo Becerra and Aída Sofía Rivera Sotelo, "¿Qué minería aurífera, por quiénes y con fines de qué desarrollo? Una mirada a la minería aurífera en la ZMI Remanso Chorrobocón," *Opera* 14 (2014): 101.

88 Fernando J. López-Vega, "Desafíos de la movilización minera interétnica en el río Inírida, Guainía, al posconflicto en Colombia," in *Extractivismos y posconflicto en Colombia: retos para la paz territorial,* eds. Astrid Ulloa y Sergio Coronado (Bogotá: Universidad Nacional de Colombia, 2016), 283.

89 Álvaro Pardo, "Minería ilegal es mucho más que mineros con dragas y retroexcavadoras. ¿Y el Estado?," *Semana Sostenible* (2013): 20–23.

90 Personal communication, December 10, 2013.

91 Veena Das, *Life and words. Violence and the Descent into the Ordinary* (Berkeley: University of California Press, 2007).

92 Personal communication, July 14, 2014.

93 Personal communication, December 10, 2013.

94 Thomas Robertson and Trisia Farrelly, "An Ethnography of Entanglements: Mercury's presence and Absence in Artisanal and Small-scale Gold Mining in Antioquia, Colombia," *Sites* 15, no. 1 (2018): 61.

158 *Indigeneity, Development and Extractivism*

95 Javier Auyero and Débora Alejandra Swistun, *Flammable. Environmental Suffering in an Argentine Shantytown* (Oxford: Oxford University Press, 2009), 10.
96 Ibid.
97 Arun Agrawal, "Environmentality. Community, Intimate Government, and the Making of Environmental Subjects in Kumaon, India," *Current Anthropology* 46, no. 2 (2005): 161–190.

References

Agrawal, Arun. "Environmentality. Community, Intimate Government, and the Making of Environmental Subjects in Kumaon, India." *Current Anthropology* 46, no. 2 (2005): 161–190. https://doi.org/10.1086/427122

Appelbaum, Nancy P. *Muddied Waters. Region, and Local History in Colombia, 1846–1948.* Durham: Duke University Press, 2003.

Auyero, Javier, and Débora Alejandra Swistun. *Flammable. Environmental Suffering in an Argentine Shantytown.* Oxford: Oxford University Press, 2009.

Bebbington, Anthony. "Underground Political Ecologies: The Second Annual Lecture of the Cultural and Political Ecology Specialty Group of the Association of American Geographers." *Geoforum* 43, no. 6 (2012): 1–11. https://doi.org/10.1016/j.geoforum.2012.05.011

Bendeck Olivella, Jorge. "el proyecto minero del Guainía y el desarrollo socioeconómico del área fronteriza." *Revista del Centro de Estudios Colombianos* 47 (1988): 52–66.

Burgos, Hugo, and Gonzalo Pesantez. "Plan nacional indigenista de Colombia: 1966–1969." *América Indígena* XXVII, no. 4 (1967): 751–781.

Caro Galvis, Catalina. "Minería en el norte del Cauca indígena. Prácticas territoriales y transformaciones socioespaciales en los resguardos indígenas nasa del municipio de Santander de Quilichao, Cauca, Colombia." In *Extractivismo minero en Colombia y América Latina*, edited by Barbara Göbel and Astrid Ulloa, 253–282. Bogotá: Ibero-Amerikanisches Institut and Universidad Nacional de Colombia, 2014.

Castillo Ardila, Ángela, and Sebastián Rubiano Galvis. *Territorios, autonomías locales y conflictos en Amazonia y Pacífico (1975–2015).* Bogotá: Ediciones Uniandes, 2019.

Conklin, Beth A., and Laura Graham. "The Shifting Middle Ground: Amazonian Indians and Eco-Politics." *American Anthropologist* 97, no. 4 (1995): 695–710. https://doi.org/10.1525/aa.1995.97.4.02a00120

Cremers, Leontien, and Marjo de Theije. "Small-Scale Gold Mining in the Amazon." In *Small-Scale Gold Mining in the Amazon. The Cases of Bolivia, Brazil, Colombia, Peru and Suriname*, edited by Leontien Cremers, Judith Kolen and Marjo de Theije, 1–16. Amsterdam: Cedla, 2013.

Das, Veena. *Life and Words. Violence and the Descent into the Ordinary.* Berkeley: University of California Press, 2007.

Gandolfo, Daniella, "Formless: A Day at Lima's Office of Formalization." *Cultural Anthropology* 28, no. 2 (2013): 278–298. https://doi.org/10.1111/cuan.12004

Göbel, Barbara, and Astrid Ulloa, eds. *Extractivismo minero en Colombia y América Latina.* Bogotá: Ibero-Amerikanisches Institut and Universidad Nacional de Colombia, 2014.

Gow, Peter. *Indigenous Modernity and the Moral Imagination.* Durham: Duke University Press, 2008.

Greene, Shane. *Customizing Indigeneity. Paths to a Visionary Politics in Peru.* Stanford: Stanford University Press, 2009.

Hansen, Thomas Blom, and Finn Stepputat. *States of Imagination. Ethnographic Explorations of the Postcolonial.* Durham: Duke University Press, 2001.

Hart, Keith. "The Informal Economy." *The Cambridge Journal of Anthropology* 10, no. 2 (1985): 54–58.

High, Mette M. "The Cultural Logics of Illegality: Living Outside the Law in the Mongolian Gold Mines." In *Change in Democratic Mongolia. Social Relations, Health, Mobile Pastoralism, and Mining*, edited by Julian Dierkes, 249–270. Leiden: Brill, 2012.

Kirsch, Stuart. "Indigenous Movements and The Risks of Counterglobalization: Tracking the Campaign against Papua New Guinea's Ok Tedi Mine." *American Ethnologist* 34, no. 2 (2007): 303–321. https://doi.org/10.1525/ae.2007.34.2.303

Kuper, Adam. *Culture: The Anthropologists' Account.* Cambridge: Harvard University Press, 1999.

López-Vega, Fernando J. "desafíos de la movilización minera interétnica en el río Inírida, Guainía, al posconflicto en Colombia." In *Extractivismos y posconflicto en Colombia: retos para la paz territorial*, edited by Astrid Ulloa and Sergio Coronado, 267–302. Bogotá: Universidad Nacional de Colombia, 2016.

Mendoza, Diana Alexandra. *Estudio de caso: minería en territorios indígenas del Guainía en la Orinoquia y la Amazonia.* Bogotá: Programa de Naciones Unidas para el Desarrollo, 2012.

Muir, Sarah. "Recursive in/formality. Time and Ideology in a Distributed Monetary System." *ANUAC* 6, no. 2 (2017): 77–83. https://doi.org/10.7340/anuac2239-625X-3073

ONIC (Organización Nacional Indígena de Colombia). "Cronología de la minería en el Guainía." *Hojas de Selva* (October–November 1990): 13.

Overing, Joana, and Alan Passes, eds. *The Anthropology of Love and Anger. The Aesthetics of Conviviality in Native Amazonia.* New York: Routledge, 2000.

Pardo, Álvaro. "Minería ilegal es mucho más que mineros con dragas y retroexcavadoras. ¿Y el estado?" *Semana Sostenible* (2013): 20–23.

Pardo, Luis Álvaro, and Aída Sofía Rivera Sotelo. "¿qué minería aurífera, por quiénes y con fines de qué desarrollo? Una mirada a la minería aurífera en la ZMI Remanso Chorrobocón." *Opera* 14 (2014): 95–117.

Peluso, Nancy, and Michael Watts, eds. *Violent Environments.* Ithaca: Cornell University Press, 2001.

Perry, Jimena. *Caminos de la antropología en Colombia: Gregorio Hernández de Alba.* Bogotá: Ediciones Uniandes, 2006.

Robertson, Thomas, and Trisia Farrelly. "An Ethnography of Entanglements: Mercury's Presence and Absence in Artisanal and Small-Scale Gold Mining in Antioquia, Colombia." *Sites* 15, no. 1 (2018): 39–69.

Salazar, Carlos Ariel, Franz Gutiérrez, and Martín Franco. *Guainía. En sus asentamientos Humanos.* Bogotá: Instituto Sinchi, 2012.

Ulloa, Astrid. *The Ecological Native: Indigenous Peoples Movements and Ecogovernmentality in Colombia.* London: Routledge, 2005.

Valdés, Mónica, "En El Guainía. Minas de oro y hambre." *Hojas de Selva* (October–November 1995): 12.

Conclusions

This book has analyzed the relationship between state-formation, Christianity and indigeneity in two departments of the Colombian Amazon. Throughout the 20th century, Catholic and evangelical missionaries endeavored to reshape Indigenous societies and identities in the Amazon region as part of, or in opposition to, processes of colonization and state-formation. Indigenous societies in the Colombian Amazon, as historical actors, developed complex and ambiguous relationships with Christianity, colonization and the state. The appropriation of evangelical Christianity was also used to challenge and thwart development schemes in the Colombian Amazon. This historical ethnography compared different modes of colonization and evangelization in the Amazon region and how they related to specific ideas of indigeneity and civilization. Not all projects of civilization were the same in Amazonia, nor was evangelization always subordinate to the state or resource extraction. This book has traced how different projects of civilization and modernity have produced different ideas about native Amazonians and how they should be governed or morally led. The expansion of state sovereignty, Christianity and the demand for raw materials (such as rubber and gold) shaped the lives of Indigenous groups in the Colombian Amazon in different ways.

The first part of this book addressed how Montfort missionaries developed their own kind of Catholic patriotism that tried to transform Tukanoans into Colombians through Catholic devotion. The daily repetition of routines associated with prayer in Montfort-Papurí (Vaupés) was combined with the public performance of sovereignty through public rituals that included the planting of huge crosses in each mission town they established and resettling Indigenous populations through the establishment of *reducciones*. The establishment of *reducciones* was important to how state sovereignty, and authority was performed in the region. Montfort missionaries were crucial to how state sovereignty was achieved in Vaupés through the control of the Indigenous communities who lived on the border with Brazil. Montfort missionaries were active in defending national interests in the region and disputing with other actors as to the exact location of the border.

Montfort missionaries also produced varied representations of the Tucano Indigenous groups they encountered as well as specific ideas about how to

DOI: 10.4324/9781003370215-7

Conclusions 161

govern them (through the establishment of *reducciones* or boarding schools, for example). Tukanoans were represented as "Indians" with no history, no documents and no writing or traditions. Montfort missionaries represented Tukanoans as "people without history." The performance of state sovereignty in Vaupés included dressing Indigenous *capitanes* in police uniforms, displaying pictures of Indigenous children at boarding schools crossing their hands and dressed all alike, hoisting flags and singing the national anthem. In this way, Montfort missionaries established a close relationship between nationalizing and civilizing Indigenous communities in Vaupés. However, Montfort missionaries had to compete with other actors such as rubber industry bosses or Salesian missionaries for Indigenous labor and loyalty. Catholic missionaries, as *protectores de indígenas* (protectors of Indians), could also interfere in the contracts and agreements established between natives under their jurisdiction and the rubber bosses.

The state-sponsored tutelage that Catholic missionaries had over Indigenous communities and territories since the end of 19th century was put into question by evangelical missionaries who traveled to the Vaupés region in the 1940s. This book shows how, unlike Catholic missionaries who developed organic relationships with the state, evangelical missionaries were seen as a *threat* to the power of the state in the Colombian Amazon, while they were simultaneously fostering new forms of Indigenous leadership and community. The fact that Indigenous conversion to evangelical Christianity became a political issue for the state shows that understandings of conversion centered only on questions of "belief" and "rationality" leave aside the political context which is also crucial.[1] Catholic missionaries, national authorities and even illegal armed groups such as the FARC. followed closely the work of Sophie Muller and New Tribes Missionaries. All of these actors were concerned with the effects of Muller's work over and upon Indigenous communities. Catholic missionaries perceived the work of Sophie Muller as an obstacle to the colonization of the region, limiting material exchange between natives and settlers. The FARC, on the other hand, perceived Muller's anti-communism as a threat to their own "work" in the region among Indigenous communities. As a response to FARC persecution, Muller had to spend the last years of her life living in Venezuela.

Clearly, New Tribes missionaries in the Colombian Amazon crafted new forms of community and indigeneity and some of these forms clashed with state-led projects of colonization. Evangelical missionaries suggested that Indigenous evangelicals should be like neither their "pagan" ancestors, nor the *colonos* that settled in the region. Evangelical Christianity shaped new ideas about indigeneity. Frictions between evangelical ideas of community and state-led projects of colonization became explicit in the 1960s when state officials tried to establish the capital of the province of Guainía in 1965. Indigenous evangelicals who lived there complained in a letter written on May 5, 1965 to the central government about the lax moral standards of those supposedly sent to "civilize" them and establish the regional government

162   *Conclusions*

there. Indigenous evangelicals rejected that the first employees of the *comisaría* forced them to drink and party; this behavior went against the teachings of their own Indigenous pastors. Nonetheless, in this same letter, Indigenous evangelicals not only demanded government protection from *chicleros* (gum extractors) but also requested education, medicines and tools, arguing that it was "our government" (not the Venezuelan government) who was responsible for attending to them. Indigenous evangelicals appropriated new languages of the state (associated with specific rights and demands) in tandem with specific forms of interaction and communication with state authorities through written letters and formal petitions, among others.

Indigenous understandings and narratives of evangelical conversion were also explored here in relation to missionary narratives of the same process. Neither missionaries nor Indigenous populations view conversion as simply rupture; both emphasize continuity in one way or another. Conversion to evangelical Christianity is partly a process of cultural and political mediation which, in this case, when also mobilized by Indigenous evangelists, created a new kind of indigeneity. In this context, Christian indigeneity incorporates both narratives of rupture with a "worldly past," as well as narratives of cultural continuity that underline Indigenous values and practices. Paraphrasing Manuela Carneiro it is possible to say that Indigenous communities in the Colombian Amazon "customized" Christianity to "their own continuity and transformation."[2]

Christian indigeneity challenges hegemonic understandings of native Amazonians and leads us to recognize other forms of historical Indigenous agency that are not based on explicit resistance to every form of evangelization or colonization. In this sense, Christian indigeneity might be understood as part of what Bruce Knauft calls "recessive agency," that is "willingly pursued actions" that put actors in a position of seeming subordination.[3] This kind of "active passivity," according to Knauft, increases "cultural and social engagement with modern institutions and activities by means of subordination," but it is always contextual. In the Colombian Amazon, indigeneity was remade through its relationships with Christianity and state-led colonization. Christian indigeneity is not only associated with specific transformations in "traditional culture," but also with changes in the existing relationship between Indigenous societies and settlers. Despite the changes that conversion to evangelical Christianity brought in the symbolic and social relationships between Indigenous societies and settlers, there are still strong continuities in the political economy of the region, since extractive economies (now in the form of coca crops and small-scale gold mining) continue to rely on Indigenous labor. One of the last governors of the province was called *el patrón* (the boss) by some of his Indigenous constituents.

As discussed in Chapter 4, differences between Catholic and Evangelical Christianity can also be traced through their divergent ways of dealing with and perceiving materiality. At the same time, different views of materiality reveal different understandings and relationships with modernity, which are closely associated with ideas about civilization (for Catholic missionaries)

Conclusions 163

and/or "worldliness" (for Indigenous evangelicals). Catholic missionaries in Vaupés relied heavily on commodities and material objects as part of their work, associating the arrival and adoption of Catholicism with the acquisition of specific kinds of objects. Catholic missionaries also used gifts and objects of different kinds to attract Indigenous groups to the mission towns, as well as rewards for agricultural or manual labor.

On the other hand, Indigenous evangelicals and churches developed an ongoing critique of materiality, commodities and money through the idea of "worldliness" (*lo mundano*), thereby producing an ambiguous relationship with modernity and condemning specific practices such as the possession of material things and "vices" such as smoking, drinking or dancing. Indigenous evangelicals developed a moral critique of modernity and produced a selective appropriation of it. The idea of "worldliness" condenses Indigenous evangelicals' understanding of, and relation to, modernity. Despite their critiques of materiality and idolatry, missionaries and Indigenous evangelicals also relied on objects such as Bibles, catechisms and songbooks (translated into Indigenous languages), flannelgraphs, images and radios for their work. In this way, this book criticizes "dematerialized" understandings of conversion to Christianity by showing how the struggle that Indigenous evangelicals conduct against worldliness had to be carried out in "this world" and needed to become materially tangible and visible. At the same time, the critiques evangelicals made to material accumulation contradicted the values and rationalities that underwrote different projects of colonization and extractivism in the region.

Finally, this book explored how the ways in which the state governed Indigenous groups changed over time as did the actors and institutions that were in charge of governing Indigenous populations. During the 1960s the role of Catholic missionaries, as intermediaries for the state between Indigenous communities and the state, was replaced by an indigenist bureaucracy whose main job was to adapt or customize development policies and programs to the cultural and social realities of Indigenous communities in the Amazon region. In this case, development did not imply "cultural assimilation"; on the contrary, the emergent indigenist bureaucracy attempted to "develop" and "integrate" Indigenous groups into the nation without assimilating them. State officials leading development policies in the 1960s emphasized that *indígenas* had their own rights and duties. This early recognition of specific rights associated with cultural differences (language, customs, land, education) constitutes a significant change regarding previous projects of "cultural assimilation" and civilization of Indigenous groups. Developmental indigenism also preceded the multicultural reform that took place in Colombia at the beginning of the 1990s. The last chapter of the book illustrates how Indigenous communities were not passive objects of development policies, but sought interactions with state functionaries at the local and national level through written correspondence in order to place their demands for development in their own terms. Furthermore, some Indigenous communities engaged in gold extraction activities, by establishing arrangements and

164   *Conclusions*

agreements with *colonos* that made informal gold mining possible. As I argue in the last chapter of this book, gold extraction not only transformed local notions of indigeneity through the figure of the ancestral Indigenous miner, but also drew settlers closer to certain ideas of ancestrality and "belonging" through the notion of the traditional miner.

I want to finish this book with the story of Filintro Antonio Rojas, who was one of the most influential and outstanding Curripaco leaders in Guainía until he passed away on December 12, 1997. That same year he published the book entitled *Ciencias naturales en la mitología Curripaco* (Natural Sciences in Curripaco Mythology), with the help of anthropologist Francisco Ortiz, who worked for the NGO Gaia Amazonas.[4] In the preface to the book, Ortiz recalls how Filintro did all kinds of jobs throughout his life: "rubber tapper (*cauchero*), carpenter, tailor, repairman, loader, topographer, teacher, *estafeta* [courier] of the guerilla, statistics collector, college student, apprentice of *payé* (shaman), lecturer, researcher and promoter of Curripaco culture."[5] In the prologue, Ortiz argues that Filintro's trajectory constitutes a "recent chapter in the history of the borders between Colombia and Venezuela, between so-called progress and tradition and, above all, between the Indigenous world and the *criollo* world."[6] Filintro's father, a former Venzuelan military officer named Natalio Rojas, who became a trader of fiber and chesnuts, had abandoned his wife (a Curripaco woman named Julia Sabana) when they were traveling through San Felipe on the Guainía River. A state official who worked for the Colombian government forced Natalio Rojas to abandon his wife under threat of being arrested if he didn't. After this, Filintro's grandmother tried to bury him, given that he was "abandoned" by his father.[7] According to Filintro: "the husband of my aunt Elena, Jesús Pepito, took me out of the hole made by my grandmother."[8]

Filintro's story can be considered a metaphor of Indigenous contemporary historical experience in the Colombian Amazon. The absence of Christianity in Filintro's biography should not be ignored or taken for granted. As I have tried to show in this book, Catholic and evangelical Christianity were just two of the forces that mediated indigeneity in the Colombian Amazon. The massive conversion of Curripacos and Puinaves to evangelical Christianity that began in the 1940s should be understood in relation to broader processes of colonization and state-formation. Relationships between Indigenous communities, settlers and state officials have historically been unequal. Filintro's research, interest and defense of "Curripaco culture" may be part of a political reaction to the effects of Christianity upon Indigenous societies. This interest is attuned to the Political Constitution of 1991 which implemented multicultural reforms, granting ethnic groups the right to defend and uphold their own culture. In this context, a clear tension emerges between multicultural notions of indigeneity and evangelically informed notions of indigeneity. While multicultural ideas of indigeneity emphasize ancestrality and continuity with the past as criteria of authenticity, evangelical ideas of indigeneity tend to emphasize, most of the time, the break with the past as

Conclusions 165

a necessary condition for becoming an Indigenous Christian. Nonetheless, Christian indigeneity established complementarities between Christian and Indigenous values, while Indigenous evangelicals were recognized as legitimate Indigenous groups by the state. This book addressed how Christian Indigeneity is just one among various pathways that Indigenous groups or individuals have constructed historically in the Colombian Amazon. In fact, this book has shown how Indigenous politics in the Colombian Amazon throughout the 20th century was forged in the midst of interactions with different actors that included Catholic and evangelical missionaries, settlers, state officials, the military and guerilla members, among others.

Notes

1 Peter van der Veer, ed. "Introduction," in *Conversion to Modernities: The Globalization of Christianity* (New York: Routledge, 1996), 10.
2 Manuela Carneiro da Cunha, "Apresentação," in *Pacificando O Branco. Cosmologias do contacto no Norte-Amazonico*, eds. Bruce Albert and Alcida Ramos (São Paulo: Editora Unesp, 2000), 7–8.
3 Bruce Knauft, *Exchanging the Past: A Rainforest World of Before and After* (Chicago: University of Chicago Press, 2008).
4 GAIA Amazonas was founded in 1990 by Martin Von Hildebrand, an anthropologist of Irish and German descent, who was born in New York and later became a Colombian citizen. Von Hildebrand was the Head of Indigenous Affairs during Virigilio Barco's presidency (1986–1990), helped in the design of *Política Amazónica* (Amazon Policy) and played a central role as Colombian representative in the negotiation of the Convention on Indigenous and Tribal Peoples (ILO Convention 169) in 1989, and in defining Indigenous rights that were later recognized in the 1991 Political Constitution.
5 Filintro Antonio Rojas, *Ciencias naturales en la mitología Curripaco* (Guainía: Fundación Etnollano, 1997), 7.
6 Ibid. *Criollo* is the word used in Venezuela to refer to the white man.
7 It is common among some Indigenous groups in Amazonia the practice of infanticide when children are born with disability or other birth defects.
8 Filintro Antonio Rojas, *Ciencias naturales en la mitología Curripaco* (Guainía: Fundación Etnollano, 1997), 7.

References

Carneiro da Cunha, Manuela. "Apresentação." In *Pacificando O Branco. Cosmologias do contacto no Norte-Amazonico*, edited by Bruce Albert and Alcida Ramos, 7–8. São Paulo: Editora Unesp, 2000.
Knauft, Bruce. *Exchanging the Past: A Rainforest World of Before and After*. Chicago: University of Chicago Press, 2008.
Rojas, Filintro Antonio. *Ciencias naturales en la mitología Curripaco*. Guainía: Fundación Etnollano, 1997.
Van der Veer, Peter. "Introduction." In *Conversion to Modernities: The Globalization of Christianity*, edited by Peter van der Veer, 2–21. New York: Routledge, 1996.

Index

Amazonia 1, 7, 9, 14, 18, 24, 68–69, 71, 73, 88, 97, 109, 112–113, 116, 133–134, 146, 160; Amazon region 3, 5–7, 130, 133, 138, 147, 160, 163; native Amazonians 5, 7–8, 15–16, 19, 24–25, 33, 35, 41, 65–66, 109, 162
agency 9, 66, 69, 108, 113–114, 122, 162

Brazil 2, 6–7, 14–16, 18–21, 25–26, 29–30, 34–35, 40–46, 69–70, 76, 91, 98, 143, 160; Brazilians 3, 15, 19, 22, 29–31, 42–44, 146

Catholicism 3, 17, 33, 58, 65–69, 163; anti-Catholicism 59–60; Catholic church 1, 8, 58–59, 69, 80, 95; Catholic patriotism 16, 33, 160; *see also* missionaries
Christianity 1, 3, 5, 8–9, 39, 46, 58, 60, 68, 79, 87–89, 91–92, 94–95, 98–101, 109–110, 113, 123, 160, 162–164; Christian 33, 35, 39–40, 58, 61, 63–64, 66, 87–89, 91–101, 110, 114–117, 119, 121–123, 132, 140, 147, 162, 165; evangelical Christianity 3, 4, 6, 8, 59, 63–69, 79–80, 87, 113, 116, 161–162, 164; holy spirit 116, 119, 121–122; Protestantism 6, 8, 58, 65, 67, 69, 79, 115; protestants 58, 65, 75, 91, 117, *see also* conversion; evangelization
civilization 7, 9, 18, 25, 36, 37, 39, 40, 46, 59–60, 62, 67–68, 73, 78–79, 88, 90–91, 96, 108–110, 123, 131–132, 137–138, 160, 163; Christian civilization 15, 19; civilize 7, 15, 41, 46; civilized 31, 37, 40, 44, 46, 67, 70, 73, 87, 89, 96–98, 101, 115, 138; civilized life 1, 15, 22; not yet civilized 1, 7, 14, 31, 46; *see also* modernity
Cold War 4, 8, 58, 79
colonization 3–7, 15, 23, 40, 60, 65, 67, 70–71, 76, 79, 89, 98, 100, 109, 123, 137–138, 160–164; *colonos*, state-led colonization 3, 71, 161–162; extractivism 67, 146, 163; *see also* civilization; development; modernity
Colombia 1–2, 4, 5, 7–8, 14–15, 17–19, 24, 26, 29–31, 33, 34–36, 42–46, 58, 61, 66, 69, 70–71, 75, 80, 92, 95, 99, 131–132, 140, 143–145, 163, 164; Colombian government 1, 3, 6, 14, 19, 43, 134, 136, 164; Colombian nation 17, 75, 95; Colombians 3, 40, 43, 44, 68, 70, 74–76, 131, 136, 160; *see also* state, Colombian state
Colombian Amazon 1–3, 5, 7–9, 41, 70, 79–80, 89, 98, 108, 113, 123, 133, 138, 140, 160–161, 164–165; *see also* Amazon region
commodities 7, 9, 15, 24, 41, 66–67, 93, 97, 108–109, 113, 115, 123, 163; gifts 15, 24–25, 69, 163; money 9, 18, 67, 74, 109, 114, 121–122, 139, 163; objects

Index 167

9, 15, 24, 67, 69, 108–109, 111–117, 119, 122–123, 163
Concordat 1, 17; Holy See 14, 17–19, 45; *see also* Catholicism, Catholic church
conversion 58–66, 68, 79, 87–97, 99–101, 111–118, 161–164; Indigenous conversion 9, 64, 66, 87, 93–94, 98, 101, 161; politics of conversion 8–9, 87, 89, 98, 100–101; *see also* Christianity; evangelization
Curripaco 3, 9, 59, 62–63, 73, 90, 94–97, 99, 101, 108–110, 112, 114, 116, 136–138, 141, 143, 164; community 62, 96–97; culture 164

development 3, 7, 9, 10, 67, 75, 79, 99–100, 130, 132, 134, 137–138, 143, 147, 152; developmental indigenism 7, 10, 130–135, 137–138, 142; development policies 9, 130, 140; development programs 7, 130, 133; *see also* colonization
Devil 59, 63, 66–69, 77–78, 90–92, 96, 108–111, 121–123
discipline 16, 24, 37, 40, 91, 96–97, 119–120; *see also* Christianity; education

education 35, 37, 46, 60, 66, 75–77, 99, 130–134, 137, 142, 152, 162–163; boarding schools 3, 6, 15, 35, 43, 47, 60, 75–76, 161; *see also* discipline
evangelization 3, 7, 15–17, 26, 33, 35, 36–38, 45–47, 60, 62–64, 69, 88, 90–94, 96–99, 111, 131, 140, 160, 162; *see also* Christianity

FARC (Revolutionary Armed Forces of Colombia) 80, 92, 143, 161
frontier 1–2, 5, 6, 7, 9, 14, 17–18, 20, 31, 33, 36–37, 39, 42, 46, 109, 132–133, 138, 143; border 2, 3, 5–7, 14–15, 18–19, 21, 25–26, 29–32, 34–35, 37, 42–44, 46, 60, 69–70, 76, 80, 116–117, 136, 145, 149, 160, 164; *see also* territory

government 3, 7, 17–19, 31–33, 35, 41–44, 59–60, 66, 70–78, 80, 88, 95, 99, 130–131, 133, 135, 140–142, 144, 146, 149, 151, 161–162; Colombian government 1, 3, 6, 14, 19, 134, 136, 164; non-governmental agencies 99, 164; *see also* sovereignty
Guainía 1–2, 8–9, 59, 62, 64, 69–71, 73–75, 77–79, 87, 89, 92, 95, 98, 100–101, 108, 114, 116, 130, 133–138, 140, 142–153, 164; Guainía river 62, 64–65, 68, 94, 96–97, 112, 143; *see* Upper Rio Negro

historical ethnography 1, 160

idolatry 17, 113, 163
indigeneity 1–5, 8, 16, 17, 33, 38–39, 46, 59–60, 79, 87, 89, 100–101, 140, 149, 152, 160–162, 164; Christian indigeneity 9, 87, 89, 98, 100, 162, 165; indigenism (*indigenismo*) 4; indigenist bureaucracy 7, 9, 130, 133–135, 163; *see also* Indigenous
Indigenous: authorities 72–73, 146–148; churches 8, 60–61, 63, 79, 91, 98, 108, 113–114, 120; communities 1, 3, 5–10, 15, 41, 46, 49, 59–60, 63–66, 68–69, 73, 75–80, 87, 89, 95–96, 98–101, 108, 111, 116–117, 130–131, 134, 137, 140, 142–143, 145–150, 152, 160–164; culture 4, 9, 73, 79, 88, 92–96, 98, 112, 123, 132, 134–135, 138; evangelicals 3, 4, 7, 8, 9, 46, 59, 60, 64, 67–70, 73, 78–80, 88–89, 93, 95–96, 99–101, 108–109, 113–117, 119, 121–124, 161–163, 165; groups 3, 7, 8, 14–19, 21, 24–25, 27, 30–31, 33, 37–38, 46, 58–59, 62, 65–69, 79–80, 87, 91, 95, 112, 130–135, 138, 149, 152, 160, 163, 165; *indígenas* 10, 15, 24–27, 31–33, 38, 40, 43–44, 46, 64, 66–70, 72, 73–74, 77–78, 130–131, 134, 136–140, 144, 161, 163;

168 *Index*

land 2, 73; leaders 9, 73–74, 89, 99, 101, 130, 136, 138–141, 145–146, 161; pastors 8, 62, 79, 87, 90, 101, 116, 117, 162; peoples 17, 38, 41, 74, 89, 92, 93, 97, 134–135, 137–138, 148–149; politics 140, 165; religion 39, 108, 111; societies 1, 4, 5, 7, 18–19, 26, 39, 73, 101, 109, 160, 162, 164; *see also* indigeneity

materiality 9, 67, 90, 108–109, 112, 114–115, 123, 162–163; material accumulation 66–67, 163; material improvement 10, 66–67, 135, 152; material possessions 9, 66, 108, 113, 115, 123; worldliness (*lo mundano*) 67, 108–109, 113, 114–116, 119, 121–124, 163; *see also* commodities

military 14, 16, 35, 59–60, 70–71, 74, 80, 147–150, 153, 164

mining 10, 109, 123, 130–131, 142–143, 145–153, 162, 164; Brazilian miners 143, 152; dredges 143–145, 150; gold extraction 10, 131, 143, 145, 146–150, 163–164; Indigenous miners 130–131, 145, 146, 147, 148, 150; miners 10, 131, 143, 145–153; mining raft 143, 146–148

missionaries 1, 3, 5, 7–8, 16–22, 24–26, 29–30, 32–46, 58–60, 63, 65–68, 74–76, 88–96, 99–101, 108–111, 115–116, 122–123, 131, 133, 162–163; Catholic 1–3, 5–6, 8–9, 17–18, 24, 41–42, 46–47, 59–61, 65–70, 79–80, 109, 130–133, 135, 160–163, 165; evangelical 1–4, 8, 46, 59–61, 64, 67, 71, 74–76, 78, 80, 87–88, 92, 95, 96, 99, 111–113, 117, 123, 132, 160, 165; Indigenous 61, 62, 95, 98, 113, 117; montfort 14–16, 19–21, 23–24, 26, 27, 29, 31, 33–35, 37, 39–42, 44–46, 59, 160–161; protestant 59, 65, 112–113; salesian 31, 44, 161; *see also* Catholicism; Christianity; evangelization

Mitú 42, 43, 45, 59, 61–62, 65, 80, 132, 133

modernity 4, 5, 9, 15, 46, 67, 89, 108, 109, 113–114, 116, 121, 123–124, 160, 162–163; *see also* civilization

Montfort-Papurí 16, 21, 25–27, 33–36, 43–45, 160

New Testament 3, 8, 35, 58–60, 63, 90, 92, 95, 110

New Tribes Mission 3, 9, 58–61, 63, 75, 78, 79, 89, 95, 108; missionaries 3, 60, 75, 77, 89–90, 95, 116, 161; Muller, S. 59–69, 76–80, 87, 89–92, 95–98, 109–112, 161

Papurí River 14–15, 20, 21–22, 24, 29–30, 35, 42–46

performance: of civilization 36; of sovereign power 16, 34, 46; of sovereignty 16, 34, 160–161

Puerto Inírida 70–71, 144, 147, 150–151; Inírida 65, 76; Inírida river 65, 69, 72, 112, 131, 135, 138, 143–145, 149

Puinave 3, 9, 59, 63, 73, 90, 92–96, 98–99, 101, 108, 110, 112–113, 115, 119, 131, 136, 141, 143, 149, 164; community 112, 145; culture 93

reducciones (mission towns) 6, 7, 14–15, 19, 25, 29, 32, 36, 46, 66, 160–161; *see also* evangelization

ritual 9, 16, 34, 36, 68, 91–93, 96–97, 108–112, 114, 160; *see also* performance

rubber 2, 5, 15, 27, 31, 40–41, 45, 98, 161; bosses 15, 19, 24, 27, 31, 40–42, 46, 73; debt peonage 41, 74; extraction 2, 19, 40, 71; industry 41, 45–46, 161; plantations 15, 31, 41–42, 45; rubber tappers 15, 40, 42, 46, 164; traders 24, 42; *see also* colonization

settlers 46, 60, 65, 73, 89, 95–96, 98, 100–101, 131, 137–138, 143, 145, 147–150, 152, 161–162, 164, 165; Brazilian miners 147, 151–152; Brazilian settlers 143;

Index 169

colonos 5, 6, 23, 60, 64–68, 70–72, 74, 76–77, 79–80, 95, 98, 109, 137–138, 141, 143, 147, 161, 164; *see also* colonization
sorcery 68, 94–95, 97, 110–112; sorcerer 109–111; witchcraft 39, 90–93, 109–112
sovereignty 2–3, 5–6, 16, 18–19, 21, 31, 34–35, 41, 46, 60, 69, 70, 76, 133, 136; national sovereignty 30, 34, 58, 71, 78–80; state sovereignty 2, 6–7, 14, 25, 33, 133, 160–161; sovereign power 16, 34–35, 47, 59; *see also* performance
state 1–10, 14, 15, 17–18, 21, 25, 27, 31, 33–34, 41, 44–46, 58–61, 65, 68–71, 73–74, 76–80, 87, 94, 109, 111, 130–152, 160–165; Colombian state 69–70, 73–74, 79; languages of the state 74, 80, 137, 141, 152, 162; nation-state 1, 3–4, 59, 60, 69, 79; state authority 4, 8; state-formation 4, 40, 76, 79, 160, 164; state-making 1, 4, 123
Summer Institute of Linguistics (SIL) 8, 58–61, 75, 78; *see also* New Tribes Mission

territory 1, 6–7, 15, 18–20, 27, 41, 44–45, 58, 69–71, 76–77, 100, 111, 141; *see also* sovereignty
The Bible 16, 24, 59–61, 64, 66, 88, 91–94, 96–97, 109, 113, 115–120, 122, 163; *see also* New Testament
tucano 2, 16, 21, 23–24, 26–27, 29, 35, 141, 160; tukanoans 27, 29, 32–33, 35–36, 38, 47, 160–161

Upper Rio Negro 2, 7, 14, 46, 63, 76, 116, 137; *see also* Guainía river

Vaupés 1–3, 6–9, 14, 15, 17, 19–21, 24–27, 31–32, 36, 38–42, 44–46, 59, 63, 65, 68–69, 74, 80, 108, 112, 131–133, 160–161, 163; Vaupés river 20, 25, 43, 61
Venezuela 2, 18, 21, 69–70, 74, 80, 113–114, 116–117, 136, 145, 149, 161–162, 164

White man 6, 9, 24, 30, 67, 78, 96–101, 112, 137, 139–140, 147–148

Printed in the United States
by Baker & Taylor Publisher Services